Current
Directions
in
MOTIVATION
AND EMOTION

READINGS FROM THE
ASSOCIATION FOR
PSYCHOLOGICAL SCIENCE

Current Directions
in
MOTIVATION
AND EMOTION

EDITED BY
Kennon M. Sheldon
University of Missouri, Columbia

Allyn & Bacon

Boston • New York • San Francisco
Mexico City • Montreal • Toronto • London • Madrid • Munich • Paris
Hong Kong • Singapore • Tokyo • Cape Town • Sydney

Acquisitions Editor: Michelle Limoges
Editorial Assistant: Lisa Dotson
Marketing Manager: Kate Mitchell
Production Supervisor: Patty Bergin
Editorial Production Service: TexTech International
Manufacturing Buyer: JoAnne Sweeney
Electronic Composition: TexTech International
Cover Designer: Joel Gendron

Library of Congress Cataloging-in-Publication Data

Current directions in motivation and emotion / edited by Kennon M. Sheldon. —1st ed.
    p. cm. — (Readings from the Association for Psychological Science)
  ISBN-13: 978-0-205-68011-5
  ISBN-10: 0-205-68011-9
  1. Motivation (Psychology)   2. Emotions. I. Sheldon, Kennon M.
(Kennon Marshall)
  BF503.C87 2010
  153.8—dc22

                                           2009016428

10 9 8 7 6 5 4 3 2 1   13 12 11 10 09

Allyn & Bacon
is an imprint of

                                 ISBN-10: 0-205-68011-9
www.pearsonhighered.com ISBN-13: 978-0-205-68011-5

Contents

Introduction

Welcome to the first APS reader on "Current Directions in Motivation and Emotion!" The creation of such a reader seems overdue, since motivation and emotion are central topics in contemporary behavioral science. If we want to know why people do what they do (i.e., what causes behavior?), we need to know what their motivation is for doing "x," and also, how they feel about doing "x." Both of these subjective factors can play a significant role in scientific explanations of behavior. However, motivation and emotion can also be non-subjective or non-conscious, as we will see below, and can be influenced by subtle forces about which people are typically unaware.

The articles in this reader are designed to supplement upper division courses on motivation and/or emotion (often, they are taught together in the same course). They illustrate much of the cutting-edge research that is currently taking place. Although many of the articles deal with rather technical concepts and issues, they have all been selected in large part because of their potential interest value to undergraduates. These articles cover important real-life concerns, such as how to achieve one's goals, how to control one's emotions and responses, and how to be a happy person more generally. They also deal with the potential downsides of tendencies that we all have, such as striving for self-esteem, perfection, or pride. It is my hope that in reading these articles, students will learn about themselves as well as about the field.

What is the difference between motivation and emotion? Actually, these topics have typically been studied in isolation from one another. Emotions have been viewed as affective responses to various circumstances and stimuli. Motivations have been viewed as attempts to make certain things happen (consciously or unconsciously). That is, emotions have been treated as outcomes, and motivations as causes. However, many of the articles in this reader reflect a growing tendency to re-think these traditional views, for example by treating emotions as forces that directly impel behavior, or motivations as responses to specifiable antecedent conditions. It is logical that motives and emotions should be both responses and causes, because they are tremendously complex phenomena, with biological and evolutionary roots but also with important real-world implications. Thus, an exciting current research trend, illustrated by several articles in this reader, is to integrate motivation and emotion concepts within the same research program. Surely, how we feel influences what we try to do, and what we try to do influences how we then feel? Psychologists are moving closer to a truly multi-faceted view of these dynamic processes.

This reader is organized into six basic sections: Three on motivation, two on emotion, and one on psychological well-being (happiness). The first section addresses *personal motivation,* that is, things that we consciously try to do. The articles concern the nature of effective goal-setting and effective self-regulation in service of goals, and also concern particular motives displayed by some or all people, towards perfectionism and self-esteem. The second section concerns *social motivation,* that is, things that we try to do in the context provided by other people. The first and second articles look at two broad social motives: to justify the political and cultural status quo, and to perform work behaviors that go beyond the call of duty. The third and fourth articles take an evolutionary perspective upon social motivation, discussing how feelings of gratitude influence peoples' willingness to behave altruistically, and how a woman's place in her own fertility cycle influences her perceptions of potential mates. The third section of the reader presents exciting new research on the *non-conscious determinants of motivation* (both individual and social), showing how the idea of money influences peoples' willingness to help others, how the color red influences peoples' ability to do well on tests, how the idea of death influences peoples' attitude towards their own bodies, and how people are automatically attuned to notice and favor the idea of themselves.

The fourth and fifth sections of the reader tackle the topic of emotion— both *personal emotions* and *non-conscious determinants of emotions.* The fourth section deals with the familiar emotions of pride and interest, considering both their causes and consequences. It also deals with positive moods and emotions more generally, as important buffers against the negative effects of stress. Also, section four deals with emotional intelligence, which has been the topic of best-selling books but which until recently has been poorly understood. The fifth section of the reader deals with evolved fear modules and evolved emotion-perceptual abilities, and also with implicit attitudes and emotions of which we are unaware.

Finally, the sixth section of the reader deals with *happiness and wellbeing* directly, consistent with the new science of "positive psychology." Of course, happiness involves positive emotions, but it is also more than that. The articles in this section consider happiness from a broad variety of perspectives, including a traditional Buddhist perspective, which asks how our growing scientific knowledge of well-being concurs with this ancient body of knowledge; a neurobiological perspective, which asks whether we each have a "happiness set-point" which we cannot escape; a socio-cultural perspective, which asks whether children of affluent parents have special difficulties, despite their enviable advantages; and a cognitive perspective, which asks whether people can correctly predict the effects of various life-changes upon their happiness levels. Hopefully students will especially benefit from this last section, as they pursue happiness in their own lives.

Section 1: Personal Motivation

I have called this first section *personal motivation* because the articles address motivational themes that we all encounter in our daily lives, as we go about trying to get what we want. The first article, on *goal-setting theory,* represents this idea well. What have researchers discovered about how goal-setting works and how it can be improved? Locke and Latham, the authors of this article, have in the past taken an applied focus to goal research, specifically within the realm of industrial-organizational psychology. For example, what kinds of goals managers should set for their employees, in order to maximize their performance: Easy, or hard? Vague, or specific? However, this article describes new directions in their research program, directions which link that program to "pure" (not just applied) research questions. This article covers a lot of issues, perhaps too briefly for some readers; however, the importance of goal-setting for everyone suggests it would be well worth following the reference section to further information.

The second article in this section addresses a very different issue, but one which is also very relevant to personal goal-pursuit. Pursuing goals often requires *self-discipline,* the ability to get ourselves to do things we don't really want to do (i.e., resist impulses to eat, or make ourselves go to the gym). Baumeister, Vohs, and Tice ask, "Is self-discipline (or self-control) like a muscle that gets tired after use?" They describe plenty of data to support this analogy, showing that acts of self-control or self-denial are costly, and can actually reduce blood glucose. So, don't forget to stop and have a snack (or have some fun) as you pursue your goals!

The third and fourth articles in this section concern two particular motivations that many people have. That is, rather than talking about general processes involved in the pursuit of any goal or motivation, they talk about two specific self-based motivations: to achieve *self-esteem,* and to achieve *perfection.* It turns out that both of these motivations are quite problematic, perhaps for similar reasons. Crocker and Knight claim that self-esteem is over-rated—yes, it feels good to have, but it doesn't help you do better. Furthermore, to the extent you do things in order to get self-esteem, you may pay a variety of costs, both psychological and physical. Their model of contingent self-esteem has many practical implications, because we all sometimes stake our sense of self-worth on how things turn out, rather than embracing a more stable and non-contingent view of our own value. Flett and Hewitt's article on "the perils of perfectionism" makes a similar point: thinking too much about achieving perfection can actually undermine one's performance. Also, by making their self-esteem contingent upon perfection, perfectionists set themselves up for misery and pay a variety of costs. So, don't be afraid to fail on occasion!

New Directions in Goal-Setting Theory

Edwin A. Locke[1]
R.H. Smith School of Business, University of Maryland

Gary P. Latham
Rotman School of Management, University of Toronto

Abstract

Goal-setting theory is summarized regarding the effectiveness of specific, difficult goals; the relationship of goals to affect; the mediators of goal effects; the relation of goals to self-efficacy; the moderators of goal effects; and the generality of goal effects across people, tasks, countries, time spans, experimental designs, goal sources (i.e., self-set, set jointly with others, or assigned), and dependent variables. Recent studies concerned with goal choice and the factors that influence it, the function of learning goals, the effect of goal framing, goals and affect (well-being), group goal setting, goals and traits, macro-level goal setting, and conscious versus subconscious goals are described. Suggestions are given for future research.

Keywords

goal setting; self-efficacy; commitment; subconscious goals

Goal-setting theory (Locke & Latham, 1990, 2002) was developed inductively within industrial/organizational (I/O) psychology over a 25-year period, based on some 400 laboratory and field studies. These studies showed that specific, high (hard) goals lead to a higher level of task performance than do easy goals or vague, abstract goals such as the exhortation to "do one's best." So long as a person is committed to the goal, has the requisite ability to attain it, and does not have conflicting goals, there is a positive, linear relationship between goal difficulty and task performance. Because goals refer to future valued outcomes, the setting of goals is first and foremost a discrepancy-creating process. It implies discontent with one's present condition and the desire to attain an object or outcome.

Goals are related to affect in that goals set the primary standard for self-satisfaction with performance. High, or hard, goals are motivating because they require one to attain more in order to be satisfied than do low, or easy, goals. Feelings of success in the workplace occur to the extent that people see that they are able to grow and meet job challenges by pursuing and attaining goals that are important and meaningful.

There are four mechanisms or mediators of the relationship between goals and performance. High goals lead to greater effort and/or persistence than do moderately difficult, easy, or vague goals. Goals direct attention, effort, and action toward goal-relevant actions at the expense of nonrelevant actions. Because performance is a function of both ability and motivation, goal effects also depend upon having the requisite task knowledge and skills. Goals may simply motivate one to use one's existing ability, may automatically "pull" stored task-relevant knowledge into awareness, and/or may motivate people to search for new knowledge.

The latter is most common when people are confronted by new, complex tasks. As we will show, such searches may or may not be successful.

Goals, in conjunction with self-efficacy (task-specific confidence; Bandura, 1997), often mediate or partially mediate the effects of other potentially motivating variables, such as personality traits, feedback, participation in decision making, job autonomy, and monetary incentives.

The key moderators of goal setting are feedback, which people need in order to track their progress; commitment to the goal, which is enhanced by self-efficacy and viewing the goal as important; task complexity, to the extent that task knowledge is harder to acquire on complex tasks; and situational constraints. With regard to the latter, Brown, Jones, and Leigh (2005) found that role overload (excess work without the necessary resources to accomplish a task) moderates goal effects; goals affected performance only when overload was low.

Goal-setting theory has high internal and external validity. As of 1990, support for goal-setting effects had been found on more than 88 different tasks, involving more than 40,000 male and female participants in Asia, Australia, Europe, and North America (Locke & Latham, 1990). Goal effects have been found in both laboratory and field settings, using both correlational and experimental designs and numerous dependent variables. Time spans have ranged from 1 minute to 25 years and effects have been obtained at the individual, group, and organizational-unit levels. Goals are effective even when they come from different sources; they can be assigned by others, they can be set jointly through participation, and they can be self-set. In the latter instance, goals are a key element in self-regulation. Goal theory is an "open" theory in that new elements are added as new discoveries are made.

ADVANCES IN GOAL THEORY

We note eight categories of studies that have moved goal theory forward. (There is no logical order in the sections that follow.)

Goal Choice

Previous research on goal choice showed that self-efficacy, past performance, and various social influences affect the level at which goals are set. Enlarging on this work and moving it into the realm of sports, Donovan and Williams (2003) found that track-and-field athletes had two sets of goals, one for the season and one for the next competition. The athletes created discrepancies between past performance and future goals by setting their current season goals higher than their best previous performance. When large negative goal–performance discrepancies occurred in the current season, goals for the season were lowered. However, goals for the next competition were typically raised in order to compensate for lower-than-desired seasonal progress. There was more goal revision if athletes attributed past performance to unstable causes, such as effort, than if they attributed it to stable causes, such as ability.

Learning Goals

Sometimes specific, difficult goals do not lead to better performance than simply urging people to do their best (Seijts & Latham, 2001). Focusing on reaching a specific performance outcome on a new, complex task can lead to "tunnel vision"—a focus on reaching the goal rather than on acquiring the skills required to reach it. In such cases, the best results are attained if a learning goal is assigned—that is, a goal to acquire the requisite task knowledge. Latham and Brown (in press), for example, found that entering MBA students who set specific difficult learning goals (e.g., learn to network, master specific course subject matter) subsequently had higher GPAs and higher satisfaction with their MBA program than did people who simply set a distal (long-term or end) performance goal for GPA at the end of the academic year. We believe that a learning goal facilitates or enhances metacognition—namely, planning, monitoring, and evaluating progress toward goal attainment. Metacognition is particularly necessary in environments in which there is minimal structure or guidance.

Framing

Assigning hard goals may not be effective when people view those goals as threatening. The concept of framing is well known in psychology, and one type of framing is in terms of gain versus loss. Whether a person appraises a high goal as a challenge versus a threat makes a difference for that person's performance. Drach-Zahavy and Erez (2002) found that, when a task was altered to pose new challenges (but with goal difficulty held constant), people who were made to view a situation as a threat (focus on failure) achieved significantly lower performance than did those who were made to view the situation as a challenge (focus on success and the usefulness of effort).

Affect

A 3-year study of people in managerial and professional jobs in Germany revealed that only those adults who perceived their goals as difficult to attain reported a change in affect. Goal progress and goal importance were strong predictors of feelings of success and well-being. Among the most interesting findings was that lack of goal attainment in one's personal life was related to greater general well-being when the person experienced goal progress on the job. Evidently, success in one realm compensated for failure in the other (Wiese & Freund, 2005).

Group Goals

Goal setting is effective with groups too. However, groups add a layer of complexity because goal conflicts may occur among the group's members. Seijts and Latham (2000) examined the effects of conflict versus no conflict between an individual's and a group's goals. In a laboratory task involving monetary incentives, they found no main effect for goal setting. However, having high personal goals that were compatible with the group's goal enhanced group performance, whereas having personal goals that were incompatible with the group's goal had a detrimental effect on how well the group performed.

Another added feature of setting goals in groups is that task-relevant information may be shared among group members. In an unpublished study, Locke and his colleagues found that dyads that share information perform better on a complex management simulation than do dyads who share less. The sharing effect is enhanced if the people in the dyads have high goals.

DeShon, Kozlowski, Schmidt, Milner, and Wiechmann (2004) were the first to compare goal effects on individuals versus on groups. On a radar-tracking simulation, the effect of individual goals on performance was fully mediated by task strategy and individual effort. Group-level goal effects were mediated only by team-related effort. Feedback to individuals led to a focus on the individual's performance, whereas feedback to the team led to a focus on the team's performance.

Goals and Traits

The effects of goal setting as a state on the effects of goal orientation as a trait were studied by Seijts, Latham, Tasa, and Latham (2004). People with a learning goal orientation tend to choose tasks in which they can acquire knowledge and skill. Those with a performance goal orientation tend to avoid tasks where others may judge them unfavorably due to possible errors they might make. Hence they tend to choose easy tasks in which they can look good in the eyes of others. Seijts et al. (2004) found that a specific high learning goal (state orientation) is effective in increasing a person's performance regardless of their trait orientation. Performance is highest on a complex task, however, when people have a learning goal orientation and also set a learning goal. In short, the beneficial effect of a learning goal orientation can be attained by inducing it as a state.

LePine (2005) conducted another intriguing goal-setting and goal-orientation study, using a decision-making simulation to study the ability of teams to adapt to changing circumstances. When conditions changed so that team members had to change the way they communicated, the teams that adapted best were those that had high goals as well as a high score on a learning-orientation trait scale. Setting high goals was actually harmful if the teams scored low on the measure of learning orientation.

In an even more complex trait-mediation study conducted in the laboratory, Lee, Sheldon, and Turban (2003) found that an "amotivated" orientation (i.e., low confidence in one's capabilities) is associated with goal-avoidance motivation. This, in turn, is associated with lower goal levels and, thereby, lower performance. In contrast, a control orientation, meaning extrinsic motivation, is associated with both avoidance and approach goals. The latter are associated with higher goal levels and higher performance. Autonomy goals, meaning intrinsic motivation, led to mastery goals. Mastery goals, in turn, enhanced mental focus; so did approach goals, which, in turn, enhanced performance. This study illustrates how motivation can be measured at different levels of abstraction, with the more specific levels mediating the more general ones.

Macro-Level Goals

Goal-setting research has also been extended from the group level to the level of the organization as a whole. A study of companies and their suppliers in China found that the relationship between a high level of a shared vision among employees and low levels of dysfunctional opportunism was partially mediated by the setting of cooperative goals. A shared vision strengthened cooperative goal setting by drawing the boundary lines of the group around the two organizations involved—namely, the company and its suppliers—thereby reducing the negative feelings that frequently occur in alliances due to perceptions of in- versus out-groups.

Baum and Locke (2004) used a longitudinal design to study the performance of small-venture entrepreneurs over a 6-year period. Growth goals, along with self-efficacy and organizational vision, were found to significantly predict future growth. These three motivators completely mediated the effects on growth of two personality traits, passion for the work and tenacity (see Fig. 1). The role of goals and self-efficacy as mediators of other motivators was also found in previous studies in which the individual was the level of analysis (Locke & Latham, 2002).

Goals and Subconscious Priming

To regulate behavior during goal-directed action, a consciously held goal does not have to be in focal awareness every second. Typically, a goal, once accepted and understood, remains in the periphery of consciousness as a reference point for guiding and giving meaning to subsequent mental and physical actions.

Intriguing findings in social psychology by Bargh and Chartrand and others (e.g., see Bargh & Williams, 2006) suggest that even goals that are subconsciously

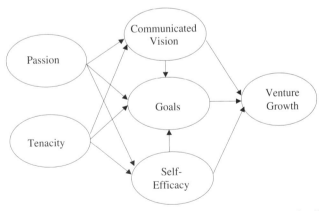

Fig. 1. The relationship of traits (passion and tenacity), vision, goals, and self-efficacy to the sales and employment growth of small ventures. Adapted from "The Relationship of Entrepreneurial Traits, Skill, and Motivation to Subsequent Venture Growth," by J.R. Baum & E.A. Locke, 2004, *Journal of Applied Psychology*, 89, p. 592. Copyright 2004, American Psychological Association. Adapted with permission.

primed (and participants report no awareness of the primed motive) affect performance. Consequently, Stajkovic, Locke, and Blair (in press) compared the effects of primed, subconscious, achievement goals with explicitly assigned, conscious, performance goals in a laboratory setting. Both priming and conscious goals had independent effects on task performance, although the conscious goal had a larger effect size. Moreover, the two types of goals had an interaction effect. Primed subjects with hard and "do your best" goals had significantly higher performance than did unprimed subjects with the same goals. Priming, however, did not enhance the effects of easy goals. In a follow-up study, Stajkovic and Locke used a 2 × 2 design in a proofreading task in which subconsciously primed speed goals and subconsciously assigned accuracy goals were crossed with explicitly assigned speed and accuracy goals. This enabled us to see what happened when subconscious goals were put in conflict with conscious goals. Using speed as the dependent variable, the two types of goals showed significant main effects, but they partly neutralized one another when they were in conflict. However, the effect of conscious speed goals was markedly greater than that of subconsciously primed speed goals. Subconscious priming had no effect at all on accuracy, but conscious goals had a strong effect.

DIRECTIONS FOR FUTURE RESEARCH

Goal setting can be used effectively on any domain in which an individual or group has some control over the outcomes. It has been applied not only to work tasks but to sports and rehabilitation and can be applied in numerous other settings. The success of goal setting depends upon taking account of the mediators and moderators that determine its efficacy and applicability.

Because goal setting is an open theory, there is no limit to the number of discoveries that can be made or to the integrations that might be made between goal theory and other theories. Future research could include studies of the effects of different types of learning goals and ways of combining them with performance goals (e.g., learning goals first, then performance goals), different types of goal framing (approach success vs. avoid failure), the relation between goals and cognition (which, by implication, entails all of cognitive psychology), goal hierarchies, and macro goal studies with organizations of different sizes. More studies of the relationship between conscious and subconscious goals would also be of interest.

Recommended Reading

Latham, G.P. (2006). *Work motivation: History, theory, research and practice.* Thousand Oaks, CA: Sage.
Locke, E.A., & Latham, G.P. (2005). Goal setting theory: Theory building by induction. In K.G. Smith & M.A. Mitt (Eds.), *Great minds in management: The process of theory development.* New York: Oxford.

Note

1. Address correspondence to Edwin A. Locke, 32122 Canyon Ridge Drive, Westlake Village, CA 91361; e-mail: elocke@rhsmith.umd.edu.

References

Bandura, A. (1997). *Self-efficacy: The exercise of control*. Stanford: W.H. Freeman.

Bargh, J., & Williams, E. (2006). The automaticity of social life. *Current Directions in Psychological Science, 15*, 1–4.

Baum, J.R., & Locke, E.A. (2004). The relationship of entrepreneurial traits, skill, and motivation to subsequent venture growth. *Journal of Applied Psychology, 89*, 587–598.

Brown, S.P., Jones, E., & Leigh, T.W. (2005). The attenuating effect of role overload on relationships linking self-efficacy and goal level to work performance. *Journal of Applied Psychology, 90*, 972–979.

DeShon, R.P., Kozlowski, W.J., Schmidt, A.M., Milner, K.R., & Wiechmann, D. (2004). Multiple-goal, multilevel model of feedback effects on the regulation of individual and team performance. *Journal of Applied Psychology, 89*, 1035–1056.

Donovan, J.J., & Williams, K.J. (2003). Missing the mark: Effects of time and causal attributions on goal revision in response to goal-performance discrepancies. *Journal of Applied Psychology, 88*, 379–390.

Drach-Zahavy, A., & Erez, M. (2002). Challenge versus threat effects on the goal-performance relationship. *Organizational Behavior and Human Performance, 88*, 667–682.

Latham, G.P., & Brown, T.C. (in press). The effect of learning, distal, and proximal goals on MBA self-efficacy and satisfaction. *Applied Psychology: An International Review*.

Lee, F.K., Sheldon, K.M., & Turban, D. (2003). Personality and the goal-striving process: The influence of achievement goal patterns, goal level, and mental focus on performance and enjoyment. *Journal of Applied Psychology, 88*, 256–265.

LePine, J.A. (2005). Adaptation of teams in response to unforeseen change: Effects of goal difficulty and team composition in terms of cognitive ability and goal orientation. *Journal of Applied Psychology, 90*, 1153–1167.

Locke, E.A., & Latham, G.P. (1990). *A theory of goal setting and task performance*. Englewood Cliffs, NJ: Prentice-Hall.

Locke, E.A., & Latham, G.P. (2002). Building a practically useful theory of goal setting and task motivation: A 35-year odyssey. *American Psychologist, 57*, 705–717.

Seijts, G.H., & Latham, G.P. (2000). The effects of goal setting and group size on performance in a social dilemma. *Canadian Journal of Behavioural Science, 32*, 104–116.

Seijts, G.H., & Latham, G.P. (2001). The effect of learning, outcome, and proximal goals on a moderately complex task. *Journal of Organizational Behavior, 22*, 291–307.

Seijts, G.H., Latham, G.P., Tasa, K., & Latham, B.W. (2004). Goal setting and goal orientation: An integration of two different yet related literatures. *Academy of Management Journal, 47*, 227–239.

Stajkovic, A.D., Locke, E.A., & Blair, E.S. (in press). A first examination of the relationships between primed subconscious goals, assigned conscious goals, and task performance. *Journal of Applied Psychology*.

Wiese, B.S., & Freund, A.M. (2005). Goal progress makes one happy, or does it? Longitudinal findings from the work domain. *Journal of Occupational and Organizational Psychology, 78*, 1–19.

The Strength Model of Self-Control

Roy F. Baumeister[1] and Dianne M. Tice
Florida State University
Kathleen D. Vohs
University of Minnesota

Abstract

Self-control is a central function of the self and an important key to success in life. The exertion of self-control appears to depend on a limited resource. Just as a muscle gets tired from exertion, acts of self-control cause short-term impairments (ego depletion) in subsequent self-control, even on unrelated tasks. Research has supported the strength model in the domains of eating, drinking, spending, sexuality, intelligent thought, making choices, and interpersonal behavior. Motivational or framing factors can temporarily block the deleterious effects of being in a state of ego depletion. Blood glucose is an important component of the energy.

Keywords

self-control; ego depletion; willpower; impulse; strength

Every day, people resist impulses to go back to sleep, to eat fattening or forbidden foods, to say or do hurtful things to their relationship partners, to play instead of work, to engage in inappropriate sexual or violent acts, and to do countless other sorts of problematic behaviors—that is, ones that might feel good immediately or be easy but that carry long-term costs or violate the rules and guidelines of proper behavior. What enables the human animal to follow rules and norms prescribed by society and to resist doing what it selfishly wants?

Self-control refers to the capacity for altering one's own responses, especially to bring them into line with standards such as ideals, values, morals, and social expectations, and to support the pursuit of long-term goals. Many writers use the terms self-control and self-regulation interchangeably, but those who make a distinction typically consider self-control to be the deliberate, conscious, effortful subset of self-regulation. In contrast, homeostatic processes such as maintaining a constant body temperature may be called self-regulation but not self-control. Self-control enables a person to restrain or override one response, thereby making a different response possible.

Self-control has attracted increasing attention from psychologists for two main reasons. At the theoretical level, self-control holds important keys to understanding the nature and functions of the self. Meanwhile, the practical applications of self-control have attracted study in many contexts. Inadequate self-control has been linked to behavioral and impulse-control problems, including overeating, alcohol and drug abuse, crime and violence, overspending, sexually impulsive behavior, unwanted pregnancy, and smoking (e.g., Baumeister, Heatherton, & Tice, 1994; Gottfredson & Hirschi, 1990; Tangney, Baumeister, & Boone, 2004; Vohs & Faber, 2007). It may also be linked to emotional problems, school underachievement, lack of persistence, various failures at task performance, relationship problems and dissolution, and more.

LIMITED RESOURCES

Folk discussions of self-control have long invoked the idea of willpower, which implies a kind of strength or energy. During the heyday of the behaviorist and cognitive revolutions, however, psychology had little use for theorizing in energy terms, and self theories in particular had scarcely mentioned energy since Freud. However, in the 1990s, research findings began to point toward an energy model of self-control. There might be something to the willpower notion after all.

The idea that self-control depended on a limited energy resource was suggested by us (Baumeister et al., 1994) based on our review of multiple research literatures. We observed that self-control appeared vulnerable to deterioration over time from repeated exertions, resembling a muscle that gets tired. The implication was that effortful self-regulation depends on a limited resource that becomes depleted by any acts of self-control, causing subsequent performance even on other self-control tasks to become worse.

The basic approach to testing the depleted-resource hypothesis was to have some research participants perform a first self-control task, while others performed a comparable but neutral task, and then all would move on to perform a second, unrelated self-control task. If self-control consumes a limited resource, then performing the first task should deplete the person's resource, leaving less available for the second task—and therefore causing poorer performance on the second task. Other theories would make different predictions. For example, if self-control mainly involved activating a cognitive schema or mental program, then the first self-control task should prime the schema and activate the self-control system, so performance on the second self-control task should improve, not worsen.

Early laboratory evidence for depleted resources in self-regulation was reported by Muraven, Tice, and Baumeister (1998) and Baumeister, Bratslavsky, Muraven, and Tice (1998). In one study, watching an emotionally evocative film while trying either to amplify or to stifle one's emotional response caused poorer performance on a subsequent test of physical (handgrip) stamina, as compared to watching the film without trying to control one's emotions. (Stamina counts as a measure of self-control because it involves resisting fatigue and overriding the urge to quit.) In another study, suppressing a forbidden thought weakened people's ability to stifle laughter afterward. In another, resisting the temptation to eat chocolates and cookies (and making oneself eat health-promoting but unappetizing radishes instead) caused participants to give up faster on a subsequent frustrating task, as compared to people who had not exerted self-control (see Fig. 1). These studies all pointed toward the conclusion that the first self-control task consumed and depleted some kind of psychological resource that was therefore less available to help performance on the second self-control task.

The term *ego depletion* was coined to refer to the state of diminished resources following exertion of self-control (or other tasks that might deplete the same resource). These ego-depletion effects are not due to a diminished a sense of self-efficacy or to the inference that one is poor at self-control. Wallace and

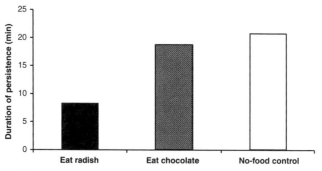

Fig. 1. Speed of giving up on an unsolvable task after eating chocolate or exerting self-control to resist chocolate in favor of radishes on a previous task (as compared to a no-food control). From Baumeister, Bratslavsky, Muraven, & Tice, 1998.

Baumeister (2002) explicitly manipulated feedback about success and failure at self-control and measured self-efficacy, but neither factor had any discernible impact on the ego-depletion patterns. Nor are these patterns due to participants refusing to exert themselves on the second task because they think they have done enough on the first task, as various findings have shown (see Baumeister, Gailliot, DeWall, & Oaten, 2006); for example, it has been found that depleted participants will subject themselves to more boredom than will nondepleted ones on a second task.

Is willpower more than a metaphor? Gailliot et al. (2007) explored the role of glucose, a chemical in the bloodstream that can be converted to neurotransmitters and thus furnishes fuel for brain activity. Acts of self-control cause reductions in blood-glucose levels, which in turn predict poor self-control on behavioral tasks. Drinking a glass of lemonade with sugar helped counteract these effects, presumably by restoring glucose in the blood. Lemonade mixed with diet sweeteners (no glucose) had no such empowering effect.

ELABORATING THE STRENGTH MODEL

The analogy between self-control and a muscle was suggested by the early findings that self-control performance deteriorates after initial exertions, just as a muscle gets tired from exertion. Other revealing aspects of self-control performance also extend the resemblance to a muscle (see Box 1).

First, just as exercise can make muscles stronger, there are signs that regular exertions of self-control can improve willpower strength (for a review, see Baumeister et al., 2006). These improvements typically take the form of resistance to depletion, in the sense that performance at self-control tasks deteriorates at a slower rate. Targeted efforts to control behavior in one area, such as spending money or exercise, lead to improvements in unrelated areas, such as studying or household chores. And daily exercises in self-control, such as improving posture, altering verbal behavior, and using one's nondominant hand for simple tasks, gradually produce improvements in self-control as measured by laboratory tasks. The finding that these improvements carry over into tasks vastly

Box 1. *Contexts, moderators, mediators, and implications of the limited-resource effect*

Responses that require self-regulation include
- Controlling thoughts
- Managing emotions
- Overcoming unwanted impulses (e.g., not eating tempting candies because of being on a diet)
- Fixing attention
- Guiding behavior
- Making many choices

Behaviors that are sensitive to depletion of self-regulatory resources include
- Eating among dieters
- Overspending
- Aggression after being provoked
- Sexual impulses
- Intelligent and logical decision making

Interpersonal processes that require self-regulatory resources include
- Self-presentation or impression management
- Kindness in response to a partner's bad behavior
- Dealing with demanding, difficult partners
- Interracial interactions

Moderators of ego depletion include
- Heightened motivation to achieve a goal
- Collectivistic cultural background

Physical indicators of ego depletion include
- Heart-rate variability
- Neural changes using electroencephalograph methods

Mediators of ego depletion include
- Subjective time perception (time perception is elongated—i.e., time moves slowly)
- Blood-glucose levels

Harmful effects of depletion may be counteracted through
- Humor and laughter
- Other positive emotions
- Cash incentives
- Implementation intentions ("if ... then" plans)
- Social goals (e.g., wanting to help people; wanting to be a good relationship partner)

different from the daily exercises shows that the improvements are not due to simply increasing skill or acquiring self-efficacy from practice.

Second, just as athletes begin to conserve their remaining strength when their muscles begin to tire, so do self-controllers when some of their self-regulatory resources have been expended. The severity of behavioral impairment during depletion depends in part on whether the person expects further challenges and demands. When people expect to have to exert self-control later, they will curtail current performance more severely than if no such demands are anticipated (Muraven, Shmueli, & Burkley, 2006).

Third, and consistent with the conservation hypothesis, people can exert self-control despite ego depletion if the stakes are high enough. Offering cash incentives or other motives for good performance counteracts the effects of ego depletion (Muraven & Slessareva, 2003). This may seem surprising but in fact it may be highly adaptive. Given the value and importance of the capacity for self-control, it would be dangerous for a person to lose that capacity completely, and so ego depletion effects may occur because people start conserving their remaining strength. When people do exert themselves on the second task, they deplete the resource even more, as reflected in severe impairments on a third task that they have not anticipated (Muraven et al., 2006).

To be sure, we think there are levels of depletion beyond which people may be unable to control themselves effectively, regardless of what is at stake. Pragmatic and ethical limitations have prevented us from showing this in laboratory work thus far. Again, the muscle analogy is relevant: Mildly tired athletes can indeed manage to summon the strength for a major exertion at decisive moments, but after a certain point fatigue becomes insurmountable.

How far the muscle analogy can be pushed remains an open question. Are there self-control states resembling sprained or injured muscles? One might speculate that burnout or other pathological states resemble the incapacities stemming from muscles that have been abused beyond their normal capacity for recovery.

Multiple lines of work have identified procedures that can moderate or counteract the effects of ego depletion. Inducing a state of positive emotion such as humor seems to have that effect (Tice, Baumeister, Shmueli, & Muraven, 2007). Having implementation intentions—formulating "if–then" statements about how to behave in a situation prior to entering it—seems to be effective most likely because such intentions operate as behavioral plans and guidelines that reduce the need for executive control (Webb & Sheeran, 2003). To be sure, none of these procedures clearly counteracts the depleted state in the sense of replenishing the depleted resource. Rather, they may all operate by inducing the person to expend more of the depleted resource. In contrast, there is some reason to think that replenishing glucose in the bloodstream does actually rectify the depletion by restoring the depleted resource (Gailliot et al., 2007).

PRACTICAL APPLICATIONS

Understanding self-control has potential applications across a broad spectrum of human behavior. At the positive end, self-control is associated with good adjustment, secure attachment, and other favorable psychological states (Tangney et al., 2004). At the negative end, poor self-control is associated with elevated rates of psychopathological complaints and symptoms, as well as increased vulnerability to various substance-abuse and eating disorders (Tangney et al., 2004). Evidence that ego depletion contributes to a variety of problem behaviors—including excessive alcohol consumption, overeating, sexual misbehavior, prejudicial discrimination, and violence—is accumulating.

Intelligent behavior is vital to human success, and it depends partly on self-control. Some processes, such as rote memory, are fairly automatic and independent of executive control, and these appear to be relatively unaffected by depletion. But logical reasoning, extrapolation, and other controlled processes depend on control by the self, and performance on these tasks dips sharply when people are depleted (Schmeichel, Vohs, & Baumeister, 2003).

Interpersonal processes also seem to hinge on self-regulatory operations, with some needing self-control more than others. Richeson and Shelton (2003) reasoned that self-control is needed for discussing delicate, sensitive issues—for instance talking about racial politics with a member of a different race—because one has to avoid saying anything that might give offense or be misinterpreted. The researchers had White participants engage in such a conversation with a Black person; afterwards, the participants showed impaired performance on the Stroop task, a classic measure of self-control in which participants are instructed to say the color in which other color words are printed (e.g., when seeing the word *green* printed in blue, the participant must override the automatic response of saying "green" in order to say "blue"). Having such a conversation with a member of one's own race does not deplete the self and impair subsequent self-control.

Presenting a desired image to others can also tax self-control strength resources (Vohs, Baumeister, & Ciarocco, 2005). After exerting effort at managing the impression they made (e.g., when trying to convey a particular image while making a recording), people showed deficits at self-control. Moreover, and conversely, after people had exerted self-control, they were less effective at managing their behavior so as to make a good impression and in fact sometimes behaved in annoying or off-putting ways.

IMPLICATIONS FOR THEORY

The existence of a single energy resource that is used for a broad range of self-control acts suggests that self theory must move beyond merely cognitive models. The self is more than a network of cognitive schemas: It is a dynamic system able to manage behavior in advanced, complex, and biologically expensive ways.

The use of the body's energy for complex action control extends beyond self-control. Recent studies indicate that the same energy is used for effortful decision making, as well as for active rather than passive responses (e.g., Vohs et al., 2007). These seem to correspond to what laypersons understand as "free will," namely the ability to override impulses, behave morally, show initiative, and behave according to rational choices (Baumeister, in press).

Most broadly, the strength model of self-control offers suggestions about how and why the human self evolved in its current form. The functional purposes of the self almost certainly include managing behavior toward fostering enlightened self-interest and facilitating group membership by garnering social acceptance. Self-control is helpful for both these goals. The role of energy suggests that self-control is a complex, biologically expensive form of behavior. Thus, we may infer that, to enable humans to create and sustain the complicated groups to which they belong, including cultural systems, evolution had to find a way to use the body's energy to control behavior in these advanced and subtle ways. For example, human beings everywhere regulate their behavior according to various rules, such as social norms, moral principles, and laws.

FURTHER DIRECTIONS

A particularly broad and important question is what other forms of behavior (beyond self-control and choice) use this limited resource: How special is this form of mental effort? We noted that success at building self-control through exercises has been inconsistent, so it is also necessary to explore why some regimens work better than others. Finding a reliable way to improve self-control would not only shed light on how the self functions but would also have practical value for therapists, coaches, educators, parents, and many others.

Identifying the biological substrates of self-control depletion (and replenishment) would be another helpful direction for further work. Better understanding of the developmental process would likewise strengthen the theory and make it more applicable to human welfare and problems.

CONCLUDING REMARKS

Psychology can contribute to society by finding ways to enable people to live healthier, more successful, and more satisfying lives. Self-control is a promising avenue to achieve this. It appears to facilitate success in life in many spheres, and, crucially, it appears amenable to improvement. Indeed, self-control can be grouped with intelligence among the (rather few) traits that are known to contribute to success in human life across a broad variety of spheres; yet unlike intelligence, self-control appears amenable to improvement from psychological interventions, even in adulthood. The strength model can illuminate how self-control operates and functions. By building on this knowledge, psychology may be able to improve the mental health and well-being of many people.

Recommended Reading

Baumeister, R.F., Schmeichel, B.J., & Vohs, K.D. (2007). Self-regulation and the executive function: The self as controlling agent. In A. Kruglanski & E.T. Higgins (Eds.), *Social psychology: Handbook of basic principles* (2nd ed., pp. 516–539). New York: Guilford. A recent and thorough overview of the research in a broad context.

Gailliot, M.T., Baumeister, R.F., DeWall, C.N., Maner, J.K., Plant, E.A., & Tice, D.M. et al. (2007). (See References). Reports experiments linking behavioral self-control measures to blood glucose.

Baumeister, R.F., Gailliot, M., DeWall, C.N., & Oaten, M. (2006). (See References). An overview of the research program on self-control with emphasis on personality implications and alternative explanations.

Acknowledgments—The authors gratefully acknowledge research support from the Templeton Foundation.

Note

1. Address correspondence to Roy F. Baumeister, Florida State University, Department of Psychology, 1107 W. Call Street, Tallahassee, FL 32306-4301; e-mail: baumeister@psy.fsu.edu.

References

Baumeister, R.F. (in press). Free will in scientific psychology. *Perspectives on Psychological Science.*

Baumeister, R.F., Bratslavsky, E., Muraven, M., & Tice, D.M. (1998). Ego depletion: Is the active self a limited resource? *Journal of Personality and Social Psychology, 74,* 1252–1265.

Baumeister, R.F., Gailliot, M., DeWall, C.N., & Oaten, M. (2006). Self-regulation and personality: How interventions increase regulatory success, and how depletion moderates the effects of traits on behavior. *Journal of Personality, 74,* 1773–1801.

Baumeister, R.F., Heatherton, T.F., & Tice, D.M. (1994). *Losing control: How and why people fail at self-regulation.* San Diego, CA: Academic Press.

Gailliot, M.T., Baumeister, R.F., DeWall, C.N., Maner, J.K., Plant, E.A., & Tice, D.M., et al. (2007). Self-control relies on glucose as a limited energy source: Willpower is more than a metaphor. *Journal of Personality and Social Psychology, 92,* 325–336.

Gottfredson, M.R., & Hirschi, T. (1990). *A general theory of crime.* Stanford, CA: Stanford University Press.

Muraven, M., Shmueli, D., & Burkley, E. (2006). Conserving self-control strength. *Journal of Personality and Social Psychology, 91,* 524–537.

Muraven, M., & Slessareva, E. (2003). Mechanisms of self-control failure: Motivation and limited resources. *Personality and Social Psychology Bulletin, 29,* 894–906.

Muraven, M., Tice, D.M., & Baumeister, R.F. (1998). Self-control as limited resource: Regulatory depletion patterns. *Journal of Personality and Social Psychology, 74,* 774–789.

Richeson, J.A., & Shelton, J.N. (2003). When prejudice does not pay: Effects of interracial contact on executive function. *Psychological Science, 14,* 287–290.

Schmeichel, B.J., Vohs, K.D., & Baumeister, R.F. (2003). Intellectual performance and ego depletion: Role of the self in logical reasoning and other information processing. *Journal of Personality and Social Psychology, 85,* 33–46.

Tangney, J.P., Baumeister, R.F., & Boone, A.L. (2004). High self-control predicts good adjustment, less pathology, better grades, and interpersonal success. *Journal of Personality, 72,* 271–322.

Tice, D.M., Baumeister, R.F., Shmueli, D., & Muraven, M. (2007). Restoring the self: Positive affect helps improve self-regulation following ego depletion. *Journal of Experimental Social Psychology, 43,* 379–384.

Vohs, K.D., Baumeister, R.F., & Ciarocco, N. (2005). Self-regulation and self-presentation: Regulatory resource depletion impairs impression management and effortful self-presentation depletes regulatory resources. *Journal of Personality and Social Psychology, 88,* 632–657.

Vohs, K.D., Baumeister, R.F., Twenge, J.M., Nelson, N.M., Rawn, C.D., Schmeichel, B.J., & Tice, D.M. (2007) *Making choices impairs subsequent self-control: A limited resource account of decision making, self-regulation, and active initiative.* Manuscript submitted for publication.

Vohs, K.D., & Faber, R.J. (2007). Spent resources: Self-regulatory resource availability affects impulse buying. *Journal of Consumer Research, 33,* 537–547.

Wallace, H.M., & Baumeister, R.F. (2002). The effects of success versus failure feedback on further self-control. *Self and Identity, 1,* 35–41.

Webb, T.L., & Sheeran, P. (2003). Can implementation intentions help to overcome ego-depletion? *Journal of Experimental Social Psychology, 39,* 279–286.

The Perils of Perfectionism in Sports and Exercise

Gordon L. Flett[1]

York University, Toronto, Ontario, Canada

Paul L. Hewitt

University of British Columbia, Vancouver, British Columbia, Canada

Abstract

Perfectionism is a multidimensional personality construct that has been linked with various forms of maladjustment. In this article, we discuss the role of perfectionism as a maladaptive factor in sports and exercise, and we describe a phenomenon we identify as the perfectionism paradox. We note that even though certain sports require athletes to achieve perfect performance outcomes, the tendency to be characterized by perfectionistic personality traits and to be cognitively preoccupied with the attainment of perfection often undermines performance and fosters a sense of dissatisfaction with performance. We review existing findings in the literature on sports and exercise and demonstrate that the extreme orientation that accompanies perfectionism is antithetical to attaining positive outcomes. Finally, future research directions are outlined.

Keywords

perfectionism; anxiety; sports; exercise; self-presentation

Research on perfectionism has increased exponentially over the past two decades. This increased attention has led to an enhanced understanding of the perfectionism construct. For instance, it is now accepted generally that perfectionism is multidimensional, and it is important, both conceptually and empirically, to distinguish the various dimensions of the construct. This multidimensional approach began with the initial work in our laboratory (see Hewitt & Flett, 1991) and in the laboratory of Frost and his associates (Frost, Marten, Lahart, & Rosenblate, 1990). Our Multidimensional Perfectionism Scale (MPS; Hewitt & Flett, 1991) assesses three dimensions of the construct—self-oriented perfectionism (i.e., excessive striving and demanding absolute perfection from the self), other-oriented perfectionism (i.e., demanding perfection from other people), and socially prescribed perfectionism (i.e., the perception that other people demand perfection from oneself). The Frost et al. (1990) Multidimensional Perfectionism Scale (FMPS) assesses six dimensions, including personal standards, organization (i.e., needing to maintain a sense of order), concern over mistakes, doubts about actions, parental expectations, and parental criticism.

Although much has been learned about the perfectionism construct, the field has not been without controversy. The most controversial issue thus far has been whether certain perfectionism dimensions are adaptive rather than maladaptive.

Some authors have concluded that some perfectionism dimensions contribute to positive rather than negative outcomes, and that it is important to distinguish between adaptive perfectionism and maladaptive perfectionism (see Slaney, Rice, & Ashby, 2002). That is, although dimensions such as socially prescribed perfectionism and excessive concern over mistakes have been associated with maladjustment, it has been suggested that other dimensions, such as self-oriented perfectionism and high personal standards, may, in fact, be positive factors (Slaney et al., 2002).

In the current article, we examine the adaptiveness versus maladaptiveness of perfectionism by reviewing findings on the role of perfectionism in sports and exercise. Research and theory on the role of perfectionism in sports and exercise is important in its own right, but it is also evident that research in this area has important implications for the adaptiveness-maladaptiveness issue. We adopt the view, consistent with our previous conceptualizations of perfectionism (Hewitt & Flett, 1991), that perfectionism is primarily a negative factor that contributes to maladaptive outcomes among athletes and exercisers. However, it is clear that this issue is complex because it cannot be denied that many sports require error-free performance in order for athletes to be successful. Nevertheless, we argue that a perfectionism paradox exists—that is, despite the fact there are many sports in which absolute perfection is required, negative, self-defeating outcomes and unhealthy patterns of behavior are evident among those athletes who are characterized by an extreme, perfectionistic personality and who are focused cognitively on attaining perfection.

We present an overview of the literature on perfectionism in sports and exercise and relate existing studies back to our central theme that perfectionism is primarily maladaptive. Several questions are addressed: (a) What motivational orientations underlie perfectionism in athletes? (b) What is the link between perfectionism and self-esteem in athletes? (c) What role do perfectionistic self-presentational concerns play in sports and exercise? We conclude by discussing factors that may protect the perfectionistic athlete from experiencing negative outcomes and by outlining some fundamental themes that need to be explored in the literature on sports and exercise behavior.

PERFECTIONISM, ANXIETY, AND FAILURE ORIENTATION

The initial investigation of dimensions of perfectionism in sports was conducted by Frost and Henderson (1991). A sample of 40 women in varsity athletics completed the FMPS, along with measures assessing sports self-confidence, sports competition anxiety, thoughts before competitions, specific reactions to mistakes during competition, and the presence of a sports success orientation (e.g., "I feel a sense of pride when I play a good game") versus a failure orientation (e.g., "My mistakes usually interfere with my play"). Frost and Henderson found that concern over mistakes, as measured on the FMPS, was associated with several negative outcomes, including anxiety, low confidence, a failure orientation, and negative reactions to mistakes during competition. High personal standards were not associated significantly with the anxiety or self-confidence measures; however, athletes high in personal-standards perfectionism reported difficulty concentrating while performing, and they experienced worries about the reactions of the audience. In addition, high personal standards were associated significantly with both a success orientation and a failure orientation. Thus, it seems that individuals striving for high personal standards have strong reactions to both positive and negative responses from other people.

PERFECTIONISM AND GOAL ORIENTATION IN SPORTS

Unfortunately, there has not been extensive research on perfectionism and motivation in sports; however, important insights were provided in research by Hall, Kerr, and Matthews (1998). They assessed the associations among perfectionism, achievement goals, and competitive anxiety in 119 high school athletes. Participants completed the FMPS and provided ratings of their perceived ability. Anxiety in competitive situations was also assessed. Participants also completed a measure of task orientation (i.e., an emphasis on mastery that is believed to facilitate success) versus ego orientation (i.e., a self-focused, competitive stance that reflects a need to protect vulnerable self-esteem) in sports. Once again, it was found that several perfectionism dimensions, including concern over mistakes, were associated with anxiety. The presence of an ego orientation was associated with high scores on all FMPS subscales, including the personal-standards subscale, although scores on this subscale also had a weaker but significant association with task orientation. Thus, athletes who are extreme perfectionists have a pervasive ego orientation, and this should have debilitating effects if they also harbor doubts about their level of ability.

PERFECTIONISM AND SELF-ESTEEM

Gotwals, Dunn, and Wayment (2003) provided further evidence of the negative aspects of an excessive concern over mistakes. A sample of 87 intercollegiate athletes completed the FMPS, along with measures of general self-esteem, perceived athletic competence, and satisfaction with sports performance. Athletes who had low self-esteem, were dissatisfied with their performance, and gave comparatively low ratings to their competence (relative to the self-ratings of other athletes) tended to be concerned about their mistakes, doubted their actions, and perceived their parents as being critical of them.

Another recent investigation showed that the association between dimensions of perfectionism and self-esteem is quite complex (Koivula, Hassmén, & Fallby, 2002). Nevertheless, among their sample of Swedish elite athletes, Koivula et al. identified a subset of perfectionistic athletes with low self-esteem and a high sense that their self-esteem was contingent on meeting standards, and these athletes had high scores not only on the FMPS subscales assessing concern over mistakes and doubts about actions, but also on the personal-standards subscale. The authors concluded that a lack of success is a severe threat to such athletes, who already are vulnerable and are relatively low in self-esteem.

PERFECTIONISM AND PERFORMANCE SUCCESS VERSUS FAILURE

Empirical research in our laboratory has demonstrated the importance of distinguishing between perfectionistic athletes who experience success and those who experience failure. Perfectionists will be particularly at risk (e.g., susceptible to psychological distress and motivational deficits; see Hewitt & Flett, 2002) to the extent that they are experiencing failure as determined by objective measures or they have developed the perception that they are failing; moreover, a repeated series of failures in ego-involving life domains will have a strong, negative impact. Recent research with a sample of golfers indicates that self-oriented perfectionism is not maladaptive for relatively successful golfers who are performing at a relatively high level, but it is associated with negative thoughts and reactions to mistakes among less successful golfers (Wieczorek, Flett, & Hewitt, 2003). The deleterious effects of performance failure for self-oriented perfectionists were also illustrated by the results of another recent experiment (see Besser, Flett, & Hewitt, 2004). A related issue is whether the perfectionist has a set of skills that make striving for perfection a somewhat realistic goal or an unrealistic goal because he or she is not capable of attaining this absolute goal.

PERFECTIONISM AND SELF-PRESENTATIONAL CONCERNS

Another key consideration when evaluating perfectionism among athletes is the extent to which they are focused excessively on self-presentational issues. Some individuals have a high concern for the impression they make on others, and when they are in social situations, they seek to portray themselves as positively as possible. Excessive self-presentational concerns can contribute to health problems, including eating disorders and a quest for bodily perfection. Although the link between perfectionism and self-presentational concerns in sports and exercise has not been investigated empirically thus far, we have identified an extreme form of perfectionistic self-presentation that may be quite relevant. Certain perfectionists are highly concerned with presenting an image of perfection to other people. Athletes with this tendency should be susceptible to a variety of negative outcomes.

With several of our colleagues, we developed the Perfectionistic Self-Presentation Scale (Hewitt et al., 2003) as a supplement to existing measures of perfectionism. Perfectionistic self-presentation involves striving to create a public image of flawlessness, either by highlighting one's success (i.e., perfectionistic self-promotion) or by minimizing one's mistakes (i.e., nondisplay or nondisclosure of imperfections). Initial research indicates that perfectionistic self-presentation is elevated in patients with eating disorders, and perfectionistic self-presentation accounts for a significant degree of various forms of psychological distress, including anxiety, depression, and negative feelings about physical appearance (see Hewitt et al., 2003).

The discovery that some individuals engage in extreme forms of perfectionistic self-presentation has a number of implications for research on sports and exercise behavior. For instance, athletes who are overly focused on perfectionistic self-presentation should be extremely self-conscious, anxious individuals who are preoccupied with public appearance and body image. Similarly, various maladaptive patterns are likely in exercisers. Some individuals may attempt to satisfy their needs for perfectionistic self-promotion by engaging in excessive, compulsive exercise. Indeed, our initial study of regular exercisers confirmed that the various dimensions of perfectionistic self-presentation are associated with compulsive exercise (Flett, Pole-Langdon, & Hewitt, 2003). These new data qualify earlier findings linking excessive exercise with dimensions of perfectionism such as self-oriented and socially prescribed perfectionism in patients with anorexia nervosa, competitive male bodybuilders, and university women (see Davis & Scott-Robertson, 2000; McLaren, Gauvin, & White, 2001) by suggesting that individual differences in perfectionistic self-presentation play a more deleterious role in exercise behavior and excessive striving than do general dimensions of perfectionism.

THE PERILS OF PERFECTIONISM:
THE ROLE OF INTERVENING FACTORS

As we noted earlier, a central tenet that has guided our work on perfectionism and maladjustment is that perfectionism renders individuals vulnerable to negative outcomes such as depression if they experience personal failure (see Hewitt & Flett, 2002). By extension, perfectionists who experience success are less likely to experience distress. Additional research has investigated factors that influence the link between perfectionism and maladjustment. Key factors that have been identified include coping styles and perceived problem-solving ability (see Hewitt & Flett, 2002). Perfectionists are at greater risk if their perfectionism is accompanied by maladaptive forms of coping (i.e., avoidance-focused coping and emotion-focused coping involving rumination and self-blame) and negative appraisals of problem-solving ability. Perceptions of self-efficacy and perceptions of self-control are also potentially important influences on the link between reactions to performance outcomes and both self-oriented and socially prescribed perfectionism. At present, research on how perfectionism combines with stress and maladaptive coping to produce negative outcomes such as psychological distress has focused on general samples of psychiatric patients and university students, and little empirical research has evaluated intervening factors in athletes.

Perfectionistic athletes will be protected, to some degree, from the "perils of perfectionism" if they experience success and if they have developed a proactive, task-oriented approach to coping with difficulties and setbacks. A key aspect of the coping process for these athletes is to develop a sense of flexibility, so that they adjust their goals in accordance with situational demands and current levels of personal functioning. Moreover, the research we have summarized indicates that perfectionistic athletes with low levels of ego orientation, a sense of self-efficacy, and relatively low sensitivity to failure should be relatively resilient. In contrast, the inherent risks are higher for perfectionistic athletes who are defensively focused on mistakes and characterized by excessive fears of failure and self-doubts.

As we have noted, another key factor that needs to be considered when evaluating the perils associated with perfectionism is the individual's actual level of skill. Demands for perfection that emanate from the self or other people seem particularly irrational when they are imposed on an athlete who simply lacks the ability to approximate perfectionistic standards. Insufficient ability should magnify feelings of dissatisfaction. Athletes who overstrive to overcompensate for deficits in ability should feel particularly dissatisfied and should be especially prone to the negative effects of perfectionism.

DIRECTIONS FOR FUTURE RESEARCH

The potential intervening factors that we have outlined have not been evaluated in the context of perfectionism in sports, and research in this area is needed. In this section, we outline four other important issues that merit investigation. Most notably, there are virtually no data available on how perfectionistic athletes cope with injuries or with diminished capabilities as they age. Presumably, the all-or-none approach that characterizes perfectionism should be a deleterious factor when an athlete is seeking to cope with such challenges, and this could lead to burnout and overtraining. Another important issue that deserves attention is the impact of perfectionistic demands on children and adolescents in sports programs. How do they cope with unrealistic pressures to be perfect? A third issue concerns how athletes respond to coaches with exceptionally high levels of other-oriented perfectionism. At what point do the perfectionistic demands of these coaches contribute to a loss of motivation in the athletes? Finally, the recent creation of sports-specific measures of perfectionism (e.g., Dunn, Causgrove Dunn, & Syrotuik, 2002) leads inevitably to questions about the predictive usefulness of general versus specific measures of perfectionism in sports and exercise contexts.

CONCLUDING REMARKS

In this article, we have summarized contemporary research on perfectionism in athletes and exercisers, and concluded that perfectionism is primarily maladaptive. Moreover, the deleterious aspects of perfectionism in this context extend to dimensions (e.g., self-oriented perfectionism) that have been identified as potentially adaptive by other researchers in other contexts. We have also outlined several factors that may mitigate the association between perfectionism and maladaptive outcomes in athletes.

We conclude by noting the possibility that scholars who disagree with our position may point to several world-class elite athletes who have a demonstrated history of extreme perfectionism (e.g., Bobby Jones, John McEnroe, and Serena Williams); perfectionism seems to have worked for these individuals. However, often such athletes have documented forms of distress that can be attributed directly to their perfectionistic ways, and success emerges only following the development of emotional self-control. This observation underscores the value of a complex research strategy that examines perfectionism in conjunction with other factors of potential significance.

Recommended Reading

Anshel, M.H., & Eom, H.-J. (2003). Exploring the dimensions of perfectionism in sport. *International Journal of Sport Psychology, 34,* 255–271.

Dunn, J.G.H., Causgrove Dunn, J., & Syrotuik, D.G. (2002). (See References)

Flett, G.L., & Hewitt, P.L. (2004). The cognitive and treatment aspects of perfectionism: Introduction to the special issue. *Journal of Rational-Emotive and Cognitive-Behavior Therapy, 22,* 229–236.

Haase, A.M., Prapavessis, H., & Owens, R.G. (2002). Perfectionism, social physique anxiety and disordered eating: A comparison of male and female elite athletes. *Psychology of Sport and Exercise, 3,* 209–222.

Hewitt, P.L., Flett, G.L., Sherry, S.B., Habke, M., Parkin, M., Lam, R.W., McMurtry, B., Ediger, E., Fairlie, P., & Stein, M. (2003). (See References)

Acknowledgments—Preparation of this article was supported by a Canada Research Chair in Personality and Health awarded to the first author and by operating grants from the Social Sciences and Humanities Research Council of Canada.

Note

1. Address correspondence to Gordon L. Flett, 214 BSB, Department of Psychology, York University, 4700 Keele St., Toronto, Ontario, M3J 1P3, Canada; e-mail: gflett@yorku.ca.

References

Besser, A., Flett, G.L., & Hewitt, P.L. (2004). Perfectionism, cognition, and affect in response to performance failure versus success. *Journal of Rational-Emotive and Cognitive-Behavior Therapy, 22,* 297–324.

Davis, C., & Scott-Robertson, L. (2000). A psychological comparison of females with anorexia nervosa and competitive male bodybuilders: Body shape ideals in the extreme. *Eating Behaviors, 1,* 33–46.

Dunn, J.G.H., Causgrove Dunn, J., & Syrotuik, D.G. (2002). Relationship between multidimensional perfectionism and goal orientations in sport. *Journal of Sport and Exercise Psychology, 24,* 376–395.

Flett, G.L., Pole-Langdon, L., & Hewitt, P.L. (2003). *Trait perfectionism and perfectionistic self-presentation in compulsive exercise.* Unpublished manuscript, York University, Toronto, Ontario, Canada.

Frost, R.O., & Henderson, K.J. (1991). Perfectionism and reactions to athletic competition. *Journal of Sport and Exercise Psychology, 13,* 323–335.

Frost, R.O., Marten, P., Lahart, C., & Rosenblate, R. (1990). The dimensions of perfectionism. *Cognitive Therapy and Research, 14,* 449–468.

Gotwals, J.K., Dunn, J.G.H., & Wayment, H.A. (2003). An examination of perfectionism and self-esteem in intercollegiate athletes. *Journal of Sport Behavior, 26,* 17–38.

Hall, H.K., Kerr, A.W., & Matthews, J. (1998). Precompetitive anxiety in sport: The contribution of achievement goals and perfectionism. *Journal of Sport and Exercise Psychology, 20,* 194–217.

Hewitt, P.L., & Flett, G.L. (1991). Perfectionism in the self and social contexts: Conceptualization, assessment, and association with psychopathology. *Journal of Personality and Social Psychology, 60,* 456–470.

Hewitt, P.L., & Flett, G.L. (2002). Perfectionism and stress in psychopathology. In G.L. Flett & P.L. Hewitt (Eds.), *Perfectionism: Theory, research, and treatment* (pp. 255–284). Washington, DC: American Psychological Association.

Hewitt, P.L., Flett, G.L., Sherry, S.B., Habke, M., Parkin, M., Lam, R.W., McMurtry, B., Ediger, E., Fairlie, P., & Stein, M. (2003). The interpersonal expression of perfection: Perfectionistic self-presentation and psychological distress. *Journal of Personality and Social Psychology, 84,* 1303–1325.

Koivula, N., Hassmén, P., & Fallby, J. (2002). Self-esteem and perfectionism in elite athletes: Effects on competitive anxiety and self-confidence. *Personality and Individual Differences, 32,* 865–875.

McLaren, L., Gauvin, L., & White, D. (2001). The role of perfectionism and excessive commitment to exercise in explaining dietary restraint: Replication and extension. *International Journal of Eating Disorders, 29,* 307–313.

Slaney, R.B., Rice, K.G., & Ashby, J.S. (2002). A programmatic approach to measuring perfectionism: The Almost Perfect Scales. In G.L. Flett & P.L. Hewitt (Eds.), *Perfectionism: Theory, research, and treatment* (pp. 63–88). Washington, DC: American Psychological Association.

Wieczorek, J., Flett, G.L., & Hewitt, P.L. (2003). *Dimensions of perfectionism, anxiety, and coping in successful versus unsuccessful golfers.* Unpublished manuscript, York University, Toronto, Ontario, Canada.

This article has been reprinted as it originally appeared in *Current Directions in Psychological Science*. Citation information for this article as originally published appears above.

Contingencies of Self-Worth

Jennifer Crocker[1] and Katherine M. Knight

University of Michigan

Abstract

We argue that the importance of self-esteem lies in what people believe they need to be or do to have worth as a person. These contingencies of self-worth are both sources of motivation and areas of psychological vulnerability. In domains of contingent self-worth, people pursue self-esteem by attempting to validate their abilities and qualities. This pursuit of self-esteem, we argue, has costs to learning, relationships, autonomy, self-regulation, and mental and physical health. We suggest alternatives to this costly pursuit of self-esteem.

Keywords

self-esteem; motivation; vulnerability; self-regulation; mental health

High self-esteem is often regarded as the holy grail of psychological health—the key to happiness, success, and popularity. Low self-esteem, on the other hand, is blamed for societal problems ranging from poor school achievement to drug and alcohol abuse. However, this rosy view of high self-esteem has detractors who argue that the objective benefits of high self-esteem are small and limited. Although high self-esteem produces pleasant feelings and enhanced initiative, it does not cause high academic achievement, good job performance, or leadership, nor does low self-esteem cause violence, smoking, drinking, taking drugs, or becoming sexually active at an early age (Baumeister, Campbell, Krueger, & Vohs, 2003). Many parents, educators, and policymakers are confused, with some holding steadfastly to the idea that low self-esteem is the root of much, if not all, evil, and others concluding that self-esteem is, at best, irrelevant.

Although high self-esteem does little to cause positive outcomes in life, and low self-esteem is not to blame for most social and personal problems, we disagree that self-esteem is irrelevant. People want to believe that they are worthy and valuable human beings, and this desire drives their behavior (Pyszczynski, Greenberg, Solomon, Arndt, & Schimel, 2004). We suggest that the importance of self-esteem lies less in whether it is high or low, and more in what people believe they need to be or do to have value and worth as a person—what we call contingencies of self-worth.

SELF-ESTEEM AND CONTINGENT SELF-WORTH

Over a century ago, William James (James, 1890) suggested that self-esteem is both a stable trait and an unstable state; momentary feelings of self-esteem fluctuate around a person's typical or trait level in response to good and bad events. James also noted that people are selective about what events affect their self-esteem: They invest their self-esteem in—that is, are ego-involved in succeeding at—some things, whereas their success at other endeavors has no impact on their self-esteem. Instability of self-esteem is the result of being ego-involved in events, or having contingent self-worth (Deci & Ryan, 1995; Kernis, 2003).

Crocker and Wolfe (2001) proposed that good and bad events in domains of contingent self-worth raise or lower momentary feelings of self-esteem around a person's typical or trait level of self-esteem, and these fluctuations in state self-esteem have motivational consequences. Increases in self-esteem feel good, and decreases in self-esteem feel bad. Therefore, regardless of whether people typically have high or low self-esteem, they seek the emotional high associated with success in domains of contingent self-worth and strive to avoid the emotional lows that accompany failure in these domains. Consequently, contingencies of self-worth regulate behavior.

Contingencies of self-worth also shape long-term and short-term goals. People want to prove that they are a success, not a failure, in domains of contingent self-worth, because that would mean they are worthy and valuable; in other words, they have self-validation goals in these domains (Crocker & Park, 2004). When they are not sure that success is possible or failure can be avoided, they will disengage from the task, deciding it doesn't matter, rather than suffer the loss of self-esteem that accompanies failure in these domains.

Students who base their self-esteem on their academic accomplishments typically have self-validation goals in this domain, viewing their schoolwork as an opportunity to demonstrate their intelligence. Because failure in domains of contingency threatens self-esteem, people try to avoid failure by increasing effort; if they are still uncertain of success, they may abandon their self-validation goal and become unmotivated, or prepare excuses that will soften the blow to self-esteem in case they fail. Making excuses or blaming others are defensive maneuvers by which people deflect the threat to self-esteem when they do fail. When failure in domains of contingency cannot be dismissed with defensive responses, self-esteem decreases. Consequently, contingencies of self-worth are both a source of motivation and a psychological vulnerability (Crocker, 2002).

We have investigated the domains in which college students commonly invest their self-esteem, including appearance, others' approval, outperforming others, academics, family support, virtue, and religious faith or God's love (Crocker, Luhtanen, Cooper, & Bouvrette, 2003). Our research indicates that contingencies of self-worth shape students' emotions, thoughts, and behavior. In a sample of college seniors applying to graduate school, the more students based their self-esteem on their academic success, the higher their self-esteem was on days they were admitted to graduate school and the lower their self-esteem was on days they were rejected (see Fig. 1; Crocker, Sommers, & Luhtanen, 2002). The more students' self-esteem is contingent on their academic success, the more it decreases on days they receive worse-than-expected grades; this is particularly true for women majoring in engineering, who face negative stereotypes about their ability (Crocker, Karpinski, Quinn, & Chase, 2003). Contingencies of self-worth are strongly related to the goal of validating one's abilities in the domain of contingency (Crocker & Park, 2004), and students report spending

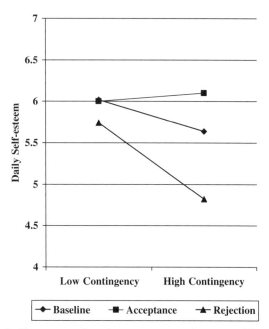

Fig. 1. Students' self-esteem on days they were accepted or rejected by a graduate school (compared to a baseline) as a function of how contingent their self-esteem was on academic success.

more time on activities that are related to their contingencies of self-worth (Crocker, Luhtanen, et al., 2003).

This approach extends or challenges existing models of self-esteem in several ways. First, our argument that the importance of self-esteem lies in what it is contingent upon stands in contrast to decades of research focused on whether trait self-esteem is high or low. Furthermore, we are not simply shifting the focus to whether people have high or low self-esteem in specific domains such as academics or athletics, but rather suggesting that regardless of people's level of domain-specific self-esteem, contingent self-worth in these domains has predictable consequences. Although our research is complementary to research that focuses on the stability of self-esteem over time (Kernis, 2003), we extend that work by showing that instability of self-esteem results from experiencing positive and negative events in those domains in which self-esteem is contingent. Other scholars have argued that people vary as to whether their self-esteem is contingent or not (Deci & Ryan, 2005; Kernis, 2003). We argue that nearly everyone has contingencies of self-worth but that people differ as to what their self-esteem is contingent on. Basing self-esteem on external factors such as appearance, others' approval, or academic achievement has more negative consequences than basing it on internal factors such as virtue or God's love. And in contrast to most researchers who argue that self-esteem is a fundamental human need that people need to pursue (Pyszczynski et al., 2004; Sheldon, 2004), we argue that pursuing self-esteem by attempting to prove that one is a success in domains of contingency is costly (Crocker & Park, 2004).

THE COSTS OF PURSUING SELF-ESTEEM

Successful pursuit of self-esteem has short-term emotional benefits, such as increased happiness and decreased anxiety (Pyszczynski et al., 2004). The emotional boosts associated with success in domains of contingency are pleasant but do not satisfy fundamental human needs for learning, relatedness, and autonomy. Rather, we think of boosts to self-esteem as analogous to sugar: tasty but not nutritious. Indeed, the boosts to self-esteem that accompany success in contingent domains can, we think, become addictive, and pursuing self-esteem by attempting to validate one's abilities has costs for learning, relatedness, autonomy, self-regulation, and, over time, physical and mental health (Crocker & Park, 2004).

Costs to Learning

When people have self-validation goals, mistakes, failures, criticism, and negative feedback are self-threats rather than opportunities to learn and improve. Consequently, when self-esteem is contingent on a domain, people either adopt performance goals to succeed and avoid failure, or they disengage entirely from the endeavor. Focusing on performance increases stress and anxiety, which can undermine learning, whereas disengagement from a domain also leads to a withdrawal of effort, which is essential to learning.

Costs to Autonomy

Autonomy refers to the sense of choice, or being the causal origin of one's behavior. When autonomy is low, people feel pressured by internal or external demands, expectations, and standards—they feel that they are "at the mercy" of people and events. When self-esteem is contingent, autonomy tends to be low. As Deci and his colleagues suggest, "The type of ego involvement in which one's 'worth' is on the line—in which one's self-esteem is contingent upon an outcome—is an example of internally controlling regulation that results from introjection. One is behaving because one feels one has to and not because one wants to, and this regulation is accompanied by the experience of pressure and tension" (Deci, Eghrari, Patrick, & Leone, 1994, p. 121).

Costs to Relationships

Pursuing self-esteem interferes with establishing and maintaining mutually supportive relationships, because people become focused on themselves at the expense of others' needs and feelings (Crocker & Park, 2004). Relationships become a means of validating the self, rather than an opportunity to give to and support others.

Costs to Self-Regulation

The pursuit of self-esteem interferes with achieving important goals both because efforts to protect self-esteem can undermine success and because the intense emotions associated with failure in contingent domains can disrupt efforts to achieve goals. The more contingent their self-worth is on academics, the more time students spend working on an easy verbal task, but the less time they spend working on a difficult verbal task; apparently, more contingent students want to work on tasks that make them feel accomplished and, hence, worthy.

Costs to Mental Health

The stress and anxiety associated with contingent self-esteem may also affect mental health. When people experience positive and negative events in domains of contingency, their self-esteem fluctuates over time; these fluctuations in self-esteem predict increases in symptoms of depression (Crocker, Karpinski, et al., 2003). We hypothesize that these fluctuations in self-esteem are accompanied by elevated cortisol levels triggered by the stress response, which is strongly linked to the development of depression.

Costs to Physical Health

Contingencies of self-worth can affect physical health directly, through stress, and indirectly, through self-destructive behavior. For example, college freshmen who base their self-esteem on their physical appearance report greater levels of alcohol consumption, drug use, unsafe sexual practices, and binge drinking (Crocker, 2002), all of which can affect physical health over time.

Do Some Contingencies Have More Costs?

The costs of pursuing self-esteem depend on what people think they need to be or do to have worth and value. Basing self-esteem on external contingencies of self-worth, such as appearance or others' approval, requires continual validation from others. Consequently, people who base their self-esteem on external sources may more chronically adopt self-validation goals and consequently experience greater costs (Crocker & Park, 2004). In a longitudinal study of college freshmen, external contingencies of self-worth at the start of college were associated with more problems such as binge drinking and symptoms of disordered eating during the freshman year, whereas internal contingencies, such as virtue or religious faith, were associated with lower levels of these problems. Thus, it matters how one pursues self-esteem. More research is needed to identify why this is the case and to find out whether people with external contingencies have chronic self-validation goals that account for these findings.

ALTERNATIVES

If the pursuit of self-esteem is costly, what is the alternative? One solution might be to replace self-validation goals with learning goals. Priming incremental theories of ability (i.e., exposing people to the idea that intelligence can be improved) eliminated the drops in self-esteem that usually accompany failure in a contingent domain (Niiya, Crocker, & Bartmess, 2004). However, incremental theories of ability do not eliminate concerns with self-esteem; rather, they shift the conditions under which failure threatens self-esteem. Specifically, Niiya and Crocker

(2004) found that, relative to less contingent students or students who do not believe that improvement is possible, highly contingent incremental theorists practice less when an upcoming task is difficult, presumably because practice followed by failure suggests lack of ability, and for highly contingent students, this implies they are worthless.

We think that adopting goals that are good for others as well as for the self may lessen the costs of contingent self-esteem. For example, instead of focusing on achieving success to boost self-esteem, focusing on how success at one's goals can contribute to others may reduce the costs of contingent self-esteem for learning, relationships, autonomy, self-regulation, and mental and physical health.

CONCLUSION

Recently, in a backlash against the self-esteem movement, researchers have suggested that rather than trying to raise self-esteem by giving indiscriminate praise or ensuring that every child receives an award or trophy, parents, educators, and athletic coaches should encourage "warranted" self-esteem, based on actual accomplishments. We think their approach validates the idea that some children deserve high self-esteem whereas others do not, and encourages the development of contingent self-esteem. Contingent self-worth is an ineffective source of motivation; although boosts to self-esteem feel good, they can become addictive, requiring ever greater success to avoid feelings of worthlessness. The resulting relentless quest for self-esteem may be narrowing and limiting, and choices may be guided by their implications for self-esteem rather than by more essential goals. Rather than trying to raise self-esteem by helping children find domains of contingency in which they can succeed, parents and educators may help children more by focusing on what they want to contribute, create, or accomplish and what they need to learn or improve in themselves to do so.

This research has implications for the treatment of depression and perhaps other disorders. Ultimately, people might benefit from shifting their motivational "driver" from self-esteem to contribution goals that are larger than the self. Helping people identify where they have invested their self-esteem and how such investment creates costs to their relationships, learning, feelings of autonomy, and ability to accomplish their goals is a crucial step in making this motivational shift, in our view.

Research on contingencies of self-worth is still in its infancy; much research examining the costs of contingencies of self-worth relative to other sources of motivation needs to be done. Developmental psychologists could explore how these contingencies develop and change across the lifespan. To what extent are contingencies of self-worth related to early attachment experience, traumatic childhood events, parenting styles, and peer influences? Cultural psychologists could examine whether there are cultural differences in contingencies of self-worth, and whether the consequences of contingent self-worth differ across cultures. The concern with validating self-worth might be a very Western, or even North American, phenomenon. Finally, research could explore how to intervene to reduce the costs of contingencies of self-worth. Are there learning orientations that reduce vulnerability of contingent self-esteem and enable people to exert effort on difficult tasks in contingent domains without protecting the self from the possibility of failure? Do goals that are larger than the self, such as contribution goals, reduce the costs of contingent self-esteem? Shifting from a focus on level of self-esteem to the contingencies on which self-esteem depends may yield new insights into the importance of self-esteem in people's lives.

Recommended Reading

Baumeister, R.F., Campbell, J.D., Krueger, J.I., & Vohs, K.D. (2003). (See References)
Crocker, J., & Park, L.E. (2004). (See References)
Crocker, J., & Wolfe, C.T. (2001). (See References)
Pyszczynski, T., Greenberg, J., Solomon, S., Arndt, J., & Schimel, J. (2004). (See References)

Note

1. Address correspondence to Jennifer Crocker, Department of Psychology, University of Michigan, Ann Arbor, MI 48109-1109; e-mail: jcrocker@umich.edu.

References

Baumeister, R.F., Campbell, J.D., Krueger, J.I., & Vohs, K.D. (2003). Does high self-esteem cause better performance, interpersonal success, happiness, or healthier lifestyles? *Psychological Science in the Public Interest, 4,* 1–44.
Crocker, J. (2002). Contingencies of self-worth: Implications for self-regulation and psychological vulnerability. *Self and Identity, 1,* 143–149.
Crocker, J., Karpinski, A., Quinn, D.M., & Chase, S. (2003). When grades determine self-worth: Consequences of contingent self-worth for male and female engineering and psychology majors. *Journal of Personality and Social Psychology, 85,* 507–516.
Crocker, J., Luhtanen, R., Cooper, M.L., & Bouvrette, S.A. (2003). Contingencies of self-worth in college students: Measurement and theory. *Journal of Personality and Social Psychology, 85,* 894–908.
Crocker, J., & Park, L.E. (2004). The costly pursuit of self-esteem. *Psychological Bulletin, 130,* 392–414.
Crocker, J., Sommers, S.R., & Luhtanen, R.K. (2002). Hopes dashed and dreams fulfilled: Contingencies of self-worth and admissions to graduate school. *Personality and Social Psychology Bulletin, 28,* 1275–1286.
Crocker, J., & Wolfe, C.T. (2001). Contingencies of self-worth. *Psychological Review, 108,* 593–623.
Deci, E.L., Eghrari, H., Patrick, B.C., & Leone, D.R. (1994). Facilitating internalization: The self-determination theory perspective. *Journal of Personality, 62,* 119–141.
Deci, E.L., & Ryan, R.M. (1995). Human autonomy: The basis for true self-esteem. In M.H. Kernis (Ed.), *Efficacy, agency, and self-esteem* (pp. 31–49). New York: Plenum.
James, W. (1890). *The principles of psychology* (Vol. 1). Cambridge, MA: Harvard University Press.
Kernis, M.H. (2003). Toward a conceptualization of optimal self-esteem. *Psychological Inquiry, 14,* 1–26.
Niiya, Y., Crocker, J., & Bartmess, E. (2004). From vulnerability to resilience: Learning orientations buffer contingent self-esteem from failure. *Psychological Science, 15,* 801–805.
Pyszczynski, T., Greenberg, J., Solomon, S., Arndt, J., & Schimel, J. (2004). Why do people need self-esteem? A theoretical and empirical review. *Psychological Bulletin, 130,* 435–468.
Sheldon, K.M. (2004). The benefits of a "sidelong" approach to self-esteem need satisfaction: A comment on Crocker and Park. *Psychological Bulletin, 130,* 421–424.

Section 1: Critical Thinking Questions

1. Do you agree that "willpower" is like a muscle, which must be rested after use? Or, might this metaphor be more misleading than revealing? If you agree with the muscle metaphor, how can the muscle be exercised and strengthened? How should we manage our goal-pursuits so that we get the most out of our self-regulatory strength?

2. Perfectionism and contingent self-esteem seem to create more problems than they solve. Where do these tendencies come from—are they taught by the environment, or are we born with them? Can you think of situations when these two traits would be beneficial, or think of counter-strategies that would prevent their "costs?"

This article has been reprinted as it originally appeared in *Current Directions in Psychological Science*. Citation information for this article as originally published appears above.

Section 2: Social Motivation

This section deals with *social motivation*. Of course, the goals that one sets or the self-esteem one tries to achieve (considered in the first section) may also have social components. But, this section's articles address motives that are specifically social, considering both the causes and consequences of these motives. The first article (by Jost and Hunyady) describes research on the *system justification* motive, in which people try to rationalize and defend the status quo. This apparently universal motive helps explain why people might endorse social or political values that go against their own best interest—because it is too upsetting to believe that the system that we all rely on has problems. Jost's research program has been controversial, because of its implication that philosophy of political conservativism is based more on personal insecurities than upon principled cognition. Readers can, of course, make up their own minds on these issues. In the second article, Borman addresses a more positive topic: *Organizational citizenship*. Some people go "above and beyond the call of duty" in the workplace—when and why does this happen, and how can it be further encouraged? Borman considers a variety of perspectives on these questions, including characteristics of the company, the workplace, the supervisor, the person being supervised, and the task being performed. Students might ask themselves if they will be "good organizational citizens" in their own future careers.

The third and fourth articles take an evolutionary perspective upon social motivation. McCullough, Kimeldorf, and Cohen suggest that human beings' unique motivation to help one another (reciprocal altruism) is enabled by the feelings of *gratitude* we each experience after somebody helps us. These feelings serve two purposes: motivating us to thank the person, delivering them an immediate small reward, and motivating us to repay the favor later on, in a "you scratch my back, I'll scratch yours" dynamic. Although this article focuses on an emotion (gratitude) and could have gone in the emotions section of the reader, I put it in the social motivation section because the feeling of gratitude serves to reinforce a very beneficial social motivation—to help others. The fourth article by Gangestad, Thornhill, and Garver-Apgar may surprise many readers, because it shows that the *sexual motivations* of both males and females change when females are in the fertile phase of their cycles. Women become more interested in "masculine" features and can be tempted to stray from their existing relationships, and men become more jealous and protective of their existing relationships, but also more likely to stray towards fertile women outside their relationships. Typically, neither sex is aware of these tendencies. Although this article could have gone in the next section on "non-conscious influences on motivation," I put it here because sexual motivation is so fundamentally social.

Antecedents and Consequences of System-Justifying Ideologies

John T. Jost[1]
New York University

Orsolya Hunyady
Adelphi University

Abstract

According to system justification theory, there is a psychological motive to defend and justify the status quo. There are both dispositional antecedents (e.g., need for closure, openness to experience) and situational antecedents (e.g., system threat, mortality salience) of the tendency to embrace system-justifying ideologies. Consequences of system justification sometimes differ for members of advantaged versus disadvantaged groups, with the former experiencing increased and the latter decreased self-esteem, well-being, and in-group favoritism. In accordance with the palliative function of system justification, endorsement of such ideologies is associated with reduced negative affect for everyone, as well as weakened support for social change and redistribution of resources.

Keywords

system justification; ideology; conservatism; status quo

In the wake of the 2004 U.S. presidential election, the satirical newspaper *The Onion* ran the following headline: "Nation's Poor Win Election for Nation's Rich" (November 11–17, 2004). The accompanying article contained a fictitious quote from the incredulous winner, President Bush, who observed that "The alliance between the tiny fraction at the top of the pyramid and the teeming masses of mouth-breathers at its enormous base has never been stronger. We have an understanding, them and us. They help us stay rich, and in return, we help them stay poor. No matter what naysayers may think, the system works" (p. 10). For many readers, this parody summarized well the apparent irrationality involved in members of disadvantaged groups' support for conservative ideology and the societal status quo.

The failure of self-interest models to explain ideology and public opinion has led political observers and analysts to search for better explanations. To investigate how and why people accept and maintain the social systems that affect them, we have developed system justification theory (Jost, Banaji, & Nosek, 2004; Jost & Hunyady, 2002). To date, the theory has shed light on such paradoxical phenomena as working-class conservatism (Jost, Glaser, Kruglanski, & Sulloway, 2003), increased commitment to institutional authorities and meritocratic ideology among the poor (Jost, Pelham, Sheldon, & Sullivan, 2003), idealization of the capitalist system (Jost, Blount, Pfeffer, & Hunyady, 2003), and minority-group members' conscious and unconscious preferences for members of majority groups (Jost, Pelham, & Carvallo, 2002).

System justification theory holds that people are motivated to justify and rationalize the way things are, so that existing social, economic, and political arrangements tend to be perceived as fair and legitimate.[2] We postulate that there is, as with virtually all other psychological motives (e.g., self-enhancement, cognitive consistency), both (a) a general motivational tendency to rationalize the status quo and (b) substantial variation in the expression of that tendency due to situational and dispositional factors. Thus, members of disadvantaged as well as advantaged groups would be expected to engage in system justification (at least to some degree) even at considerable cost to themselves and to fellow group members.

TYPES OF SYSTEM-JUSTIFYING IDEOLOGIES

There are a number of ideologies that people adopt to justify the status quo in our society. Over the years, researchers have identified several distinct but related system-justifying ideologies, including the Protestant work ethic, meritocratic ideology, fair market ideology, economic system justification, belief in a just world, power distance, social dominance orientation, opposition to equality, right-wing authoritarianism, and political conservatism. These ideologies are listed and described in Table 1; some focus purely on social and cultural issues, whereas others concern economic matters. The fact that these belief systems reliably correlate with one another—at least in Western capitalist societies—suggests that they may serve a similar ideological function, namely to legitimize existing social arrangements (e.g., Jost, Blount, et al., 2003; Jost & Thompson, 2000; Sidanius & Pratto, 1999). In this article, we will review evidence indicating that these system-justifying ideologies (a) share similar cognitive and motivational antecedents and (b) produce similar consequences for individuals, groups, and systems.

Under a dramatically different socio-economic system than in North America and Western Europe (a system such as communism, for example), the contents of system-justifying ideologies would differ, but the social and psychological processes would be similar. That is, we expect that many of the antecedents of procapitalist ideology in the West would be the same as antecedents of procommunist ideology under a communist regime (see Kossowska & van Hiel, 2003). In both contexts, people tend to anchor on the status quo and are prone to exaggerating the fairness and legitimacy of their own system. Because most of the research to date on the antecedents and consequences of system-justifying ideologies has been conducted in Western, capitalist societies, this is the context that provides the empirical foundation for our conclusions.

ANTECEDENTS AND CONSEQUENCES
OF SYSTEM JUSTIFICATION

Why would people legitimize and support social arrangements that conflict with their own self-interest? There are hedonic benefits to minimizing the unpredictable, unjust, and oppressive aspects of social reality. As Lerner (1980) put it, "People want to and have to believe they live in a just world so that they can go

Table 1. *System-justifying ideologies, their descriptive contents, and illustrative references*

Ideology	Descriptive content	Sample illustrative reference(s)
Protestant work ethic	People have a moral responsibility to work hard and avoid leisure activities; hard work is a virtue and is its own reward.	Jost & Hunyady (2002)
Meritocratic ideology	The system rewards individual ability and motivation, so success is an indicator of personal deservingness.	Jost, Pelham, et al. (2003)
Fair market ideology	Market-based procedures and outcomes are not only efficient but are inherently fair, legitimate, and just.	Jost, Blount, et al. (2003)
Economic system justification	Economic inequality is natural, inevitable, and legitimate; economic outcomes are fair and deserved.	Jost & Thompson (2000)
Belief in a just world	People typically get what they deserve and deserve what they get; with regard to outcomes, what "is" is what "ought" to be.	Jost & Burgess (2000); Lerner (1980)
Power distance	Inequality is a natural and desirable feature of the social order; large power differences are acceptable and legitimate.	Jost, Blount, et al. (2003)
Social dominance orientation	Some groups are superior to others; group-based hierarchy is a good thing.	Jost & Thompson (2000); Sidanius & Pratto (1999)
Opposition to equality	Increased social and economic equality is unattainable and undesirable; it would be detrimental for society.	Jost & Thompson (2000); Kluegel & Smith (1986)
Right-wing authoritarianism	People should follow conventional traditions and established authorities and stop getting rebellious ideas.	Altemeyer (1998); Jost, Glaser, et al. (2003)
Political conservatism	Traditional institutions in society should be preserved; social and economic inequality is acceptable and natural.	Jost, Glaser, et al. (2003)

about their daily lives with a sense of trust, hope, and confidence in their future" (p. 14). But there are also social and political costs of system justification, insofar as people who rationalize the status quo are less likely to improve upon it. Many people who lived under feudalism, the Crusades, slavery, communism, apartheid, and the Taliban believed that their systems were imperfect but morally defensible and, in many cases, better than the alternatives they could envision. Popular support helped prolong those regimes, much as it helps prolong our current system. In this section, we first consider in greater detail the factors (both dispositional and situational) that make system-justifying ideologies appealing. Then we summarize the ramifications of these ideologies—both favorable and unfavorable—for individuals, groups, and the system as a whole.

Antecedents of System Justification

As with many psychological tendencies, there are both dispositional and situational sources of variation in the expression of system justification. Several are listed in Table 2. People who possess heightened needs to manage uncertainty and threat are especially likely to embrace conservative, system-justifying ideologies (including right-wing authoritarianism, social dominance orientation, and economic system justification). More specifically, uncertainty avoidance; intolerance of ambiguity; needs for order, structure, and closure; perception of a dangerous world; and fear of death are all positively associated with the endorsement of these ideologies. Cognitive complexity and openness to experience are negatively associated with their endorsement (Jost, Glaser, et al., 2003). There is a good match between needs to reduce uncertainty and threat and system justification, because preserving the status quo allows one to maintain what is familiar while rejecting the uncertain prospect of social change. For many people, the devil they know seems less threatening and more legitimate than the devil they don't.

There are other dispositional findings that suggest a motivational basis to system justification. Jost, Blount, et al. (2003) found that self-deception (measured as an individual difference variable) predicts endorsement of fair market ideology and support for capitalism. Scores on the fair market ideology scale—operationally defined as the tendency to believe that market-based procedures and outcomes are inherently fair and legitimate—are moderately to strongly correlated with endorsement of other system-justifying ideologies, including conservatism, opposition to equality, right-wing authoritarianism, belief in a just world, and economic system justification (which also tend to be correlated with one another). The observation that self-deception and feelings of threat are associated with the degree of system justification indicates that there is a motivational (or "hot") component to otherwise "cold" judgments concerning the legitimacy of political and economic institutions.

With regard to situational variables, the appeal of conservative, system-justifying beliefs is enhanced under conditions of high system threat and mortality salience (e.g., Jost, Glaser, et al., 2003; Landau, et al., 2004). Our experiments demonstrate that threats to the legitimacy of the social system lead people to increase their use of stereotypes to justify inequality between groups (e.g., Jost & Hunyady, 2002) and—especially if they are high in self-deception—to defend the capitalist

Table 2. *Some cognitive-motivational antecedents of system-justifying ideologies*

Antecedent	Conceptual/operational definition
Needs for order, structure, and closure (+)	Preference for a decision-making environment that is orderly, well structured, and unambiguous; a desire to make decisions quickly and to stick with them
Openness to experience (−)	An orientation that is creative, curious, flexible, and sensation seeking; an affinity for situations involving novelty, diversity, and change
Perception of a dangerous world (+)	Heightened sensitivity to potential dangers in the social environment, including threats of violence, crime, terrorism, and evildoing
Death anxiety/mortality salience (+)	Existential awareness of and fear associated with the prospect of one's own death; anxiety arising from mortality concerns
System instability and threat (+)	Actual or perceived threat to the legitimacy or stability of the social, economic, or political system; an attack (symbolic or material) on the status quo

Note. (+) Indicates that the variable is positively associated with the endorsement of system-justifying ideologies; (−) indicates that it is negatively associated with system justification.

status quo more vigorously (Jost, Blount, et al., 2003). The fact that the 9/11 terrorist attacks simultaneously evoked mortality salience and system threat may help to explain why they precipitated relatively strong increases (among liberals as well as conservatives) in patriotism and support for the Bush administration and its policies. In general, threats to the system—as long as they fall short of toppling the status quo—lead people to bolster existing arrangements by endorsing system-justifying ideologies. Experiments by Kay, Jimenez, and Jost (2002) suggest that, when regime change seems inevitable, people will begin to rationalize the new arrangements almost immediately.

Consequences of System Justification

From a social psychological point of view, there are both advantages and disadvantages of engaging in system justification (see Jost & Hunyady, 2002). In Table 3 we have listed some of the consequences for individuals, for groups, and for the social system as a whole. There is evidence that, at the individual level, system-justifying beliefs and ideologies serve the palliative function of decreasing negative affect and increasing positive affect and satisfaction with one's situation (Jost, Pelham, et al., 2003; Kluegel & Smith, 1986). Studies by Wakslak, Jost, Tyler, and Chen (2005) further demonstrate that endorsement of system justification is associated with reductions in moral outrage, guilt (especially but not exclusively among the advantaged), and frustration (especially but not exclusively among the disadvantaged).

At the same time, however, members of disadvantaged groups are faced with a potential conflict between needs to justify the status quo and competing motives to enhance their own self-esteem and group status. Consequently, members of

Table 3. *Several consequences of endorsement of system-justifying ideologies for members of advantaged and disadvantaged groups*

Variable	Operational definition(s)	Consequences of system justification for advantaged	Consequences of system justification for disadvantaged
Positive and negative affect	Self-report ratings of (a) happiness, satisfaction, contentment, and general positive affect; and (b) frustration, anger, guilt, shame, discomfort, and general negative affect	Increased positive affect, decreased negative affect	Increased positive affect, decreased negative affect
Self-esteem, subjective well-being	Scores on self-report measures of individual self-esteem, depression, and neuroticism	Increased self-esteem, subjective well-being	Decreased self-esteem, subjective well-being
In-group versus out-group favoritism	Favorability of (implicit and explicit) attitudes toward one's own group relative to the favorability of attitudes toward other groups	Increased in-group favoritism	Increased out-group favoritism (decreased in-group favoritism)
Perceived legitimacy of authorities and institutions	Trust and approval of the government, support for restricting criticism of the government, belief in the fairness of the economic system	Increased perceptions of legitimacy	Increased perceptions of legitimacy
Support for social change and redistribution of resources	Support for policies of redistribution in educational and employment contexts; willingness to support community service programs to help the disadvantaged	Decreased support for social change	Decreased support for social change

disadvantaged groups (such as blacks) who reject egalitarian alternatives to the status quo tend to suffer in terms of subjective well-being as indexed by levels of self-esteem and depression (Jost & Thompson, 2000). This conflict is not present for members of advantaged groups, who have no problem reconciling the desire to see the system as fair and just with the desire to see themselves and their fellow group members in favorable terms.

There are also important consequences of system justification for attitudes toward social groups. To the extent that they endorse system-justifying ideologies, members of both advantaged and disadvantaged groups tend to perpetuate the status quo by evaluating the advantaged group more favorably than the disadvantaged group on implicit (unconscious) as well as explicit (conscious) measures. Evidence summarized by Jost et al. (2004) indicates that acceptance of system-justifying ideologies (including the belief in a just world, economic system justification, social dominance orientation, and political conservatism) is associated with (a) increased in-group favoritism among members of advantaged groups (such as whites, Northerners, and heterosexuals), and (b) increased out-group favoritism among members of disadvantaged groups (such as blacks, Southerners, and homosexuals; see Fig. 1).

In addition, there are clear consequences of system justification for the perceived legitimacy and stability of the over-arching social system. Survey research by Jost, Pelham, et al. (2003) suggests that motives to rationalize the status quo may lead those who suffer the most under current circumstances to defend existing authorities and institutions, to support limitations on rights to criticize the government, and to imbue the economic system with legitimacy. Work by Jost, Blount, et al. (2003) showed that endorsement of fair market ideology was

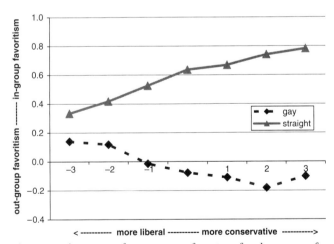

Fig. 1. Implicit in- and out-group favoritism as a function of endorsement of conservative versus liberal ideologies among gay ($n = 3,264$) and straight ($n = 14,038$) respondents. Endorsement of conservative ideology was associated with increased in-group favoritism among straight respondents but with decreased in-group favoritism (and increased out-group favoritism) among gay respondents. Similar results were obtained for explicit measures of favoritism as well as for racial comparisons (black vs. white). Adapted from Jost, Banaji, and Nosek (2004).

associated with the tendency to minimize the seriousness of ethical scandals involving business corporations.

Finally, Wakslak et al. (2005) found that increased system justification (either in terms of ideological endorsement or the temporary activation of a Horatio Alger "rags to riches" mindset) undermines support for the redistribution of resources and the desire to help the disadvantaged by alleviating negative emotional states. That is, system justification leads to a significant reduction in emotional distress, both in general and with respect to the particular affective states of moral outrage, guilt, and frustration. Because moral outrage inspires efforts to remedy injustice and participate in social change, the lessening of moral outrage triggered by system justification ultimately contributes to a withdrawal of support for social change.

CONCLUSION

The picture that emerges from the research we have summarized is of man as an "ideological animal." Although there are important situational and dispositional sources of variability in the system-justification tendency, most people possess at least some motivation to see the social, economic, and political arrangements that affect them as fair and legitimate. We will end by mentioning some practical implications and directions for future research.

Practical Implications

It is often assumed that liberal and left-wing parties enjoy a "natural advantage" in democratic political systems over conservative, right-wing parties because the poor outnumber the rich. This is derived from the notion that ideologies are rationally adopted according to economic and political self-interest. In this article, we have reviewed evidence that ideological endorsement is a product of motivated social cognition rather than "cold logic." At least two practical consequences follow for political parties and leaders in the U.S. system.

First, although liberals may possess weaker needs for system justification than conservatives in general, even liberals want to feel good about most aspects of their own system. Thus, liberals (as well as conservatives) value patriotism; trust and respect most authorities; and believe that democracy and capitalism are the only acceptable political and economic forms, respectively. However, because liberals are more open than conservatives are to modest change (reform) in the system, they consistently leave themselves open to political charges that they are (a) not supportive enough of the current system (i.e., unpatriotic, nontraditional, unconventional), or (b) the same as conservatives, only weaker (i.e., "Republican lite").

Second, the political advantages associated with conservative, system-justifying agendas may be especially pronounced under conditions of uncertainty and threat. This may be the case even if conservative politicians are themselves responsible for increasing levels of threat. Analysis of public opinion data, for example, indicates that President Bush's approval ratings increased after each incident in which terror alert levels were raised during his first term.

Future Research

In addition to identifying antecedents and consequences of system justification across time and place, we need to make further progress on disentangling the various cognitive and motivational mechanisms involved in justifying the status quo. In this article, we have focused on conscious endorsement of ideologies, but there are unconscious mechanisms as well. Stereotypes, for example, can provide support for existing forms of intergroup relations whether they are consciously endorsed or not. Our research suggests that even incidental exposure to complementary stereotypes—in which members of advantaged and disadvantaged groups are seen as possessing both strengths and weaknesses—increases the perception that society is fair and just. In future work, it would be useful to determine whether the system-justifying potential of specific stereotype contents (e.g., Southerners are "poor but honest," blacks are "aggressive but athletic," and professors are "smart but absentminded") can explain their emergence and popularity.

In this article, we have reviewed evidence suggesting that there are dispositional and situational sources of variability in the individual's need for system justification and that this need may be satisfied through the endorsement of different ideologies (as well as through other means, including stereotyping). These qualities of flexibility and substitutability of means suggest that system justification may operate as a goal. If so, it may exhibit other goal-like properties, such as persistence and resumption following interruption. We expect that the strength of an individual's motivation to restore the system's legitimacy following system threat would steadily increase until the goal is attained and that interruption of goal pursuit would lead people to redouble their system-justification efforts. Experiments directly investigating these possibilities would shed valuable light on the motivational dynamics of system-justification processes.

Recommended Reading

Altemeyer, R.A. (1998). (See References)

Glick, P., & Fiske, S.T. (2001). An ambivalent alliance: Hostile and benevolent sexism as complementary justifications for gender inequality. *American Psychologist, 56,* 109–118.

Jost, J.T., Banaji, M.R., & Nosek, B.A. (2004). (See References)

Jost, J.T., Glaser, J., Kruglanski, A.W., & Sulloway, F. (2003). (See References)

Pratto, F., Sidanius, J., Stallworth, L.M., & Malle, B.F. (1994). Social dominance orientation: A personality variable predicting social and political attitudes. *Journal of Personality and Social Psychology, 67,* 741–763.

Notes

1. Address correspondence to John T. Jost, Department of Psychology, New York University, 6 Washington Place, 5th Floor, New York, NY 10003; e-mail: john.jost@nyu.edu.

2. Unfortunately, space constraints prohibit discussion of how system justification theory differs from cognitive dissonance, just world, social identity, social dominance, and terror management theories, but interested readers are directed elsewhere (esp. Jost et al., 2004, pp. 881–888, 911–912; Jost & Hunyady, 2002, pp. 114–118).

References

Altemeyer, R.A. (1998). The other 'authoritarian personality'. *Advances in Experimental Social Psychology, 30*, 47–91.

Jost, J.T., Banaji, M.R., & Nosek, B.A. (2004). A decade of system justification theory: Accumulated evidence of conscious and unconscious bolstering of the status quo. *Political Psychology, 25*, 881–919.

Jost, J.T., Blount, S., Pfeffer, J., & Hunyady, G. (2003). Fair market ideology: Its cognitive-motivational underpinnings. *Research in Organizational Behavior, 25*, 53–91.

Jost, J.T., & Burgess, D. (2000). Attitudinal ambivalence and the conflict between group and system justification motives in low status groups. *Personality and Social Psychology Bulletin, 26*, 293–305.

Jost, J.T., Glaser, J., Kruglanski, A.W., & Sulloway, F. (2003). Political conservatism as motivated social cognition. *Psychological Bulletin, 129*, 339–375.

Jost, J.T., & Hunyady, O. (2002). The psychology of system justification and the palliative function of ideology. *European Review of Social Psychology, 13*, 111–153.

Jost, J.T., Pelham, B.W., & Carvallo, M. (2002). Non-conscious forms of system justification: Cognitive, affective, and behavioral preferences for higher status groups. *Journal of Experimental Social Psychology, 38*, 586–602.

Jost, J.T., Pelham, B.W., Sheldon, O., & Sullivan, B.N. (2003). Social inequality and the reduction of ideological dissonance on behalf of the system: Evidence of enhanced system justification among the disadvantaged. *European Journal of Social Psychology, 33*, 13–36.

Jost, J.T., & Thompson, E.P. (2000). Group-based dominance and opposition to equality as independent predictors of self-esteem, ethnocentrism, and social policy attitudes among African Americans and European Americans. *Journal of Experimental Social Psychology, 36*, 209–232.

Kay, A., Jimenez, M.C., & Jost, J.T. (2002). Sour grapes, sweet lemons, and the anticipatory rationalization of the status quo. *Personality and Social Psychology Bulletin, 28*, 1300–1312.

Kluegel, J.R., & Smith, E.R. (1986). *Beliefs about inequality*. New York: Aldine de Gruyter.

Kossowska, M., & Van Hiel, A. (2003). The relationship between need for closure and conservative beliefs in Western and Eastern Europe. *Political Psychology, 24*, 501–518.

Landau, M.J., Solomon, S., Greenberg, J., Cohen, F., Pyszczynski, T., Arndt, J., Miller, C.H., Ogilvie, D.M., & Cook, A. (2004). Deliver us from evil: The effects of mortality salience and reminders of 9/11 on support for President George W. Bush. *Personality and Social Psychology Bulletin, 30*, 1136–1150.

Lerner, M.J. (1980). *The belief in a just world*. New York: Plenum.

Nation's poor win election for nation's rich (2004, November 11–17). *The Onion*, pp. 1, 10.

Sidanius, J., & Pratto, F. (1999). *Social dominance*. New York: Cambridge University Press.

Wakslak, C., Jost, J.T., Tyler, T.R., & Chen, E. (2005). *System justification and the alleviation of emotional distress*. Manuscript in preparation.

The Concept of Organizational Citizenship

Walter C. Borman[1]
Personnel Decisions Research Institutes, Inc.,
Tampa, Florida, and University of South Florida

Abstract

This article describes the construct of citizenship performance and summarizes some of the industrial-organizational psychology research on organizational citizenship. Citizenship performance is defined as behaviors that go beyond task performance and technical proficiency, instead supporting the organizational, social, and psychological context that serves as the critical catalyst for tasks to be accomplished. The research reviewed addresses these topics: (a) the weights supervisors place on task and citizenship performance when making judgments about organization members' overall performance; (b) whether personality predicts citizenship performance better than task performance; (c) links between citizenship performance and organizational effectiveness; and (d) relations between organizational characteristics such as justice in the workplace and citizenship performance. Citizenship on the part of organization members is important in contemporary organizations. Because of current trends, such as increased global competition, greater use of teams, continuing downsizing initiatives, and more emphasis on customer service, citizenship performance is likely to be important in the foreseeable future, as well.

Keywords

industrial-organizational psychology; job performance; citizenship behavior; personality

Perhaps the most important dependent variable in industrial and organizational psychology is job performance. For all of the main applications of this branch of psychology, such as employee training and job redesign, the focus is almost always on improving job performance. This emphasis on job performance means that it is quite important how performance is defined.

Historically, job performance has had as its central core task activities. These kinds of activities are typically identified in job analyses that focus on tasks and estimate their importance, frequency, and the like (e.g., closing the sale for a sales job, filing project papers for a clerical job). Task performance can be defined as the proficiency with which these tasks are performed.

Recently, there has been considerable interest in a class of job performance that contributes importantly to organizational effectiveness but falls outside the domain of task performance. My colleagues and I call this type of performance *contextual* or *citizenship performance* (Borman & Motowidlo, 1993). We define citizenship performance as behaviors that are not directly related to the main task activities but are important because they support the organizational, social, and psychological context that serves as the critical catalyst for tasks to be accomplished. Such behaviors include volunteering to carry out tasks that are not formally a part of the job; persisting with extra effort when necessary to complete tasks successfully; helping and cooperating with other people on the job; following reasonable organizational rules and procedures even when they are personally inconvenient; and endorsing, supporting, and defending organizational objectives.

There are at least two important distinctions between task and citizenship performance. First, task activities are typically different for different jobs, whereas citizenship activities are similar across jobs. Volunteering, persisting, helping others, and the other citizenship behaviors just mentioned are likely to be important for most if not all jobs. Second, people's knowledge, skills, and abilities typically predict their level of task performance. Predictors of citizenship performance are more likely to be volitional and predispositional. Thus, for citizenship performance, motivational characteristics and dispositional variables such as personality should be the primary predictors.

ORIGINS OF THE CITIZENSHIP PERFORMANCE CONCEPT

As early as 1938, Barnard referred to the need for cooperation between organization members in sharing information to make the organization run smoothly. Katz (1964) emphasized helping and cooperating behaviors as useful for organizational functioning. More recently, Smith, Organ, and Near (1983) introduced the notion of organizational citizenship behavior and defined it as discretionary behavior that goes beyond one's official role and is intended to help other people in the organization or to show conscientiousness and support toward the organization.

Similarly, my colleagues and I (Borman, Motowidlo, Rose, & Hanser, 1983) developed a model of soldier effectiveness proposing that successful performance reflects more than technical proficiency. Targeted toward first-term soldiers in the U.S. Army, the model made a case for the importance of behaviors related to teamwork, discipline, and commitment in contributing to organizational effectiveness. Finally, Brief and Motowidlo (1986) introduced the closely related concept of prosocial organizational behavior, defined as behavior that is directed toward individuals, groups, or organizations with the intention of promoting their welfare. Table 1 summarizes a three-category taxonomy that attempts to summarize and integrate parsimoniously all these concepts (Borman et al., 2001).

FOUR STREAMS OF RESEARCH ON CITIZENSHIP PERFORMANCE

Research on citizenship performance has focused on (a) the weights experienced supervisors place on task and citizenship performance when judging organization members' overall performance or overall worth to the organization; (b) whether personality predicts citizenship performance better than task performance; (c) links between citizenship performance and organizational effectiveness; and (d) the influence of organizational characteristics on citizenship performance.

Supervisors' Use of Task and Citizenship Performance in Making Global Judgments About Subordinates

Major personnel decisions with long-term effects, such as decisions involving promotions, raises, and even downsizing, are likely to be largely determined by supervisors' global judgments about subordinates' performance and effectiveness.

Table 1. *Conceptual model of citizenship performance*

Personal support
　Helping others by offering suggestions, teaching them useful knowledge or skills, directly performing some of their tasks to help out, and providing emotional support for their personal problems
　Cooperating with others by accepting suggestions, informing them of events they should know about, and putting team objectives ahead of personal interests
　Showing consideration, courtesy, and tact in relations with others, as well as motivating and showing confidence in them

Organizational support
　Representing the organization favorably by defending and promoting it, as well as expressing satisfaction and showing loyalty by staying with the organization despite temporary hardships
　Supporting the organization's mission and objectives, complying with reasonable organizational rules and procedures, and suggesting improvements

Conscientious initiative
　Persisting with extra effort despite difficult conditions
　Taking the initiative to do all that is necessary to accomplish objectives even if not normally a part of own duties, and finding additional productive work to perform when own duties are completed
　Developing own knowledge and skills by taking advantage of opportunities within the organization and outside the organization, using own time and resources, when necessary

But such judgments are important in the short term as well; for example, work assignments are probably often made on the basis of these kinds of perceptions. Because supervisors' global perceptions and judgments likely have a substantial effect on decision making and on subordinates' organizational life, the question arises, what are the factors and cues that supervisors use to make these judgments? And, in the context of the current discussion, what are the relative weights supervisors give to task and citizenship performance?

Several studies have addressed this issue. In one such study (Motowidlo & Van Scotter, 1994), each of more than 300 U.S. Air Force personnel was rated by supervisors on overall performance, task performance, and citizenship performance. The authors found a correlation of .43 between task and overall performance and a correlation of .41 between citizenship and overall performance. Although the methodologies vary across studies, this is the typical finding: Supervisors weight task and citizenship performance roughly equally when making overall performance judgments (Podsakoff, MacKenzie, Paine, & Bachrach, 2000). Thus, citizenship performance is valued by supervisors just as strongly as technical proficiency.

Personality as a Predictor of Citizenship Performance

My colleagues and I (Motowidlo, Borman, & Schmit, 1997) hypothesize that cognitive ability is the primary predictor of task performance and that personality measures predict citizenship performance better than task performance. In fact, studies for the most part confirm this pattern, although the differences are some-times not so clear-cut (Hurtz & Donovan, 2000). The most consistent personal-ity predictor of citizenship performance is conscientiousness and some of its subcomponents (e.g., dependability).

Such findings have important implications for what industrial-organizational psychology can add to the science of personnel selection. If investigators can dis-cover reliable relations between workers' characteristics and their performance on the job, then it will be possible to develop a more complete understanding of the knowledge, skill, ability, and personality requirements for task and citizen-ship performance.

The correlations between citizenship performance and supervisory judgments of overall performance and between personality and citizenship performance, taken together, also have implications for reinterpreting Barrick and Mount's (1991) influential analysis of the literature on personality correlations with job performance. Their analysis showed a consistent moderate correlation between conscientiousness and overall performance, in almost all cases measured by rat-ings of overall performance. In light of the results discussed here, it is quite pos-sible that this correlation reflects primarily a relation between conscientiousness and citizenship performance.

Links Between Citizenship Performance and Organizational Effectiveness

There are many reasons to expect high levels of citizenship performance on the part of organization members to contribute to organizational effectiveness. Such behavior might enhance co-workers' or supervisors' productivity, help coordinate activities, increase the stability of organizational performance, and help the orga-nization attract and retain employees. However, only recently has such specula-tion been supported by empirical studies. Podsakoff et al. (2000) reviewed four studies that examined correlations between mean levels of rated citizenship per-formance within organizational units and various indices of organizational effec-tiveness for these same units. The studied samples ranged from 30 restaurants to 306 sales teams, and effectiveness indices included financial efficiency indicators, customer service ratings, and performance quality ratings. Across the studies, the relationships between citizenship performance and organizational effectiveness were substantial. A median of 19% of the variance in organizational effectiveness was accounted for by average levels of citizenship. An additional study (Koys, 2001) with a longitudinal design suggested that citizenship performance on the part of organization members may cause organizational effectiveness. Accord-ingly, it seems likely that citizenship behaviors can contribute to the effective-ness of organizations.

Organizational Factors and Citizenship Performance

If citizenship performance is important and "a good thing," then the question might be raised, how can it be fostered in organizations? There has been some research indicating that high levels of citizenship performance are associated with certain organizational characteristics that organizations themselves can influence. Analyses (Podsakoff et al., 2000) show that levels of citizenship performance tend to be enhanced in organizations that set group goals, demonstrate a high degree of procedural justice (i.e., have procedures and processes that are seen as fair), design jobs to be intrinsically satisfying, and have leaders who provide a supportive environment and who themselves exhibit citizenship behavior. The magnitude of these relationships is typically not very large, but correlations consistently range from .20 to .35. It is interesting to contemplate the flip side of these findings. If an organization does not have these characteristics (e.g., it provides a nonsupportive, unjust, destructively competitive environment), citizenship behavior is not likely to occur, nor, in my judgment, should it be expected from the organization's members.

CONCLUDING REMARKS

I have tried to make the case that citizenship performance is important for contemporary organizations. Experienced supervisors seem to weight citizenship performance at least as highly as task performance when judging their subordinates' overall effectiveness. And there are conceptual and empirical links between citizenship performance on the part of organization members and those organizations' effectiveness.

Research on this performance domain has shown that, for the most part, personality tends to predict citizenship performance better than task performance. Thus, using personality measures to select people likely to be good organizational citizens may have some merit. Organizational variables are also associated with citizenship performance. A supportive and just work environment, group goal setting, and a boss who is a good organizational citizen all appear to contribute to citizenship performance.

Most of the interest in organizational citizenship has occurred in the past 15 years. However, the question might be asked, is this construct likely to continue to be important in the future? Four contemporary trends suggest that the answer is yes. First, as global competition continues to raise the effort level required of organization members, citizenship performance, especially organizational support and conscientious initiative (see Table 1), will become increasingly important. Second, as team-based organizations become even more popular, there will be increased need for the personal-support component of citizenship performance. Third, citizenship performance, and especially conscientious initiative, will be needed as downsizing continues to make adaptability and willingness to exhibit extra effort more critical. And finally, as customer service and client satisfaction are increasingly emphasized, all three dimensions of citizenship performance will be more important.

Recommended Reading

Borman, W.C., & Motowidlo, S.J. (1993). (See References)
Organ, D.W. (1988). *Organizational citizenship behavior: The good soldier syndrome.* Lexington, MA: Lexington Books.
Podsakoff, P.M., MacKenzie, S.B., Paine, J.B., & Bachrach, D.G. (2000). (See References)

Note

1. Address correspondence to Walter C. Borman, Personnel Decisions Research Institutes, 100 South Ashley Dr., Suite 375, Tampa, FL 33602; e-mail: wally.borman@pdri.com.

References

Barnard, C.I. (1938). *The functions of the executive*. Cambridge, MA: Harvard University Press.

Barrick, M.R., & Mount, M.K. (1991). The Big Five personality dimensions and job performance: A meta-analysis. *Personnel Psychology, 44,* 1–26.

Borman, W.C., Buck, D.E., Hanson, M.A., Motowidlo, S.J., Stark, S., & Drasgow, F. (2001). An examination of the comparative reliability, validity, and accuracy of performance ratings made using computerized adaptive rating scales. *Journal of Applied Psychology, 86,* 965–973.

Borman, W.C., & Motowidlo, S.J. (1993). Expanding the criterion domain to include elements of contextual performance. In N. Schmitt & W.C. Borman (Eds.), *Personnel selection* (pp. 71–98). San Francisco: Jossey-Bass.

Borman, W.C., Motowidlo, S.J., Rose, S.R., & Hanser, L.M. (1983). *Development of a model of soldier effectiveness* (Institute Report No. 95). Minneapolis, MN: Personnel Decisions Research Institute.

Brief, A.P., & Motowidlo, S.J. (1986). Prosocial organizational behaviors. *Academy of Management Review, 11,* 710–725.

Hurtz, G.M., & Donovan, J.J. (2000). Personality and job performance: The big five revisited. *Journal of Applied Psychology, 85,* 869–879.

Katz, D. (1964). The motivational basis of organizational behavior. *Behavioral Science, 9,* 131–146.

Koys, D.J. (2001). The effects of employee satisfaction, organizational citizenship behavior, and turnover on organizational effectiveness: A unit-level, longitudinal study. *Personnel Psychology, 54,* 101–114.

Motowidlo, S.J., Borman, W.C., & Schmit, M.J. (1997). A theory of individual differences in task and contextual performance. *Human Performance, 10,* 71–83.

Motowidlo, S.J., & Van Scotter, J.R. (1994). Evidence that task performance should be distinguished from contextual performance. *Journal of Applied Psychology, 79,* 475–480.

Podsakoff, P.M., MacKenzie, S.B., Paine, J.B., & Bachrach, D.G. (2000). Organizational citizenship behaviors: A critical review of the theoretical and empirical literature and suggestions for future research. *Journal of Management, 26,* 513–563.

Smith, C.A., Organ, D.W., & Near, J.P. (1983). Organizational citizenship behavior: Its nature and antecedents. *Journal of Applied Psychology, 68,* 653–663.

This article has been reprinted as it originally appeared in *Current Directions in Psychological Science*. Citation information for this article as originally published appears above.

An Adaptation for Altruism?:
The Social Causes, Social Effects,
and Social Evolution of Gratitude

Michael E. McCullough[1], Marcia B. Kimeldorf,
and Adam D. Cohen
University of Miami

Abstract

People feel grateful when they have benefited from someone's costly, intentional, voluntary effort on their behalf. Experiencing gratitude motivates beneficiaries to repay their benefactors and to extend generosity to third parties. Expressions of gratitude also reinforce benefactors for their generosity. These social features distinguish gratitude from related emotions such as happiness and feelings of indebtedness. Evolutionary theories propose that gratitude is an adaptation for reciprocal altruism (the sequential exchange of costly benefits between nonrelatives) and, perhaps, upstream reciprocity (a pay-it-forward style distribution of an unearned benefit to a third party after one has received a benefit from another benefactor). Gratitude therefore may have played a unique role in human social evolution.

Keywords

gratitude; emotion; evolution; morality; pro-social behavior; reciprocity; altruism

Emotions are discrete, time-limited, affective responses to significant environmental changes. Once activated, emotions are thought to coordinate thought, physiology, and behavior so that people can respond to reality in self-protective and self-enhancing ways (Ekman, 1992). Discovering what a particular emotion *does*—the environmental inputs that activate it and its effects on behavior, for instance—is therefore regarded by many emotion researchers as a royal road to discovering what it is *for*—that is, why humans evolved to experience that emotion.

Gratitude—a positive emotion that typically flows from the perception that one has benefited from the costly, intentional, voluntary action of another person—is an interesting test bed for considering this functional approach to emotion. Western social theorists from Seneca and Cicero to Adam Smith and David Hume, to modern social scientists such as Robert Frank and Robert Trivers, have apprehended the importance of gratitude for creating and sustaining positive social relations (Bartlett & DeSteno, 2006; Harpham, 2004; McCullough, Kilpatrick, Emmons, & Larson, 2001). Oddly, though, psychological science largely neglected gratitude until the 21st century. Fortunately, recent research has explored gratitude's distinct social causes and effects. These studies may help to shed light on gratitude's evolutionary history.

GRATITUDE AS A PROSOCIAL EMOTION

Gratitude is a pleasant emotion, but it is different from simple happiness because gratitude is typically preceded by the perception that one has benefited from another person's generosity. Because gratitude is predicated upon receiving a benefit from another social agent, McCullough et al. (2001) proposed that gratitude possesses three psychological features that are relevant to processing and responding to prosocial behavior: It is a (a) benefit detector and both a (b) reinforcer and (c) motivator of prosocial behavior.

Gratitude as a Benefit Detector

First, McCullough and colleagues proposed that gratitude is an affective readout that alerts people that they have benefited from another person's prosocial behavior. Gratitude is responsive to four types of information about the benefit-giving situation: (a) the benefit's costliness to the benefactor, (b) its value to the beneficiary, (c) the intentionality with which it was rendered, and (d) the extent to which it was given even without relational obligations to help (for example, parents' obligations to help their children). Recent experiments support this characterization of gratitude as a benefit detector. For example, Tsang (2006a) found that, consistent with the proposition that gratitude increases proportionally with the benefactor's intentionality, participants experienced more gratitude toward benefactors who helped them out of benevolent rather than self-serving motives.

Gratitude as a Reinforcer of Prosocial Behavior

McCullough et al. (2001) also proposed that gratitude reinforces prosocial behavior because expressions of gratitude (for example, saying "thanks") increase the likelihood that benefactors will behave prosocially again in the future. Reviewing previous studies, McCullough and colleagues concluded that benefactors who are thanked for their efforts are willing to give more and work harder on behalf of others when future opportunities arise than are benefactors who have not been thanked. Writing "thank you" on a restaurant bill even raises servers' tips.

Why would saying "thanks" reinforce prosocial behavior—and even tipping? Perhaps because the beneficiary's expression of thanks acknowledges to the benefactor that he or she has noticed a kindness and, thus, might be prone to reciprocate when a future opportunity to do so arises. In other words, expressing gratitude may make beneficiaries seem like safe targets for future investments.

Gratitude as a Motivator of Prosocial Behavior

This leads to gratitude's third prosocial characteristic: It motivates people to behave prosocially after receiving benefits. In 2001, when McCullough and colleagues reviewed the literature, gratitude's efficacy as a motivator of future prosocial behavior was the most speculative of their proposals about gratitude's effects. More recent research has confirmed their speculation. McCullough, Emmons, and Tsang (2002) found that people who scored higher on self- and peer-report measures of the "grateful disposition" also scored higher on measures of prosocial behaviors during the previous month (and overall) than did people who scored lower on the gratitude measures. In addition, Bartlett and DeSteno (2006) discovered that participants made to feel grateful toward a benefactor exerted more effort to help the benefactor on an unrelated task (i.e., completing a boring and cognitively taxing survey) than did nongrateful participants. They were also more likely to help a stranger (that is, someone who had not helped them) than were nongrateful participants. This latter finding shows that gratitude's effects on prosocial behavior were not simply caused by reminding people of the norm of reciprocity (the norm that dictates that one should return help for help received).

Likewise, Tsang (2006b) found that people who received a benefit due to the intentional effort of a partner not only were more grateful than were people who received the benefit by chance but also were more likely to behave generously toward their partner in response. Finally, Emmons and McCullough (2003) found that participants who wrote daily for 2 weeks about things for which they were grateful reported offering more emotional support and (with near-statistical significance) tangible help to others than did participants who wrote about their daily hassles or about ways in which they were more fortunate than others.

Gratitude may motivate prosocial behavior by influencing psychological states that support generosity and cooperation. For example, Dunn and Schweitzer (2005, Study 3) found that participants who described a time in the past when they felt grateful toward someone (thereby creating grateful emotion in the present) subsequently reported higher levels of trust toward a third party than did participants who were asked to describe a time they felt angry, guilty, or proud. Similarly, Jackson, Lewandowski, Fleury, and Chin (2001) found that having participants recall a real-life gratitude-inducing experience caused them to attribute another person's good fortune to stable causes that were under the fortunate person's control. In other words, gratitude causes one to give people credit for their accomplishments. Trust and a readiness to give people credit for their accomplishments are important lubricants for positive social interaction, so psychological effects such as these may explain how gratitude promotes prosocial behavior.

DISTINGUISHING GRATITUDE FROM OTHER EMOTIONS

In light of its prosocial characteristics, functional emotion theorists would likely speculate that gratitude was shaped by evolutionary pressures for generosity and helping. However, if gratitude's prosocial characteristics were not unique to gratitude (for example, if gratitude were indistinguishable in these respects from emotions such as happiness and indebtedness), then the proposition that gratitude was designed specifically to facilitate social exchange would be weakened. Fortunately for the functionalist approach, research shows that gratitude is quite distinct from several kindred emotions in its phenomenology, causes, and effects.

Gratitude Versus Other Positive Emotions

Psychologists have long held that positive emotions such as happiness and amusement can promote prosocial behavior. What may distinguish gratitude from other positive emotions in this respect is that gratitude stimulates helping even when it is costly to the helper. Bartlett and DeSteno (2006) found that participants in an experimentally induced state of gratitude voluntarily spent more time completing a boring survey as a favor to their benefactor than did participants in an amused emotional state (see also Tsang, 2006b). Additionally, as noted above, Jackson et al. (2001) showed that gratitude causes people to give other people who encounter good fortune more credit for their good fortune than does simple happiness.

Gratitude Versus Obligation and Indebtedness

Gratitude is also distinct from obligation and indebtedness. Although people often use obligation-related phrases (e.g., "I owe you one") and gratitude-related phrases (e.g., "I'm grateful to you") interchangeably, they are distinct and have distinct psychological effects. For example, obligation feels negative and uncomfortable, whereas gratitude is usually associated with contentment and well-being (McCullough et al., 2001).

Moreover, feeling obligated after receiving a favor does not uniquely predict compliance with a request to perform a favor for the benefactor after controlling for gratitude statistically. In contrast, gratitude predicts compliance even after controlling for indebtedness (Goei & Boster, 2005; Goei, Roberto, Meyer, & Carlyle, 2007). Tsang (2007) also found that gratitude was a better mediator of the association between receiving a gift of large value and reciprocating a favor than was indebtedness.

In a related finding, Watkins, Scheer, Ovnicek, and Kolts (2006) showed that people anticipate feeling indebted and obligated, but not grateful, when benefactors help them with an explicit expectation of a return favor (that is, when the help has "strings attached"). Indeed, the greater one's gratitude for a benefit, the greater one's desire to help, praise, and be near the benefactor. Conversely, the greater one's indebtedness, the greater one's distress and desire to avoid the benefactor (Watkins et al., 2006).

THE SOCIAL EVOLUTION OF GRATITUDE

Researchers have noted that gratitude appears to be cross-culturally and linguistically universal (McCullough et al., 2001), and Darwin himself (1871/1952) posited (albeit without appealing to any systematic evidence) that gratitude was observable in the behavior of nonhuman primates. There is also reason to believe that gratitude evolved independently of language because some nonverbal behaviors (e.g., handshakes) are useful for communicating gratitude (Hertenstein, Keltner, App, Bulleit, & Jaskolka, 2006). These observations, plus the recently discovered facts about gratitude's causes and effects, raise the possibility that gratitude evolved to facilitate social exchange. Indeed, many of psychology's recent discoveries about gratitude can be reconciled with two hypotheses from evolutionary biology about the selection pressures that sculpted gratitude into its modern form.

Gratitude and the Evolution of Reciprocal Altruism

The first of these hypotheses is that gratitude evolved to facilitate reciprocal altruism. In introducing the theory of reciprocal altruism, Trivers (1971) proposed that "the emotion of gratitude has been selected to regulate human response to altruistic acts and that the emotion is sensitive to the cost/benefit ratio of such acts" (p. 49). Research confirms both of Trivers's proposals: Gratitude regulates people's responses to benefits by motivating them to acknowledge those benefits verbally and nonverbally and by motivating them to extend benefits to their benefactors in kind. Trivers was also correct in proposing that gratitude is sensitive to the costs and benefits associated with altruistic acts (McCullough et al., 2001; Tsang, 2007).

Trivers's theory is also congenial to two other findings about gratitude. The first is that people anticipate feeling more grateful to strangers, acquaintances, and friends who benefit them than to genetic relatives (i.e., siblings and parents) who provide the same benefit (Bar-Tal, Bar-Zohar, Greenberg, & Hermon, 1977). The second is that gratitude increases people's trust in third parties, but only when they lack a high degree of familiarity with those third parties (Dunn & Schweitzer, 2005).

Both phenomena make sense if gratitude evolved expressly in response to selection pressure for reciprocal altruism. Because people share, on average, 50% of their genes in common with their offspring and siblings, it is in one's genetic self-interest to expend resources to benefit a genetic relative (kin altruism) as long as the value of the benefit to the beneficiary, weighted by the degree of relatedness, exceeds the cost to the benefactor (Hamilton, 1964). Concerns about reciprocity are superfluous, then, to the selection pressures that gave rise to kin altruism. For this reason, specialized adaptations for reciprocal altruism—gratitude possibly being one of them—should not be activated by the prospect of receiving benefits from genetic relatives. This may explain why gratitude toward kin is apparently less intense than is gratitude toward nonkin. Furthermore, the fact that gratitude increases trust in strangers, but not in well-known acquaintances, makes sense if gratitude evolved to help people convert acquaintanceships with nonkin into relationships that can support reciprocal altruism.

Gratitude and the Evolution of Upstream Reciprocity

A second (admittedly more speculative) evolutionary hypothesis is that gratitude evolved to stimulate not only direct reciprocal altruism but also what Nowak and Roch (2006) have called "upstream reciprocity": passing benefits on to third parties instead of returning benefits to one's benefactors (for example, on occasions when one's benefactors do not need helping). On the basis of computer simulations, Nowak and Roch concluded that a gratitude that motivates organisms to direct benefits toward third parties in this gratuitous fashion can enhance fitness, provided the population has already evolved for direct reciprocity. (To better appreciate the possible adaptive advantage of upstream reciprocity, note that upstream reciprocators will sometimes undeservingly benefit from other upstream reciprocators' benevolent actions.) In fact, Nowak and Roch came to the surprising conclusion that if this "pay it forward" sort of gratitude evolves within a population that is already adapted for direct reciprocity, natural selection will reduce the benefit–cost ratio required for altruism to stabilize within the population, thereby making altruism more efficient. Another interpretation is that gratitude-motivated upstream reciprocity appears to facilitate the evolution of higher levels of altruism than would be possible without it.

Thus, Nowak and Roch suggest, modern gratitude may have been shaped by selection pressure for upstream reciprocity. If the Nowak-Roch model turns out to be correct, then Bartlett and DeSteno's (2006) finding that gratitude increases people's willingness to help third parties may not be the "incidental effect" that Bartlett and DeSteno (2006) presumed, but rather, an intrinsic part of gratitude's adaptive design.

DIRECTIONS FOR FUTURE RESEARCH

Three avenues for future research seem especially promising. First, if gratitude evolved to facilitate altruism among nonrelatives, as Trivers (1971) and Nowak and Roch (2006) proposed, then benefits delivered by kin should produce less gratitude, and therefore less direct and upstream reciprocity, than should benefits delivered by nonkin. Moreover, gratitude is probably more valuable for establishing reciprocal relationships than for maintaining them: Once a long chain of successful reciprocal exchanges has occurred, a gratitude-based acknowledgment of a benefactor's altruistic act and a gratitude-motivated intent to reciprocate would be superfluous because actions (e.g., both parties' long histories of mutual trustworthiness) would speak louder than words. Exploration of relational boundary conditions such as these would shed further light on gratitude's possible adaptive design.

Second, Nowak and Roch's (2006) model of upstream reciprocity needs fuller attention. If their model is correct, then the motivation to respond to the receipt of benefits by passing them on to undeserving third parties is not an incidental effect of gratitude but, rather, an intrinsic design feature.

Third and finally, we recommend research on whether the effects of gratitude on psychological well-being (Emmons & McCullough, 2003; McCullough et al., 2002) are due to real (or even merely perceived) changes in people's social relationships. As many have noted, positive social relations are conducive to health and well-being, so given gratitude's pervasive relational effects, gratitude's links to health and well-being may be partially due to those relational effects.

CONCLUSION

Gratitude appears well-designed for signaling and motivating the exchange of benefits. Gratitude's unique social characteristics suggest that it may have been instrumental in the evolution of humans' prodigious tendencies to cooperate with nonkin. Research on gratitude that is informed by evolutionary theorizing can be a time machine that helps us to make inferences about the social forces in our evolutionary past that turned us into the exquisitely cooperative creatures we are today.

Recommended Reading

Cosmides, L., & Tooby, J. (1992). Cognitive adaptations for social exchange. In J. Barkow, L. Cosmides, & J. Tooby (Eds.), *The adapted mind* (pp. 163–228). New York: Oxford University Press. A "modern classic" that outlines a strategy for identifying psychological adaptations for social exchange.

Emmons, R.A., & McCullough, M.E. (Eds.). (2001). *The psychology of gratitude*. New York: Oxford University Press. A readable collection of chapters on gratitude by leading scholars in philosophy, the social sciences, and the life sciences.

McCullough, M.E., Kilpatrick, S.D., Emmons, R.A., & Larson, D.B. (2001). (See References). A more leisurely and wide-ranging review of research and theory on gratitude through the end of the 20th century.

Nowak, M., & Roch, S. (2006). (See References). An important introduction to the logic and evolutionary plausibility of natural selection for upstream reciprocity.

Trivers, R.L. (1971). (See References). A landmark theoretical work that provides a blueprint of the psychological system that might have supported the evolution of reciprocal altruism in humans.

Acknowledgments—This research was supported by National Institute of Mental Health Grant R01MH071258 and support from the Center for the Study of Law and Religion at Emory University and the John Templeton Foundation. We gratefully acknowledge our colleagues Rob Kurzban and Debra Lieberman for thoughtful suggestions on earlier drafts of this article.

Note

1. Address correspondence to Michael E. McCullough, Department of Psychology, University of Miami, P.O. Box 248285, Coral Gables, FL 33124-0751; e-mail: mikem@miami.edu.

References

Bar-Tal, D., Bar-Zohar, Y., Greenberg, M.S., & Hermon, M. (1977). Reciprocity behavior in the relationship between donor and recipient and between harm-doer and victim. *Sociometry, 40*, 293–298.

Bartlett, M.Y., & DeSteno, D. (2006). Gratitude and prosocial behavior: Helping when it costs you. *Psychological Science, 17*, 319–325.

Darwin, C. (1952). *The descent of man, and selection in relation to sex*. Chicago, IL: University of Chicago Press. (Original work published 1871)

Dunn, J.R., & Schweitzer, M.E. (2005). Feeling and believing: The influence of emotion on trust. *Journal of Personality and Social Psychology, 88*, 736–748.

Ekman, P. (1992). An argument for basic emotions. *Cognition and Emotion, 6*, 169–200.

Emmons, R.A., & McCullough, M.E. (2003). Counting blessings versus burdens: An experimental investigation of gratitude and subjective well-being in daily life. *Journal of Personality and Social Psychology, 84*, 377–389.

Goei, R., & Boster, F.J. (2005). The roles of obligation and gratitude in explaining the effect of favors on compliance. *Communication Monographs, 72*, 284–300.

Goei, R., Roberto, A., Meyer, G., & Carlyle, K. (2007). The effects of favor and apology on compliance. *Communication Research, 34*, 575–595.

Hamilton, W.D. (1964). The genetical evolution of social behaviour (parts I & II). *Journal of Theoretical Biology, 7*, 1–52.

Harpham, E.J. (2004). Gratitude in the history of ideas. In R.A. Emmons & M.E. McCullough (Eds.), *The psychology of gratitude* (pp. 19–36). New York: Oxford.

Hertenstein, M.J., Keltner, D., App, B., Bulleit, B.A., & Jaskolka, A.R. (2006). Touch communicates distinct emotions. *Emotion, 6*, 528–533.

Jackson, L.A., Lewandowski, D.A., Fleury, R.E., & Chin, P.P. (2001). Effects of affect, stereotype consistency, and valence of behavior on causal attributions. *Journal of Social Psychology, 141*, 31–48.

McCullough, M.E., Emmons, R.A., & Tsang, J. (2002). The grateful disposition: A conceptual and empirical topography. *Journal of Personality and Social Psychology, 82*, 112–127.

McCullough, M.E., Kilpatrick, S.D., Emmons, R.A., & Larson, D.B. (2001). Is gratitude a moral affect? *Psychological Bulletin, 127,* 249–266.

Nowak, M., & Roch, S. (2006). Upstream reciprocity and the evolution of gratitude. *Proceedings of the Royal Society of London, Series B: Biological Sciences, 274,* 605–609.

Trivers, R.L. (1971). The evolution of reciprocal altruism. *Quarterly Review of Biology, 46,* 35–57.

Tsang, J. (2006a). The effects of helper intention on gratitude and indebtedness. *Motivation and Emotion, 30,* 198–204.

Tsang, J. (2006b). Gratitude and prosocial behaviour: An experimental test of gratitude. *Cognition and Emotion, 20,* 138–148.

Tsang, J. (2007). Gratitude for small and large favors: A behavioral test. *Journal of Positive Psychology, 2,* 157–167.

Watkins, P.C., Scheer, J., Ovnicek, M., & Kolts, R. (2006). The debt of gratitude: Dissociating gratitude and indebtedness. *Cognition and Emotion, 20,* 217–241.

This article has been reprinted as it originally appeared in *Current Directions in Psychological Science*. Citation information for this article as originally published appears above.

Adaptations to Ovulation: Implications for Sexual and Social Behavior

Steven W. Gangestad[1] and Christine E. Garver-Apgar
Department of Psychology
Randy Thornhill
Department of Biology, University of New Mexico

Abstract

In socially monogamous species in which males heavily invest in offspring, there arises an inevitable genetic conflict between partners over whether investing males become biological fathers of their partners' off-spring. Humans are such a species. The ovulatory-shift hypothesis proposes that changes in women's mate preferences and sexual interests across the cycle are footprints of this conflict. When fertile (mid-cycle), women find masculine bodily and behavioral features particularly sexy and report increased attraction to men other than current partners. Men are more vigilant of partners when the latter are fertile, which may reflect evolved counteradaptations. This adaptationist hypothesis has already generated several fruitful research programs, but many questions remain.

Keywords

mating; evolutionary psychology; attraction

Human sex can result in conception only about 20% of the time: from 5 days before ovulation to the day of ovulation. Yet unlike in humans' close primate relatives, human females lack conspicuous sexual swellings that vary across the cycle, and people have sex throughout the cycle. Continuous receptivity, however, need not imply that women's sexual interests or preferences remain constant. Indeed, it would be surprising if selection had not forged psychological adaptations in one or both sexes to be sensitive to conception risk—and recent research confirms this expectation. The ways people are sensitive to it provide keys to understanding how selection shaped human sexual relations. In short, romantic relationships take shape out of people's adaptive design for cooperating with partners—often lovingly—in pursuit of shared interests, in conjunction with each sex's adaptive design for pursuing its own interests (or those of same-sex ancestors) that conflict with those of partners.

EVOLUTIONARY BACKGROUND: MATE CHOICE FOR GENES

Over evolutionary time, natural selection sifts through available genetic variants, saving those that promote success within a species' niche and discarding others. Our genes are typically "good genes" that have passed a test of time. But some aren't. Genes mutate. Though each gene is copied correctly 99.99+% of the time, sperm or eggs commonly contain one or more new copying errors. Because mutations typically have minor effects (much as slight impurities in a tank of gas subtly compromise car performance), most survive multiple generations before being eliminated. On average, an individual probably has several tens if not hundreds of mutations. Additionally, although the world to which humans must adapt is constant in many ways (e.g., its gravitational fields), in other subtle-but-profound ways it is not. Pathogens constantly evolve to better thrive in the human body, and humans must change merely to keep pace. Despite selection on thousands of ancestral generations to resist pathogens, humans do not possess sure-fire defenses against them.

The ubiquity of maladapted genes may explain why sex evolved. A gene mutated in an asexual, cloning organism persists in all descendants. Sexual organisms pass on just half of their genes to offspring, and what may make sex worthwhile is that offspring need not get all maladapted genes; some offspring get fewer than either parent.

Through good fortune and bad, not everyone has the same number of mal-adapted genes. The best way to minimize mal-adapted genes in offspring is to mate with someone lacking them. While mate choosers cannot directly compare DNA copying errors in suitors, they can do so indirectly—for precisely the reason that choosing mates with good genes is important: Genes affect their bearers' performance. Selection ensures that mate choosers evolve to be attuned and attracted to elements of performance that are sensitive to poorly adapted genes within the species—whether it be growth, the ability to physically dominate or outwit others, or possessing "good looks."

TRADE-OFFS BETWEEN MATERIAL
AND GENETIC BENEFITS

In relatively few species do both females and males intensively nurture offspring. Humans may be one. While questions remain about how and to what extent men nurture their own offspring in foraging societies, in most societies men and women typically form socially monogamous pairs and men attempt to direct resources (meat, protection, direct care, money) to mates and offspring. Chimpanzees, bonobos, and gorillas don't share this pattern and are probably poor models of human sexual relations. As many bird species form social pairs, however, theories about their mating may offer insight into how selection shaped human sexual psychologies.

Many socially monogamous birds are not sexually monogamous. On average across species, 10 to 15% of offspring are fathered by males other than social partners—so-called "extra-pair" males. Multiple reasons that females seek extra-pair mates are being investigated, but one is that male assistance in raising offspring doesn't eliminate selection pressure on females to obtain good genes. Not all females can pair up with males with high genetic fitness. Those who don't could potentially benefit from getting social partners' cooperation in raising offspring but getting other males' genes. This pattern has been elegantly demonstrated in the collared flycatcher. A large male forehead patch advertises good genes. Females don't prefer large-patched males as social partners, as they work less hard at the nest. Small-patched males, however, are more likely to be cuckolded and large-patched males the biological fathers. Indeed, females time extra-pair copula-tions to occur during peak fertility, favoring paternity by extra-pair partners.

More generally, in socially monogamous species in which pairs have males as close neighbors, an inevitable conflict between the sexes arises. All else being equal, females mated to males not possessing the best genes could benefit by getting genes from someone else. At the same time, selection operates on invest-ing males to prevent cuckoldry (e.g., by mate guarding or being able to recognize offspring not their own). Selection hence operates on each sex against the inter-ests of the other sex; thus "sexually antagonistic adaptations" evolve. Depending on which sex evolves more effective adaptations (which may depend on ecologi-cal factors affecting the ease with which males guard their mates, the relative value of good genes, the amount of assistance males give females, etc.), the actual extra-pair sex rate may be high (20% or more) or low (5% or less). Even when it is low, however, the genetic conflict exists and sexually antagonistic adaptations may evolve.

THE OVULATORY-SHIFT HYPOTHESIS

We (Gangestad & Thornhill, 1998) proposed to look for human adaptations that are footprints of these selection forces, based on the fact we began with: Women are fertile during a brief window of their cycles. If ancestral females benefited from multiple mating to obtain genetic benefits but at some potential cost of los-ing social mates, selection may have shaped preferences for indicators of those benefits to depend on fertility status: maximal at peak fertility and less pro-nounced outside the fertile period. Cycle shifts should furthermore be specific to when women evaluate men as short-term sex partners (i.e., their "sexiness") rather than as long-term, investing mates (Penton-Voak et al., 1999). The logic is that costs do not pay when benefits cannot be reaped.

Over a dozen recent studies show that female preferences clearly do shift. At mid-cycle, normally ovulating, non-pill-using women particularly prefer physical symmetry, masculine facial and vocal qualities, intrasexual competitiveness, and various forms of talent.

The scent of symmetrical men. Asymmetry on bilateral traits that are symmet-rical at the population level (e.g., finger lengths, ear dimensions, wrist width) reflects developmental instability, perturbations due to mutations, pathogens, toxins, and other stresses. Developmental instability, in turn, could affect numer-ous other features of men, including their scent. In four studies, men wore tee-shirts for two nights and women rated the attractiveness of the shirts' scents. All studies found that, when they were fertile, women particularly preferred the scent of symmetrical men (see Fig. 1). When women were not fertile, they had no preference for symmetrical men's scents. Although the chemical mediating this effect has not been identified, data and theory suggest the existence of androgen-derived substances, the scent of which women evaluate more posi-tively when fertile.

Masculine faces. Male and female faces differ in various ways. Most notably, men have broader chins and narrower eyes (due to development of the brow

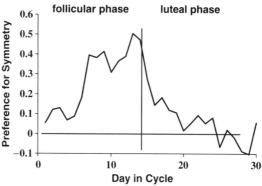

Fig. 1. Women's preference for the scent of symmetrical men as a function of their day in the cycle ($N = 141$). The vertical line corresponds to women's average day of ovulation. The follicular and luteal phases precede and follow ovulation, respectively. Each woman's ratings of scent attractiveness (a sum of ratings of pleasantness and sexiness) were measured against men's physical symmetry. Data are compiled from three separate studies: Gangestad & Thornhill (1998), Thornhill & Gangestad (1999), and Thornhill et al. (2003).

ridge). Men vary, however, in the extent to which they possess masculine facial features. Women's preference for more masculine faces is more pronounced when they are fertile than when they are infertile, particularly when they rate men's sexiness, not their attractiveness as long-term mates (e.g, Penton-Voak et al., 1999; Johnston, Hagel, Franklin, Fink, & Grammer, 2001).

Behavioral displays of social presence and intrasexual competitiveness. We (Gangestad, Simpson, Cousins, Garver-Apgar, & Christensen, 2004) had women view videotapes of men being interviewed for a potential lunch date. Men independently rated as confident and who acted toward their male competitors in condescending ways were found more sexy by women when the women were fertile than they were when the women were not fertile (see Fig. 2).

Vocal masculinity. When rating men's short-term attractiveness, women find masculine (deep) voices more attractive at mid-cycle than they do at other times (Puts, 2005).

Talent versus wealth. Haselton and Miller (in press) found that, when faced with trade-offs between talent (e.g., creativity) and wealth, women choose talent more often when fertile than they do when nonfertile, but only when evaluating men's short-term mating attractiveness.

All of these characteristics may well have been indicators of good genes ancestrally. Not all positive traits are sexier mid-cycle, however. Traits particularly valued in long-term mates (e.g., promising material benefits) do not appear to be especially attractive to fertile women. For instance, follow-up analyses showed that while the women in the Gangestad et al. (2004) study found arrogant, confrontative, and physically attractive men particularly sexy mid-cycle, their attraction to men perceived to be kind, intelligent, good fathers, and likely to be financially successful—traits particularly valued in long-term mates— didn't change across the cycle. And men judged to be faithful were rated as less sexy mid-cycle than at other times (see also Thornhill et al., 2003).

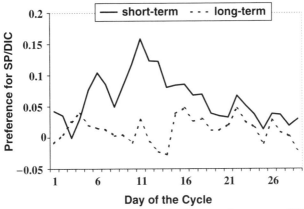

Fig. 2. Women's preference for men who display social presence (SP) and direct intrasexual competitiveness (DIC) as short-term partners (solid line) and as long-term partners (dotted line), as a function of day of their cycle ($N = 238$). From Gangestad et al. (2004).

SHIFTS IN WOMEN'S SEXUAL INTERESTS

Patterns of women's sexual interests also shift across the cycle. In one study, normally ovulating women reported thoughts and feelings over the previous 2 days twice: once when fertile (as confirmed by a luteinizing hormone surge, 1–2 days before ovulation) and once when infertile. When fertile, women reported greater sexual attraction to and fantasy about men other than their primary partners than they did at other times—but their level of attraction to primary partners at this time was no greater than it was when they were infertile (Gangestad, Thornhill, & Garver, 2002; cf. Pillsworth, Haselton, & Buss, 2004).

In fact, however, the ovulatory-shift hypothesis expects a more finely textured pattern. On average, ancestral women could have garnered genetic benefits through extra-pair mating, but those whose primary partners had good genes could not. Selection thus should have shaped interest in extra-pair men mid-cycle to itself depend on partner features; only women with men who, relatively speaking, lack purported indicators of genetic benefits should be particularly attracted to extra-pair men when fertile. We (Gangestad, Thornhill, & Garver-Apgar, 2005) tested this prediction in a replication and extension of Gangestad et al. (2002). Romantically involved couples participated. Again, individuals privately filled out questionnaires twice, once when the female was fertile and once during her luteal phase. Men's symmetry was measured. Once again, women reported greater attraction to extra-pair men and not their primary partners when fertile. Effects, however, were moderated by the symmetry of women's partners. At high fertility, women with relatively asymmetrical partners were more attracted to extra-pair men—and less attracted to their own partners—than when they were infertile. No such effects were found during the luteal phase. Controlling for relationship satisfaction, another important predictor of women's attraction to extra-pair men, did not diminish the effect of partner symmetry. (See also Haselton & Gangestad, in press.)

MALE COUNTERSTRATEGIES ACROSS THE CYCLE

If women have been under selection to seek good genes mid-cycle, men should have been under selection to take additional steps to prevent them from seeking extra-pair sex at this time. Multiple studies indicate that they do so by being more vigilant, proprietary, or monopolizing of mates' time during those times (e.g., Gangestad et al., 2002; Haselton & Gangestad, in press).

There are several candidate cues of fertility status men might use. Three studies found that men find the scent of ovulating women particularly attractive (e.g., Thornhill et al., 2003) and one found that men judge women's faces more attractive mid-cycle. If women's interests change across the cycle, their behavior might too. Whatever the cues, women are unlikely to have been designed through selection to send them. As noted at the outset, women do not have obvious sexual swellings mid-cycle, and they have sex throughout the cycle. These features may well be due to selection on women to suppress signs of fertility status. Men, nonetheless, should be selected to detect byproducts of fertility status not fully suppressed. Consistent with this idea, we (Gangestad et al., 2002) found that enhanced male vigilance of partners mid-cycle (as reported by women) was predicted by enhanced female interest in extra-pair men and not their partners. Men may be particularly vigilant of their partners mid-cycle, when their partners least want them to be.

ADDITIONAL OVULATORY ADAPTATIONS AND BYPRODUCTS

Women's preferences and biases may shift not only toward certain men, but away from clearly undesirable mating options (e.g., incest, rape; e.g., Chavanne & Gallup, 1998). Fessler and Navarrete (2003) assessed women's disgust in several domains: maladaptive sex such as incest and bestiality, food aversiveness, and filth. Only disgust to maladaptive sex rose with fertility.

Women can identify male faces as male more quickly when fertile (e.g., Macrae, Alnwick, Milne, & Schloerscheidt, 2002). This effect is perhaps a byproduct of greater salience of masculine features in male faces associated with their preference when women are fertile. Adaptive ovulatory shifts in preferences, sexual interests, and biases may produce a variety of other byproducts.

CONCLUSION

In any socially monogamous species in which males heavily invest in offspring, there is an inevitable genetic conflict between partners over where the female obtains genes for her off-spring. Changes across the ovulatory cycle in women's and men's behavior may contain telltale signs of this conflict.

Many questions remain unanswered. Which female mate preferences strengthen mid-cycle; which don't? Is the pattern consistent with the good-genes hypothesis? Some preferences may be for compatible genes, ones that complement those of the mate chooser (e.g., dissimilar major histocompatibility complex [MHC] genes). Are preferences for compatibility maximal mid-cycle (see Thornhill et al., 2003)? How do male-partner features (e.g., symmetry, MHC dissimilarity) or relationship characteristics (e.g., satisfaction) affect female sexual interest mid-cycle? Do cycle shifts endure across women's reproductive lifespan? Are they robust across human populations? How, precisely, do men behave differently toward fertile partners and what cues mediate changes? Do women resist partners' proprietary actions more mid-cycle? What proximate mechanisms (e.g., hormones) mediate cycle shifts? (Changes in female preferences for the scent of symmetrical men are best predicted by corresponding changes in women's testosterone [positively] and progesterone [negatively], but other candidates [e.g., estrogen, luteinizing hormone] are possible.) Do men's hormones (e.g., testosterone) fluctuate in response to female partners' ovulatory status?

An evolutionary approach uniquely views ovulation as a highly important event around which psychological adaptations might evolve. Alternative nonevolutionary approaches could not have predicted a priori or accounted for these findings. More generally, then, the ovulatory-shift hypothesis illustrates the heuristic value of an adaptationist perspective, guiding researchers to explore domains otherwise unexplored and generating fruitful predictions not offered by other approaches.

Recommended Reading

Gangestad, S.W., Thornhill, R., & Garver-Apgar, C.E. (in press). Adaptations to ovulation. In D.M. Buss (Ed.), *Evolutionary Psychology Handbook*. Boston: Allyn-Bacon.

Jennions, M.D., & Petrie, M. (2000). Why do females mate multiply?: A review of the genetic benefits. *Biological Reviews, 75,* 21–64.

Kappeler, P.M., & van Schaik, C.P. (Eds.) (2004). *Sexual selection in primates: New and comparative perspectives*. Cambridge, U.K.: Cambridge University Press.

Rice, W.R., & Holland, B. (1997). The enemies within: Intragenomic conflict, interlocus contest evolution (ICE), and the intraspecific Red Queen. *Behavioral Ecology and Sociobiology, 41,* 1–10.

Note

1. Address correspondence to Steve Gangestad, Department of Psychology, University of New Mexico, Albuquerque, NM 87111; email: sgangest@unm.edu.

References

Chavanne, T.J., & Gallup, G.G. (1998). Variation in risk taking behavior among female college students as a function of the menstrual cycle. *Evolution and Human Behavior, 19,* 27–32.

Fessler, D.M.T., & Navarrete, C.D. (2003). Domain-specific variation in disgust sensitivity across the menstrual cycle. *Evolution and Human Behavior, 324,* 406–417.

Gangestad, S.W., Simpson, J.A., Cousins, A.J., Garver-Apgar, C.E., & Christensen, P.N. (2004). Women's preferences for male behavioral displays change across the menstrual cycle. *Psychological Science, 15,* 203–207.

Gangestad, S.W., & Thornhill, R. (1998). Menstrual cycle variation in women's preference for the scent of symmetrical men. *Proceedings of the Royal Society of London, B, 262,* 727–733.

Gangestad, S.W., Thornhill, R., & Garver, C.E. (2002). Changes in women's sexual interests and their partners' mate retention tactics across the menstrual cycle: Evidence for shifting conflicts of interest. *Proceedings of the Royal Society of London, B, 269,* 975–982.

Gangestad, S.W., Thornhill, R., & Garver-Apgar, C.E. (2005). Female sexual interests across the ovulatory cycle depend on primary partner developmental instability. *Proceedings of the Royal Society of London, B, 272,* 2023–2027.

Haselton, M.G., & Gangestad, S.W. (in press). Conditional expression of female desires and male mate retention efforts across the human ovulatory cycle. *Hormones and Behavior.*

Haselton, M.G., & Miller, G.F. (in press). Evidence for ovulatory shifts in attraction to artistic and entrepreneurial excellence. *Human Nature.*

Johnston, V.S., Hagel, R., Franklin, M., Fink, B., & Grammer, K. (2001). Male facial attractiveness: Evidence for hormone mediated adaptive design. *Evolution and Human Behavior, 23,* 251–267.

Macrae, C.N., Alnwick, K.A., Milne, A.B., & Schloerscheidt, A.M. (2002). Person perception across the menstrual cycle: Hormonal influences on social-cognitive functioning. *Psychological Science, 13,* 532–536.

Penton-Voak, I.S., Perrett, D.I., Castles, D., Burt, M., Kobayashi, T., & Murray, L.K. (1999). Female preference for male faces changes cyclically. *Nature, 399,* 741–742.

Pillsworth, E.G., Haselton, M.G., & Buss, D.M. (2004). Ovulatory shifts in female sexual desire. *Journal of Sex Research, 41,* 55–65.

Puts, D.A. (2005). Mating context and menstrual phase affect women's preference for male voice pitch. *Evolution and Human Behavior, 26,* 388–397.

Thornhill, R., & Gangestad, S.W. (1999). The scent of symmetry: A human pheromone that signals fitness? *Evolution and Human Behavior, 20,* 175–201.

Thornhill, R., Gangestad, S.W., Miller, R., Scheyd, G., McCollough, J., & Franklin, M. (2003). MHC, symmetry and body scent attractiveness in men and women (*Homo sapiens*). *Behavioral Ecology, 14,* 668–678.

Section 2: Critical Thinking Questions

1. What do you think of the idea that political conservatism is motivated by a need for "system justification?" Most academics have a liberal orientation—does Jost's research constitute an unfair attack on the right? What about research efforts to increase organizational citizenship—is this just an attempt to get people to do more than they're paid to do? Or, are workers actually better off if they can take this attitude? If so, why?

2. Evolutionary perspectives on human behavior are criticized as being very difficult to prove—after all, we can't go back in time to see how we actually evolved. How persuasive do you find these articles' arguments regarding altruism and sexual motivation? If you accept the evolutionary arguments, does this mean that human behavior is somewhat hard-wired? (i.e., are men and women "programmed" to look outside of their relationships at certain times? Can we program others to do what we want just by making them feel grateful?)

This article has been reprinted as it originally appeared in *Current Directions in Psychological Science.* Citation information for this article as originally published appears above.

Section 3: Non-Conscious Influences on Motivation

This section deals with both personal and social motivation, considering a variety of factors that might have *non-conscious influence* upon both types of motivation. The first two articles concern situational factors, and are excellent examples of "priming" research. Vohs, Meade, and Goode show that priming the concept of *money* (in a way that participants don't notice) has large effects on social motivation, making people want to work harder, but also making them less helpful and less willing to connect and cooperate with others. Strikingly, people don't even have to be trying to get money themselves for these effects to occur—merely activating the concept of money does it. If reciprocal altruism (discussed in the previous section) is the root of much human good, then it appears that money may indeed be the root of some (but of course not all) "evil." Elliott and Maier address an experience that we all fear: Getting back a paper full of red marks! They show that subtly priming the color *red* affects peoples' cognitive and test performance, even if the color has nothing to do with critical remarks or grading. It is likely that both "money" and "red" have effects because of peoples' past conditioning, and these articles show that motivators should think carefully before embedding these potent symbols within a social situation or context.

The third and fourth articles also address non-conscious influences on motivation, but focus on factors that come from within, rather than from the situation. Goldenberg first describes *terror management theory,* the provocative idea that much of our behavior is driven by the urgent (but non-conscious) need to deny or cope with the knowledge of our own eventual death. She then describes data showing that when people are primed with thoughts of death, they become much more uncomfortable with "bodily" issues such as sex, excretion, and physical appearance. Why? Because we would rather believe that humans have some kind of immortality compared to animals, but these issues remind us of our animal nature. If you are new to terror management theory, these ideas are worth thinking deeply about! The fourth article by Pelham, Carvallo, and Jones discusses our *implicit egotism,* that is, our tendency to like anything that is like us. This tendency is also non-conscious, and even applies to such surprising personal characteristics as the first letter of our names. To an extent far exceeding chance, people prefer professions, cities, states, and romantic partners whose names start with the same letter as their own! Pelham and colleagues have done a nice job of ruling out alternative explanations for these fascinating findings.

71

Merely Activating the Concept of Money Changes Personal and Interpersonal Behavior

Kathleen D. Vohs[1]
Department of Marketing, Carlson School of Management, University of Minnesota

Nicole L. Mead
Department of Psychology, Florida State University

Miranda R. Goode
Sauder School of Business, University of British Columbia

Abstract

Money plays a significant role in people's lives, and yet little experimental attention has been given to the psychological underpinnings of money. We systematically varied whether and to what extent the concept of money was activated in participants' minds using methods that minimized participants' conscious awareness of the money cues. On the one hand, participants reminded of money were less helpful than were participants not reminded of money, and they also preferred solitary activities and less physical intimacy. On the other hand, reminders of money prompted participants to work harder on challenging tasks and led to desires to take on more work as compared to participants not reminded of money. In short, even subtle reminders of money elicit big changes in human behavior.

Keywords

money; self; competency; performance; helping; interpersonal relationships

Money changes people. Although this statement seems to be a truism, little work has been done to test the psychological underpinnings of money. We examined the potential cognitive, motivational, emotional, and behavioral changes that result from the activation of the idea of money in people's minds. We found that even subtle reminders of money produce robust changes in behavior. Money-related concepts have been studied in psychology, sociology, marketing, anthropology, and health sciences, and this research hints at money having dual effects. These studies have found that money is bad for the interpersonal self but can be good for the personal self (Vohs, Mead, & Goode, 2006).

On the former point, research is clear that the love of money is often the start of trouble—relationship trouble, mostly. Americans who highly value money have poorer relationships than do those who take a more moderate approach to money (e.g., Kasser & Ryan, 1993). People's mental health is also harmed when they value both family relationships and the possession of material objects, because these two values conflict and cause mental stress (Burroughs & Rindfleisch, 2002). (Intriguingly, people who value material objects but not family do not have mental health repercussions.) Hence, wanting money or what money can buy impairs relationship-related outcomes.

However, life seems to be better when people have money than when people lack money. Evidence that has been widely discussed and debated (Diener & Seligman, 2004) suggests that having more money is associated with more frequent positive emotions and less frequent negative emotions than having less money is (although methodological factors may contribute to the effect; Kahneman, Krueger, Schkade, Schwarz, & Stone, 2006). Other work shows that having money is good for personal health. Studies of socioeconomic status (of which income is a major determinant) consistently indicate that financial strain has negative effects on mortality (Adler & Snibbe, 2003). Financial strain is accompanied by heightened depression, ill physical health, and lower feelings of control (Price, Choi, & Vinokur, 2002). Recent work revealed that having money protects people from unfortunate and unforeseen perturbations in life, mainly because money allows for control over the outcomes (Johnson & Krueger, 2006). In short, having money confers benefits to people's lives.

We found it somewhat puzzling that wanting money seems to make life worse, but having money makes life better; after all, few (if any) other major wants or needs have this quality. So we developed a pair of hypotheses to reveal more about the psychological effects of money.

PREDICTING THE DUAL EFFECTS OF MONEY

Common uses of money include procurement of goods and being rewarded for successful task completion (Lea & Webley, 2006). In some cases, people exchange resources in a manner that is sensitive to the contribution that each person makes to the exchange (i.e., ratio-based exchange, for which money is the quintessential, but not only, mechanism). That is, person A may have performed a task that yields an output that person B finds exceptionally valuable. In return for being allowed to own or use the output of that task, B may give A some money. When people trade resources on the basis of equity, the more that B values the output, the more money B should give A in a proportional sense. This type of exchange defines what is known as a market-pricing mode, one of the four fundamental ways of relating to others socially (Fiske, 1991). Market pricing underlies cost/benefit analyses, in that a person considers what he or she will receive in return before enacting a given behavior. Because money is the most typical form of market pricing, over time, the mere presence of money should elicit a market-pricing orientation toward the world.

This framework led to two hypotheses. Our first hypothesis was that money is linked to a focus on personal inputs and outputs, which may manifest behaviorally as an emphasis on personal performance. This prediction came from the fact that people use money to procure goods and services to enable them to meet personal needs, which they can do far more efficiently with money than they could without it. A secondary source of support comes from the fact that money rewards successful task completion, which means that money often follows from performance efforts. Hence, we predicted that reminding people of the concept of money would encourage individual performance efforts.

Although promoting personal performance may be beneficial for getting ahead, it may not be the best for getting along with others. If money conjures up a market-pricing mode, in which people think of life in transactional terms with inputs and expected outputs, then one might expect problems when it comes to socially relating to others. Indeed, the mode that underlies the connectedness found in warm and intimate relationships is located at the opposite end of the relational-model spectrum (Fiske, 1991), suggesting that behaviors elicited by one mode may clash with the other mode. Hence, our second hypothesis was that being reminded of money would make people less sensitive to the needs of others than they would be without that reminder.

We used the term *self-sufficiency* to describe the inner state that accompanies a market pricing mode. Self-sufficiency is defined as an emphasis on behaviors of one's own choosing accomplished without active involvement from others. Being in a self-sufficient state would mean being hesitant to allow others to involve the self in their activities (for more information on the term self-sufficiency, see Vohs et al., 2006).

TESTING THE MIXED EFFECT OF MONEY

Research on concepts related to money (e.g., materialism, desire for money, wealth, financial strain) yielded some important ideas about the possible effects of money, but it was unclear whether money was the sole driving force. There are many differences between wealthy and nonwealthy people and between people who value material goods and those who do not, and these differences may have been driving the effects in extant research. Therefore, we took our hypotheses to the laboratory and used experimental manipulations to change how strongly or weakly the concept of money was activated in participants' minds. We randomly assigned participants to the different conditions, thereby eliminating concerns that different types of people could produce the effects. Together, these two features allowed us to make causal claims about whether money per se determines the observed effects. Additionally, we used subtle reminders, or *primes,* to uncover natural mental associations by minimizing the salience of the manipulations, such that participants were likely unaware of the presence of monetary cues.

The methods we used can be categorized into four broad classes. In one manipulation, participants played the board game Monopoly, after which participants moved on to a new task. But before the new task began, we gave participants in the high-money condition $4,000 of play money and gave participants in the low-money condition $200, which we simply said was "for later." Participants in the control condition also played the game but afterwards were given no play money. A second manipulation asked participants to think about life with abundant or restricted finances. A third manipulation had participants organize phrases that were or were not related to money ("I cashed a check" versus "I wrote the letter"). A fourth manipulation involved participants sitting near images of cash or neutral images. All of these manipulations yielded similar effects.

We first investigated the effects of money on social relationships by testing helpfulness toward others. We predicted that reminders of money would detract from helpfulness due to its suspected role in straining social relationships. Moreover, helpfulness is a socially valuable motive that we predicted would reflect changes in underlying preferences related to sociality. We measured helpfulness in four experiments that varied whether the helping opportunity involved offering time or offering money. In one experiment, participants were reminded of money via the Monopoly game method mentioned earlier. Later, the experimenter took the participant across the laboratory ostensibly to perform a task in another room, and at a certain moment when the participant walked by, a confederate (a woman who worked for the laboratory, unbeknownst to participants) also walked by and spilled 27 pencils in front of the participant. Participants who had been strongly reminded of money were less helpful than either set of participants who had been weakly reminded of money (i.e., the low-money and control groups) in that they picked up fewer pencils. In another experiment, participants first were reminded of money (or not) via a linguistic puzzle and then met a confused peer (actually another confederate working for the lab). The confused peer asked for help in understanding instructions for a task on which she was working. Participants not reminded of money spent 120% more time helping the confused student than did those who had been reminded of money.

Although we had observed multiple instances of reduced helpfulness among participants reminded of money, we wondered whether we had given money-reminded participants a suitable opportunity to help. Perhaps being helpful by giving money is preferred among people who have been reminded of money. Prior to the manipulation, we paid participants for their participation by giving them eight quarters ($2). Participants were nonconsciously reminded of money or neutral constructs and then given a private opportunity to donate to the University Student Fund. Consistent with our findings on helping in terms of time, we found that participants who had been unobtrusively reminded of money donated less money than did neutral participants. In fact, participants who had been reminded of money donated only 39% of their payment, compared with 67% donated by participants in the control group.

To widen the scope of the findings, three additional experiments tested whether participants who were reminded of money preferred differing amounts of social contact. In one experiment, participants were reminded of money, nature, or no specific content, by being exposed to one of three screensavers (see Fig. 1); participants in the control group were exposed to a blank screen. The screensavers were displayed on a computer screen on top of the desk at which participants were seated. Afterward, participants were told that the next task involved a getting-acquainted conversation with a participant who was down the hall. As the experimenter left the room, ostensibly to retrieve the would-be conversation partner, she pointed to a chair in the corner of the room and told the participant to pull that chair toward the participant's own chair for the upcoming interaction. Distance between the chairs was taken as a tacit sign of preferred social intimacy. Participants who had been reminded of money put more physical distance between themselves and the unacquainted interaction partner than did participants who were not reminded of money (Fig. 1).

We also considered the idea that money prompts separateness from strangers but not from friends and loved ones. In one experiment, we exposed participants to money reminders by having them complete questionnaires while seated at a desk placed underneath a poster of hard currency or a watercolor print (Fig. 2, see p. 78). Afterwards, participants were given a list of leisure activities and asked

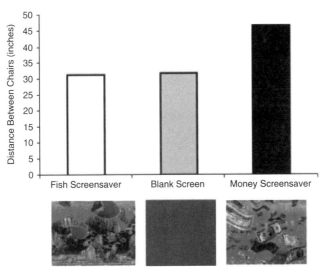

Fig. 1. Distance between chairs (in inches) as a function of prior exposure to a fish screensaver, no screensaver, or a money screensaver. Participants' placement of their chair relative to an unacquainted participant's chair was considered to be an indicator of preferred social distance. Participants sat at a desk to complete a packet of questionnaires, and one of the two screensavers or a blank screen could be seen in their visual periphery. Screenshots of the two screensavers can be seen below each bar graph; both are commercially available at www.geliosoft.com.

to indicate which they would find enjoyable. The list was organized such that participants were forced to choose between activities for one person (e.g., reading a favorite novel) and shared activities (e.g., going to a café with a friend). To test whether being with loved ones would trump the tendency for money to prompt social separateness, the list specifically mentioned activities with friends, family, and loved ones. Nonetheless, participants who had been reminded of money preferred solo leisure activities more than did neutral participants.

Given frequent use of money as an incentive for good performance or dedicated effort, we conducted three experiments related to task performance and persistence. When offered the choice to work on a task alone or with another person, participants who had been reminded of money were three times more likely to choose to work alone than were those not so reminded (84% versus 28%; Fig. 3, see p. 79). To work with someone else presumably meant sharing some of the work (or at the very least doing the task oneself, in which case the workload would be the same as if completed by oneself), so we can safely assume that participants who chose to work alone recognized that they would be taking on more work. Thus, participants who nonetheless opted to work alone must have desired to be alone so much that they were willing to be responsible for the entire job.

In two additional experiments involving performance-related behavior, participants were given difficult or impossible tasks; help was available from either the experimenter or a peer (respectively). Time spent working on the challenging tasks before requesting help was the dependent measure. Consistent with our earlier experiments, we found that participants reminded of money worked 48%

Fig. 2. Posters used to prime money (top) and neutral concepts (bottom). Participants sat at a desk to complete a packet of questionnaires, and one of these posters could be seen out of their visual periphery.

longer, averaged across both experiments, before asking for help than did participants who were not reminded of money.

In summary, we found that small reminders of money produced large changes in behavior. Compared to neutral conditions, when the construct of money was activated, participants behaved in ways that were both more desirable (persistence on challenging tasks; taking on more work for oneself) and more undesirable (reduced helpfulness; placing more distance between the self and others)—in short, a mixed bag that echoes people's ambivalence toward money and the divergent findings observed in extant research.

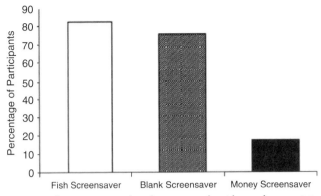

Fig. 3. Percentage of participants who chose to work with another participant (versus alone) on an upcoming task as a function of whether they had been exposed earlier to a fish screensaver, a blank screen, or a money screensaver. (See Fig. 1 for screensaver shots.)

KNOWNS AND UNKNOWNS

The effects of money on behavior are large and consistent, but also diverse. Our most pressing question is: Why does being reminded of money have the effects that it does?

Self-sufficiency may or may not prove to be the best explanation for the data. We have no validated indicator of self-sufficiency, and therefore it is crucial to consider constructs instead of, or in addition to, self-sufficiency. Here, we think it best to describe some of our null findings, which bear on some of the alternate explanations for the observed effects and, given that they occurred in experiments that showed other statistically significant results, may be relevant. One such null finding is that participants reported being in similar emotional states regardless of whether they had been reminded of money. A lack of emotion differences assuages concerns that money renders people distrusting of others, anxious, or prideful, which in turn would account for our findings. Others have interpreted our findings as demonstrating that money makes people selfish. The idea that money leads to greed or selfishness seems to be part of modern Western cultural lore but does not seem to fit our data: A selfish person likely would have immediately asked for help when given a tough assignment (cf. aforementioned findings) and would have rejected the notion of accepting more work than was necessary (cf. Fig. 3).

We are eager to explore the idea that money leads to a perspective on the world that emphasizes inputs and outputs with an expectation of equity (cf. Fiske, 1991)—a perspective that would emphasize performance and, consequently, may harm interpersonal sensitivity. In light of our findings that money enhances performance strivings, the link between money and feelings of personal control, which surface repeatedly from studies on income, should be explored. Unpublished findings from our laboratory suggest that the market-pricing explanation is promising in that, after people are reminded of money, they show improved memory of exchange-related information, prefer exchange-based relationships, and follow equity rules.

CONCLUSION

Money is a constant in modern life, yet there has been a dearth of basic experimental research on money's psychological underpinnings. We encourage scientists to turn their attention toward the cognitive, motivational, and behavioral consequences of money, because the centrality of money in people's lives shows no sign of waning.

Recommended Reading

Diener, E., & Seligman, M.E.P. (2004). (See References). A discussion of the role of money and nonmonetary factors in well-being in the context of public policy.
Kahneman, D., Krueger, A., Schkade, D., Schwarz, N., & Stone, A. (2006). (See References). An argument that the statistical relationship between income and happiness is due to an attentional bias.
Lea, S.E.G., & Webley, P. (2006). Money as tool, money as drug: The biological psychology of a strong incentive. *Behavioral and Brain Sciences, 29,* 161–209. A comprehensive theory of money as a powerful incentive.
Vohs, K.D., Mead, N.L., & Goode, M.R. (2006). (See References). Discusses the experiments summarized in the current report, along with an expanded self-sufficiency theory of money.

Note

1. Address correspondence to Kathleen D. Vohs, University of Minnesota, Carlson School of Management, Department of Marketing, 3-150 321 19th Ave. So., Minneapolis, MN 55455; e-mail: kvohs@umn.edu.

References

Adler, N.E., & Snibbe, A.C. (2003). The role of psychosocial processes in explaining the gradient between socioeconomic status and health. *Current Directions in Psychological Science, 12,* 119–123.
Almond, R. (2004). "I can do it (all) myself": Clinical technique with defensive narcissistic self-sufficiency. *Psychoanalytical Psychology, 21,* 371–384.
Bergman, M.M. (1991). Computer-enhanced self-sufficiency: I. Creation and implementation of a text writer for an individual with traumatic brain injury. *Neuropsychology, 5,* 17–23.
Burroughs, J.E., & Rindfleisch, A. (2002). Materialism and well-being: A conflicting values perspective. *Journal of Consumer Research, 29,* 348–370.
Diener, E., & Seligman, M.E.P. (2004). Beyond money. *Psychological Science in the Public Interest, 5,* 1–31.
Fiske, A.P. (1991). *Structures of social life: The four elementary forms of human relations.* New York: Free Press.
Johnson, W., & Krueger, R.F. (2006). How money buys happiness: Genetic and environmental processes linking finances and life satisfaction. *Journal of Personality and Social Psychology, 90,* 680–691.
Kahneman, D., Krueger, A., Schkade, D., Schwarz, N., & Stone, A. (2006). Would you be happier if you were richer? A focusing illusion. *Science, 312,* 1908–1910.
Kasser, T., & Ryan, R.M. (1993). A dark side of the American dream: Correlates of financial success as a central life aspiration. *Journal of Personality and Social Psychology, 65,* 410–422.
Lea, S.E.G., & Webley, P. (2006). Money as tool, money as drug: The biological psychology of a strong incentive. *Behavioral and Brain Sciences, 29,* 161–209.

Price, R.H., Choi, J.N., & Vinokur, D.A. (2002). Links in the chain of diversity following job loss: How financial strain and loss of personal control lead to depression, impaired functioning, and poor health. *Journal of Occupational Health Psychology, 7*, 302–312.

Vohs, K.D., Mead, N.L., & Goode, M.R. (2006). The psychological consequences of money. *Science, 314*, 1154–1156.

This article has been reprinted as it originally appeared in *Current Directions in Psychological Science*. Citation information for this article as originally published appears above.

Color and Psychological Functioning

Andrew J. Elliot[1]
University of Rochester

Markus A. Maier
University of Munich, Munich, Germany

Abstract

Color is a ubiquitous perceptual experience, yet little scientific information about the influence of color on affect, cognition, and behavior is available. Accordingly, we have developed a general model of color and psychological functioning, which we present in this article. We also describe a hypothesis derived from this model regarding the influence of red in achievement contexts. In addition, we report a series of experiments demonstrating that a brief glimpse of red evokes avoidance motivation and undermines intellectual performance, and that it has these effects without conscious awareness or intention. We close with thoughts on the need for rigorous scientific work on color psychology.

Keywords

color; red; avoidance; approach; motivation

Every visual stimulus processed by the human perceptual system contains color information. Given the prevalence of color, one would expect color psychology to be a well-developed area. Surprisingly, little theoretical or empirical work has been conducted to date on the influence of color on psychological functioning, and the work that has been done has been driven mostly by practical concerns, not scientific rigor. As such, although the popular and applied literatures are replete with statements regarding the content of color associations and their presumed impact on behavior (e.g., "Green is peaceful and helps people relax"), the lack of theory and carefully controlled experimentation makes clear conclusions about color associations and their implications elusive (Levy, 1984; Whitfield & Wiltshire, 1990).

Given the disparity between the ubiquity of color stimuli and the dearth of extant theory and research on color psychology, we have developed a general model of color and psychological functioning. In this article, we set a conceptual and empirical context for our model, present the model, and describe one main hypothesis derived from it. Then, we overview a research program designed to test various aspects of this hypothesis. Finally, we briefly describe a second hypothesis generated from our model, and close with thoughts on the need for rigorous scientific work on color psychology.

EXTANT THEORETICAL AND EMPIRICAL WORK

Most existing work on color and psychological functioning is applied, as opposed to theoretically based. The questions that drive this type of research include: What colors influence retail behavior? What colors influence food preference?

What colors influence worker mood and productivity? What colors influence physical health and aggressive behavior? What color preferences are associated with different personality types? Such research simply seeks to establish relations between color stimuli and affect, cognition, or behavior for pragmatic purposes; it seeks neither to explain why such relations occur nor to test basic principles regarding psychological functioning.

Of the existing research that is theoretically based, most has been loosely guided by Goldstein's (1942) proposal that red and yellow are naturally experienced as stimulating and disagreeable, that these colors focus people on the outward environment, and that they produce forceful, expansive behavior, whereas green and blue are experienced as quieting and agreeable, focus people inward, and produce reserved, stable behavior. Subsequent researchers have tended to interpret Goldstein's proposal in terms of wavelength and arousal: Longer-wavelength colors like red are experienced as arousing, and shorter-wavelength colors like green are experienced as calming (e.g., Stone & English, 1998).

Aside from Goldstein's proposal and its derivatives, most theoretical statements about color rely on general associations. Different colors are presumed to have different associations, and viewing a color is thought to trigger psychological responses consistent with these associations. For example, Frank and Gilovich (1988) posited that black is associated with evil and death and, therefore, leads to aggressive behavior. Likewise, Soldat, Sinclair, and Mark (1997) proposed that red and blue are associated with happiness and sadness, respectively, and therefore lead to cognitive processing and behavior consistent with those emotions. Such models tend to focus on one or two colors/associations and typically propose general links between colors and functioning across situations.

Existing research on these proposals tends to be sparse and spotty, occasionally supporting some hypotheses but not others. Although the popular and even scientific literatures commonly state as fact that long-wavelength colors are arousing and short-wavelength colors are calming, the actual data simply are not supportive. Frank and Gilovich's (1988) proposal is supported by some data, but that proffered by Soldat et al. (1997) is not. Furthermore, the extant research on color and psychological functioning in general is plagued by several weaknesses. First, perhaps due to the applied nature of the work, many studies have neglected to follow basic experimental procedures such as experimenter blindness to hypothesis and condition. Second, many of the manipulations in these studies have been uncontrolled (e.g., presenting color on an office wall for 4 days) or have altered participants' typical perceptual experience (e.g., presenting color via overhead lights). Third, and most important, almost no extant research has examined the effect of hue while controlling for lightness (similar to brightness) and chroma (similar to saturation), despite the fact that these other color attributes can themselves influence psychological functioning.

A MODEL OF COLOR AND PSYCHOLOGICAL FUNCTIONING AND A HYPOTHESIS DERIVED FROM THE MODEL

We (Elliot, Maier, Moller, Friedman, & Meinhardt, 2007) have developed a general model of color and psychological functioning, the core premises of which are stated in the following. First, colors can carry specific meanings. Color is not just about aesthetics—it also communicates specific information. Second, color meanings are grounded in two basic sources: learned associations that develop from repeated pairings of colors with particular messages, concepts, or experiences; and biologically based proclivities to respond to particular colors in particular ways in particular situations. Some color associations may emerge from learning alone, but color theorists suspect that many such associations emerge from evolutionarily ingrained responses to color stimuli (Mollon, 1989). Research indicates that colors often serve a signal function for nonhuman animals (e.g., the redness of fruit signals readiness for eating), thereby facilitating fitness-relevant behavior (Hutchings, 1997). If, as we suspect, humans are "prepared" to respond to color stimuli in a similar fashion, then at least some color associations may represent a cognitive reinforcing or shaping of biologically based response tendencies. Third, the mere perception of color evokes evaluative processes. Color computations occur at an early level within the visual system, and evaluative processes are so fundamental that they are present, at least in rudimentary form, in all animate life (Schneirla, 1959). By "evaluative processes" we mean basic mechanisms that discern whether a stimulus is hostile or hospitable (Elliot & Covington, 2001). Fourth, the evaluative processes evoked by color stimuli produce motivated behavior. Color stimuli that carry a positive meaning produce approach responses, whereas those that carry a negative meaning produce avoidance responses. Fifth, color typically exerts its influence on psychological functioning in an automatic fashion; the full process from evaluation of the color stimulus to activation and operation of motivated behavior typically takes place without conscious intention or awareness. Given that the influence of color tends to be nonconscious in nature, color effects tend to persist, even when they are deleterious. Sixth, color meanings and effects are contextual. A given color has different implications for feelings, thoughts, and behaviors in different contexts (e.g., achievement contexts, relational contexts).

Our research to date has focused primarily on the color red in achievement contexts. Our hypothesis is that red carries the meaning of danger in such contexts, specifically the psychological danger of failure (Elliot, Maier, Moller, et al., 2007). One source of this red–danger link is presumed to be teachers' use of red ink to mark students' mistakes and errors. This specific association is likely grounded in a more general societal association between red and danger where negative possibilities are salient, such as stop signs and warning signals. These learned associations may be bolstered by or even derived from an evolutionarily ingrained predisposition across species to interpret red as a signal of danger in competitive contexts. For example, in primates, red on the chest or face (due to a testosterone surge) signals the high status, and thus danger, of an opponent (Setchell & Wickings, 2005). Thus, through both specific and general associative processes that may themselves emerge from biologically based proclivities, red carries the meaning of failure in achievement contexts, warning that a dangerous possibility is at hand. This warning signal is posited to produce avoidance-based motivation that primarily has negative implications for achievement outcomes. The influence of red in achievement contexts is presumed to take place outside of individuals' conscious awareness.

OUR EMPIRICAL WORK ON RED IN ACHIEVEMENT CONTEXTS

We began our empirical work with four experiments designed to test the effect of red on intellectual performance (Elliot, Maier, Moller, et al., 2007, Experiments 1–4). In the first experiment, participants completed an anagram test that contained a red, green, or black subject number in the upper right-hand corner. Green provided a chromatic contrast to red, its opposite in several color models, and green has some general associations with approach motivation. Black, an achromatic color, served as a neutral control. At the end of this and all experiments in this research program, participants received a careful debriefing that probed their awareness of the purpose of the experiment. Results indicated that participants shown red solved fewer anagrams than those shown green or black; those shown green or black did not differ. Participants were unaware of the purpose of the experiment. Additional experiments replicated this finding using different achromatic controls (white, gray), a different method of presenting color (on a test cover; see Figs. 1 & 2), and color stimuli equated on all color parameters except hue (this was true in all experiments reported below). In some of these subsequent experiments, participants' motivation and perceived competence were assessed with self-report measures; null results were obtained on these measures, indicating that participants were unaware of the effect color had on their motivation and performance.

Given that our initial experiments showed no effect of red on conscious reports of avoidance motivation, we conducted two additional experiments to examine the effect of red on nonconscious avoidance motivation (Elliot, Maier, Moller, et al., 2007, Experiments 5–6). Both of these experiments manipulated color using the test-cover procedure described above. In one experiment, after the color manipulation and before (ostensibly) taking a test, participants selected the number of easy and moderately difficult items they wanted on the test; selection of easy items is a classic indicator of avoidance motivation. Results indicated that participants shown red selected more easy items than those shown green or

Fig. 1. An example test cover used in our experiments.

85

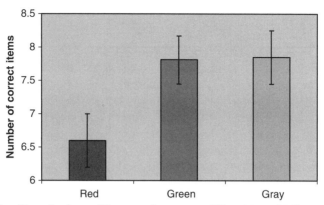

Fig. 2. The effect of color on IQ test performance in Elliot, Maier, Moller, et al. (2007, Experiment 4): Mean number of correctly solved items by color on the cover of the test (means are adjusted for general ability, premanipulation performance, and gender). Confidence intervals (95%) are indicated by vertical lines. "Red" participants performed significantly worse than "green" participants and "gray" participants, who did not differ from each other.

gray; participants shown green or gray did not differ. In the other experiment, after the color manipulation and prior to (ostensibly) taking a test, participants' prefrontal cortical activity was assessed using electroencephalography (EEG); right (relative to left) prefrontal cortical activity indicates that avoidance motivation has been activated in the brain. Results indicated that participants shown red evidenced more right prefrontal cortical activity than those shown green or gray; participants shown green and gray did not differ.

In a separate set of experiments, we examined the effect of red on physically enacted avoidance behavior (Elliot, Maier, Binser, Friedman, & Pekrun, 2007). In a first experiment, participants were shown red or green on the cover of an analogies test that they would (ostensibly) take in an adjacent lab. Participants shown red, relative to those shown green, knocked fewer times on the door of the adjacent lab as they anticipated taking the test. In a second experiment, participants were shown red, green, or gray on the cover of an IQ test that they would (ostensibly) take. A sensor was placed on participants to assess their body movement upon presentation of the test cover. Participants shown red moved their bodies away from the test cover to a greater degree than did those shown green or gray; those shown green or gray did not differ (see Fig. 3). Debriefing indicated that the effect of red in these experiments occurred without participants' awareness.

Finally, we conducted four experiments designed to test whether nonconscious avoidance motivation mediates the deleterious effect of red on intellectual performance (Maier, Elliot, & Lichtenfeld, 2007). In the final experiment in this series, participants were shown red or gray on the cover of an IQ test and then completed a visual-matching task assessing local (relative to global) processing of stimuli. Local processing represents an often rigid constricting of attention to the "trees" as opposed to the "forest" and is a well-established indicator of avoidance motivation. After the visual-matching task, participants completed an

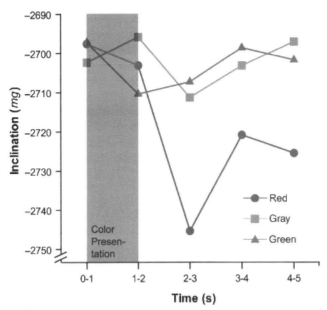

Fig. 3. The effect of color on body movement in Elliot, Maier, Binser, Friedman, and Pekrun (2007, Experiment 2). Mean inclination of the upper body over time in milli g (mg) units as related to the color on the cover of the IQ test. Negative mg values indicate angle adjustment away from the test cover.

IQ test. Results indicated that participants shown red performed worse and evidenced more local processing than did those shown gray. Furthermore, local processing was shown to mediate the direct effect of red on performance—that is, red led to more local processing, which in turn undermined performance.

OTHER CONTEXTS AND COLORS

All of the research that we have overviewed has been conducted in achievement contexts, but we are currently examining a second hypothesis that focuses on the color red in relational contexts (Elliot & Niesta, 2007). We posit that in relational situations, specifically those involving sexual attraction, red carries the meaning of love, passion, and sexual readiness. These associations are likely grounded in the use of red hearts to symbolize romance on Valentine's Day; the use of red lipstick, rouge, and lingerie to heighten attractiveness; and the use of red light to signal sexual availability in brothels. These learned associations may be bolstered by or even derived from the biologically ingrained use of red to attract mating partners during estrus in many nonhuman female mammals (Mollon, 1989). Thus, through associative processes that may themselves emerge from evolutionarily based proclivities, red signals love, passion, and sexual readiness, and the perception of red is presumed to produce approach-motivated behavior outside of individuals' conscious awareness.

Color effects on psychological functioning are not thought to be constrained to red. Other colors undoubtedly impact affect, cognition, and behavior as well, and research to examine such possibilities is needed. A core premise of our model is that color effects are context specific, and it will be important to attend carefully to this issue in subsequent research. Thus, in the United States, green may be linked with money and facilitate spending in consumer contexts, but green (especially blue-green) may be associated with mold and quash one's appetite in culinary contexts. Likewise, in the United States, black may be linked with evil/death and lead to aggression in zero-sum competitive contexts, but black may be associated with eroticism and enhance arousal in sexual contexts. Furthermore, although we believe that some color meanings and effects (such as those that are the focus of our work thus far) are biologically based and pancultural, it is likely that at least some color meanings and effects are entirely learned and vary by culture (e.g., black has negative associations in the United States that are not present in other countries lacking a history of prejudice against African Americans). As such, "context" must be considered not only in terms of domain but also in terms of culture.

CONCLUSION

Our research both provides a conceptual framework to guide research in the neglected area of color psychology and illustrates how rigorous empirical work in this area may be conducted. We think that this is a highly promising research area in which many pressing questions await empirical consideration (e.g., How do color associations develop, and how does this development differ when biologically based predispositions are present versus absent? How potent are color effects in real-world contexts containing a wide variety of color stimuli? What is the duration of color priming?). The scientific study of color and psychological functioning is not an easy enterprise, as it requires careful assessment and calibration of lightness and chroma, as well as hue. However, we believe such efforts pale in comparison to the benefits of documenting the influence of a ubiquitous feature of the perceived social environment on important affective, cognitive, and behavioral processes outside of conscious awareness. Social-cognitive research on priming focuses extensively on the effects of lexical, contextual, and relational stimuli on psychological functioning; we think the time has come to broaden this focus to include color stimuli.

Recommended Reading

Elliot, A.J., Maier, M.A., Moller, A.C., Friedman, R., & Meinhardt, J. (2007). (See References)
Fehrman, K.R., & Fehrman, C. (2004). *Color: The secret influence* (2nd ed.). Upper Saddle River, NJ: Prentice Hall.
Whitfield, T.W., & Wiltshire, T.J. (1990). Color psychology: A critical review. *Genetic, Social & General Psychology Monographs, 116,* 387–412.

Note

1. Address correspondence to Andrew Elliot, Department of Clinical and Social Sciences in Psychology, University of Rochester, Rochester, NY, 14227; e-mail: andye@psych.rochester.edu.

References

Elliot, A.J., & Covington, M.V. (2001). Approach and avoidance motivation. *Educational Psychology Review, 13,* 73–92.

Elliot, A.J., Maier, M.A., Moller, A.C., Friedman, R., & Meinhardt, J. (2007). Color and psychological functioning: The effect of red on performance attainment. *Journal of Experimental Psychology: General, 136,* 154–168.

Elliot, A.J., Maier, M.A., Binser, M.J., Friedman, R., & Pekrun, R. (2007). The effect of red on avoidance behavior in achievement contexts. Manuscript submitted for publication.

Elliot, A.J., & Niesta, D. (2007). [The effect of red on sexual attraction]. Unpublished raw data.

Frank, M.G., & Gilovich, T. (1988). The dark side of self and social perception: Black uniforms and aggression in professional sports. *Journal of Personality and Social Psychology, 54,* 74–85.

Goldstein, K. (1942). Some experimental observations concerning the influence of colors on the function of the organism. *Occupational Therapy and Rehabilitation, 21,* 147–151.

Hutchings, J. (1997). Color in plants, animals, and man. In K. Nassau (Ed.), *Color for Science, Art, and Technology* (pp. 222–246). Amsterdam: Elsevier.

Levy, I.B. (1984). Research into the psychological meaning of color. *American Journal of Art Therapy, 23,* 58–62.

Maier, M.A., Elliot, A.J., & Lichtenfeld, S. (2007) Nonconscious avoidance motivation mediates the negative effect of red on intellectual performance. Manuscript submitted for publication.

Mollon, J.D. (1989). "Tho'she kneel'd in that place where they grow . . ." *Journal of Experimental Biology, 146,* 21–38.

Schneirla, T. (1959). An evolutionary and developmental theory of biphasic processes underlying approach and withdrawal. In M. Jones (Ed.), *Nebraska Symposium on Motivation* (pp. 1–42). Lincoln: University of Nebraska Press.

Setchell, J.M., & Wickings, E.J. (2005). Dominance, status signals, and coloration in male mandrills (*Mandrillus sphinx*). *Ethology, 111,* 25–50.

Soldat, A.S., Sinclair, R.C., & Mark, M.M. (1997). Color as an environmental processing cue: External affective cues can directly affect processing strategy without affecting mood. *Social Cognition, 15,* 55–71.

Stone, N.J., & English, A.J. (1998). Task type, posters, and workspace color on mood, satisfaction, and performance. *Journal of Environmental Psychology, 18,* 175–185.

Whitfield, T.W., & Wiltshire, T.J. (1990). Color psychology: A critical review. *Genetic, Social & General Psychology Monographs, 116,* 387–412.

This article has been reprinted as it originally appeared in *Current Directions in Psychological Science*. Citation information for this article as originally published appears above.

Implicit Egotism

Brett W. Pelham[1] and Mauricio Carvallo
University at Buffalo, State University of New York

John T. Jones
U.S. Military Academy, West Point

Abstract

People gravitate toward people, places, and things that resemble the self. We refer to this tendency as implicit egotism, and we suggest that it reflects an unconscious process that is grounded in people's favorable self-associations. We review recent archival and experimental research that supports this position, highlighting evidence that rules out alternate explanations and distinguishes implicit egotism from closely related ideas such as mere exposure. Taken together, the evidence suggests that implicit egotism is an implicit judgmental consequence of people's positive self-associations. We conclude by identifying promising areas for future research.

Keywords

implicit; egotism; self-esteem

Researchers have long known that how people view themselves plays an important role in virtually every aspect of their daily lives, including phenomena as diverse as personal achievement, interpersonal attraction, and even physical well-being. In recent years, however, researchers have argued that people's conscious self-evaluations provide an incomplete view of the self-concept. Specifically, researchers have argued that people's implicit (i.e., unconscious) self-evaluations also influence their judgment and behavior (Greenwald & Banaji, 1995; Hetts & Pelham, 2001). Implicit self-evaluations are not beliefs that a Freudian homunculus has banished to the unconscious. Instead, such beliefs are probably best conceptualized as part of the cognitive or adaptive unconscious (Kihlstrom, 1987). Presumably, some implicit self-evaluations consist of beliefs that were once conscious but have become highly automatized. Other implicit self-evaluations might be unconscious because they were formed prior to the individual's acquisition of language. Although few researchers have acknowledged the possibility, it may also be that implicit self-evaluations are a product of defensive processes to which people have little or no conscious access. Finally, implicit self-evaluations may be a product of classical conditioning or implicit learning, that is, associative learning that occurs in the absence of conscious awareness. Thus, just as puppies do not know why they salivate, people may not always know why they trust a stranger who sounds vaguely like Garrison Keillor.

It is now well documented that people possess implicit self-evaluations—that is, unconscious associations about the self. It is also well-documented that most implicit self-associations are highly favorable. Two decades ago, Nuttin (1985) showed that people like the letters that appear in their own names much more than other people like these same letters—a phenomenon Nuttin called the *name-letter effect*. Nuttin also showed that people who preferred the letters in their own names were typically unaware of the basis of this preference. Similarly, Beggan (1992) showed that once people are given an object people evaluate the object more favorably than they would otherwise—a phenomenon called the *mere-ownership effect*. Give Ivan a puppy, and he will overestimate the puppy's worth, presumably because the puppy has become an extension of the self.

It is now well established that people possess positive implicit associations about themselves. Until very recently, however, it was unclear whether people's implicit self-associations ever predict meaningful social behaviors (but see Dijksterhuis, 2004; Shimizu & Pelham, 2004; Spalding & Hardin, 1999). To address this question, we investigated the role of implicit self-associations in major life decisions. Our primary hypothesis was simple. If Dennis adores the letter *D*, then it might not be too far-fetched to expect Dennis to gravitate toward cities such as Denver, careers such as dentistry, and romantic partners such as Denise. Pelham, Mirenberg, and Jones (2002) referred to this unconscious tendency to prefer things that resemble the self as *implicit egotism*. In a series of articles (Jones, Pelham, Carvallo, & Mirenberg, 2004; Pelham, Mirenberg, & Jones, 2002; Pelham, Carvallo, DeHart, & Jones, 2003), we reported the results of numerous archival studies (i.e., studies relying on public records such as birth, marriage, or death records) and experiments suggesting that implicit egotism influences major life decisions. As suggested by the list in Table 1, (see p. 92) which summarizes many of our recent studies, implicit egotism appears to influence a wide variety of important decisions. In the remainder of this report, we address some of the strengths and limitations of our research on implicit egotism and then offer some suggestions for future research.

STUDYING IMPLICIT EGOTISM

In our initial article (Pelham et al., 2002), we argued that implicit egotism influences both where people choose to live and what people choose to do for a living. For instance, in Study 1 of this article, we identified four common female first names that strongly resembled the name of a Southeastern state. The names were Florence, Georgia, Louise, and Virginia, corresponding with the states Florida, Georgia, Louisiana, and Virginia. We then consulted Social Security Death Index (SSDI) records (kept since the advent of the Social Security system) to identify women who had died while living in each of the four relevant Southeastern states. This design yielded a 4 × 4 matrix of name–state combinations, and a total sample size of more than 75,000 women. Women named Florence, Georgia, Louise, and Virginia were all disproportionately likely (on average, 44% above chance values) to have resided in the state that closely resembled their first name.

Ruling Out Confounds

This study raised many concerns about possible confounds. One concern was the possibility that these women disproportionately resided in states whose names resembled their own first names simply because they had been named after the states in which they had been born (and had never moved). Although SSDI

Table 1. *A selective summary of the most comprehensive studies providing support for implicit egotism*

Pelham, B.W., Mirenberg, M.C., & Jones, J.K. (2002):

1. Four most common female first names that resemble Southeastern state names
2. Four most common male first names that resemble Southeastern state names
3. Eight largest U.S. states and surnames resembling these state names
4. Eight largest Canadian cities and surnames resembling these city names
5. Four most common male and female names that resemble the occupations "dentist" and "lawyer"
6. All U.S. cities that prominently feature number words in the names (matched with numbers corresponding to people's day and month of birth)

Pelham, B.W., Carvallo, M., DeHart, T., & Jones, J.T. (2003):

1. The 30 most common European American surnames and all U.S. cities that include the surname anywhere in the city name (e.g., Johnson City, Johnsonville, Fort Johnson, etc.)
2. The three most common U.S. surname pairs (e.g., Smith–Johnson) and street names that include these surnames (each pair was replicated individually in each U.S. state)
3. Three sets of surnames chosen to avoid spurious name–street matches (e.g., Hill–Park) and street names that included these names or words (each pair also replicated individually in each U.S. state)

Jones, J.T., Pelham, B.W., Carvallo, M., & Mirenberg, M.C. (2004):

1. Matches for first letter of surname in two large counties, covering approximately 150 years
2. Single initial surname matches for parents of every birth occurring in Texas in 1926
3. Systematic surname match studies of four large Southeastern states over about 150 years
4. Nationwide joint telephone listing study of 12 systematically chosen male and female first names
5. Laboratory experiments involving (a) birthday numbers, and (b) first three letters of surname
6. Subliminal conditioning study using participants' full names as conditioning stimuli

---

records do not indicate where the deceased were born, these records do indicate the state in which they resided when they applied for social security cards (typically as adults). Using these records, we were able to focus on people who got their social security cards in one state and died while residing in another—that is, people who had moved into the states in which they died. An analysis of these interstate immigrants yielded clear and consistent evidence for implicit egotism.

Another concern about this study is that the results might reflect explicit rather than implicit egotism. It would be extremely surprising if Virginia failed to notice the resemblance between her first name and the state name that appeared on her driver's license. Archival research methods do not always lend themselves well to documenting implicit effects. Nonetheless, we have tried. In other studies summarized in the same article (Pelham et al., 2002), we focused on names that, unlike Georgia and Virginia, shared only their first few letters with the states or cities to which people with those names gravitated. When Samuel Winters moves to Winnipeg, for example, it seems unlikely that he will conclude that the first few letters of his surname are the reason for his move.

Watering down a manipulation in this fashion tends to water down the size of the effect obtained. But to our surprise, implicit egotism proved to be sufficiently robust that it survived systematic tests involving relatively subtle manipulations. We were able to show, for example (Pelham et al., 2002; Study 6), that people disproportionately inhabit cities whose names feature their birthday numbers. Just as people born on February 2 (02-02) disproportionately inhabit cities with names such as Two Harbors, people born on May 5 (05-05) disproportionately inhabit cities with names such as Five Points. This birthday-number study also illustrated that implicit egotism is not limited to name-letter preferences. Presumably, any meaningful self-attribute can serve as a source of implicit egotism. Another finding that seems likely to reflect implicit preferences comes from studies of street addresses. Whereas people whose surname is Street tend to have addresses that include the word Street (e.g., Lincoln Street), people whose surname is Lane tend to have addresses that include the word Lane (e.g., Lincoln Lane; Pelham et al., 2003).

Moderators of Implicit Egotism

Can archival studies such as these shed any light on the psychological mechanisms behind implicit egotism? We believe so. To the degree that archival studies yield support for meaningful moderators of implicit egotism, such studies can suggest, albeit indirectly, that implicit egotism is based on self-evaluation. For example, laboratory research has shown that women show stronger first-name preferences than men do (perhaps because many women realize that their first name is the only name they will keep forever). In keeping with this established finding in the laboratory research, behavioral first-name preferences have also proven to be stronger for women than for men (Pelham et al., 2002).

The distinctiveness of a person's name also appears to moderate the strength of implicit egotism. Implicit egotism is more pronounced for rare (i.e., more self-defining) than for common names. The fact that rare names do a better job of distinguishing their owners from other people than common names do suggests that implicit egotism is grounded in identity. By definition, people with rare names are also exposed to their own names slightly less often than are people with common names (e.g., Zeke meets other people named Zeke less often than John meets other people named John). The fact that implicit egotism is stronger among those with statistically rare names also suggests that implicit egotism is not grounded exclusively in the mere exposure effect, that is, the tendency for people to prefer stimuli to which they have been exposed more often (see also Jones et al., 2002, where this issue is addressed in other ways).

The Problem of Sampling

One of the limitations of archival research on implicit egotism is that it is often impossible to sample people randomly in such studies. The researcher is usually forced to sample names systematically. In some studies, we tackled this problem by sampling surnames and city or street names from all 50 U.S. states (Pelham et al., 2003). For example, by systematically sampling the same common surname pairs (e.g., Smith–Johnson, Williams–Jones) in all 50 U.S. states, we were able to document robust name–street matching in six different nationwide samples. Thus, we were able to show, for instance, that the surname pair Smith–Johnson yielded supportive data for 45 out of 50 individual U.S. states.

Another way in which we have tackled the sampling problem is by sampling names exhaustively within large geographical units. In studies of interpersonal attraction, we were sometimes able to sample entire states or counties. For example, using exhaustive statewide birth records, Jones et al. (2004) were able to show that people are disproportionately likely to marry others who happen to share their first or last initial. (Moreover, in samples in which it has been possible to determine people's ethnicity, we have also been able to control for ethnic matching (the tendency for people to marry others of their own ethnic group) by testing our hypothesis within specific ethnic groups (e.g., among Latinos only)). Although archival studies of interpersonal attraction raise their own methodological problems, we have gone to great lengths to rule out alternative explanations, including not only ethnic matching but also age-group matching and proximity. For instance, we ruled out the possibility that people married those who were seated near them in high school (based on surname) by showing that our findings remained robust among couples whose ages differed by 5 years or more. Our studies have consistently yielded evidence for implicit egotism.

Assessing Implicit Egotism in the Laboratory

Thomas Edison once said that genius is 1% inspiration and 99% perspiration. With a little inspiration and a great deal of perspiration, researchers who rely on archival research methods can go a long way toward ruling out alternate explanations for a particular effect. But as Edison's contemporary, the methodologist R.A. Fisher, might have put it, neither inspiration nor perspiration is a match for randomization. The researcher who wishes to rule out numerous alternate explanations for a phenomenon, while gaining insights into its underlying mechanisms, must occasionally conduct experiments. In our research on implicit egotism and interpersonal attraction (Jones et al., 2004), we have done exactly that.

In one experiment, we introduced participants to a bogus interaction partner whose arbitrarily assigned experimental code number (e.g., 02-28) either did or did not happen to resemble their own birthday number. Participants were more attracted to the stranger when his or her code number resembled their own birthday number. This study suggests that implicit egotism is not merely a corollary of the principle that people are attracted to others who are similar to them. After all, participants did not think that their interaction partner actually shared their birthday. In a second experiment, we found that implicit egotism is most likely to emerge under conditions of self-concept threat (i.e., when people have been forced to think about their personal weaknesses). Men who had just experienced a mild self-concept threat (by writing about their personal flaws as a potential dating partner) were especially attracted to a woman in a "Yahoo personals" ad when her screen name happened to contain the first few letters of their surname (e.g., Eric Pelham would prefer STACEY_PEL to STACEY_SMI). Together with past research suggesting that self-concept threats temporarily increase people's positive associations to the self, this study suggests that implicit egotism is grounded in self-evaluation (Beggan, 1992; Jones et al., 2002).

In a third experiment on interpersonal attraction (Jones et al., 2004, Study 7), we found the most direct evidence yet for the underpinnings of implicit egotism. Male and female participants evaluated an attractive young woman on the basis of her photograph. The woman was depicted wearing a jersey that prominently featured either the number 16 or the number 24 (see Fig. 1). Prior to evaluating the woman, participants took part in 30 trials of a computerized decision-making task in which they made simple judgments about strings of random letters. At the beginning of each judgment trial, a row of Xs appeared briefly in the center of the computer monitor, to focus participants' attention. This task was actually a subliminal conditioning task: The row of Xs was always followed (for 14 ms) by either the number 16 or the number 24. One of these two numbers (16 or 24)

Fig. 1. Stimulus person from subliminal conditioning study (Jones, J.T., Pelham, B.W., Carvallo, M., & Mirenberg, M.C., 2004). Participants evaluated this woman after the number on her jersey (16 or 24) had or had not been subliminally paired with their own names.

was always followed by the individual participant's own full name (for 14 ms), and the other number was always followed by one of several gender-matched control names. Participants liked the woman more, and evaluated her more favorably, when her jersey number had been subliminally paired with their own names. Implicit egotism appears to be implicit.

FROM IMPLICIT EGOTISM
TO IMPLICIT SELF-EVALUATION

We believe that we have established beyond a reasonable doubt that implicit egotism influences important decisions. Thus, we believe that future research should attempt to identify meaningful boundary conditions (i.e., predictable limitations) of implicit egotism. Along these lines, some questions that seem ripe for investigation involve close relationships, culture, and implicit self-esteem.

Do name-letter preferences apply exclusively to the self, or do the names of people to whom one is close also affect one's preferences? Do such preferences grow stronger as relationships grow closer? If Bill truly loves Virginia, will he be highly interested in moving to Virginia, just as she might be? Given recent developments in the psychology of culture, it might also be profitable to assess cultural influences on implicit egotism. One might expect that in collectivistic cultures (i.e., ones that celebrate collective as opposed to individual identities), name-letter preferences would be exaggerated for collective aspects of the self (e.g., surnames might have a greater effect than fore-names). We are currently planning studies to test this idea. We have also begun to address the implications of implicit egotism for more mundane decisions. Specifically, we (Brendl, Chatto-padhyay, Pelham, & Carvallo, in press) recently found that people prefer products (e.g., teas, crackers, chocolate candies) whose names share one or more letters with their own names.

If unconscious self-evaluations influence both mundane and important daily decisions, it is important to understand the origins and nature of these implicit self-evaluations—that is, to understand implicit self-esteem. Do negative social interactions early in life cause some people to develop low implicit self-esteem? Apparently they do. In three separate studies, DeHart, Pelham, and Tennen (in press) asked parents, their adult children, or both to report on parent–child interactions in the family when the children were growing up. Both the children's and their parents' reports of how nurturing the parents had been were associated with the adult children's levels of implicit self-esteem. This association still held true after controlling for participants' levels of explicit self-esteem. Studies such as these raise the question of whether we have observed consistent evidence for implicit egotism merely because most people are fortunate enough to possess positive implicit associations to the self. It is possible that our typical findings would be reversed among people who possess truly negative self-associations (i.e., for those with very low levels of implicit self-esteem). Such findings might have implications not only for theories of self-regulation but also for clinical theories of the etiology of depression and self-destructive behaviors. Of course, broad speculations such as these await empirical scrutiny. However, we hope that our research on implicit egotism will inspire researchers to take a closer look at the nature of implicit self-esteem. A complete understanding of the self-concept may hinge, in part, on a better understanding why Jack loves both Jackie and Jacksonville.

Recommended Reading

Fazio, R.H., & Olson, M.A. (2003). Implicit measures in social cognition research: Their meaning and uses. *Annual Review of Psychology, 54,* 297–327.
Koole, S.L., & Pelham, B.W. (2003). On the nature of implicit self-esteem: The case of the name letter effect. In S. Spencer, S. Fein, & M. Zanna (Eds.), *Motivated social perception: The Ontario Symposium on Personality and Social Psychology* (Vol. 9, pp. 93–116). Mahwah, NJ: Erlbaum.
Wilson, T.D., & Dunn, E.W. (2004). Self-knowledge: Its limits, value and potential for improvement. *Annual Review of Psychology, 55,* 493–518.

Acknowledgments—We thank the many friends and colleagues who have encouraged us to pursue this research.

Note

1. Address correspondence to Brett Pelham, Department of Psychology, SUNY, Buffalo, Buffalo, NY 14260; e-mail: brettpel@buffalo.edu.

References

Beggan, J.K. (1992). On the social nature of nonsocial perception: The mere ownership effect. *Journal of Personality and Social Psychology, 62,* 229–237.
Brendl, C.M., Chattopadhyay, A., Pelham, B.W., & Carvallo, M. (in press). Name letter branding: Valence transfers when product specific needs are active. *Journal of Consumer Research.*
DeHart, T., Pelham, B.W., & Tennen, H. (in press). What lies beneath: Early experiences with parents and implicit self-esteem. *Journal of Experimental Social Psychology.*
Dijksterhuis, A. (2004). I like myself but I don't know why: Enhancing implicit self-esteem by subliminal evaluative conditioning. *Journal of Personality and Social Psychology, 86,* 345–355.
Greenwald, A.G., & Banaji, M.R. (1995). Implicit social cognition: Attitudes, self-esteem, and stereotypes. *Psychological Review, 102,* 4–27.
Hetts, J.J., & Pelham, B.W. (2001). A case for the non-conscious self-concept. In G. Moskowitz (Ed.), *Cognitive social psychology: The Princeton Symposium on the Legacy and Future of Social Cognition* (pp. 105–123). Mahwah, NJ: Erlbaum.
Jones, J.T., Pelham, B.W., Carvallo, M., & Mirenberg, M.C. (2004). How do I love thee? Let me count the Js: Implicit egotism and interpersonal attraction. *Journal of Personality and Social Psychology, 87,* 665–683.
Jones, J.T., Pelham, B.W., Mirenberg, M.C., & Hetts, J.J. (2002). Name letter preferences are not merely mere exposure: Implicit egotism as self-regulation. *Journal of Experimental Social Psychology, 38,* 170–177.
Kihlstrom, J.F. (1987). The cognitive unconscious. *Science, 237,* 1445–1452.
Nuttin, J.M. (1985). Narcissism beyond Gestalt and awareness: The name letter effect. *European Journal of Social Psychology, 15,* 353–361.
Pelham, B.W., Carvallo, M., DeHart, T., & Jones, J.T. (2003). Assessing the validity of implicit egotism: A reply to Gallucci. *Journal of Personality and Social Psychology, 85,* 800–807.
Pelham, B.W., Mirenberg, M.C., & Jones, J.K. (2002). Why Susie sells seashells by the seashore: Implicit egotism and major life decisions. *Journal of Personality and Social Psychology, 82,* 469–487.
Shimizu, M., & Pelham, B.W. (2004). The unconscious cost of good fortune: Implicit and explicit self-esteem, positive life events, and health. *Health Psychology, 23,* 101–105.

Spalding, L.R., & Hardin, C.D. (1999). Unconscious unease and self-handicapping: Behavioral consequences of individual differences in implicit and explicit self-esteem. *Psychological Science, 10,* 535–539.

Section 3: Critical Thinking Questions

1. The articles in this section go to considerable lengths to show subtle effects of various primes. How important are such primes in daily life, do you think? Do you behave differently when the ideas of money, the color red, or death are in your mind? Is it even possible to answer this question, or are such influences forever beneath our awareness? What if motivators consciously use knowledge of priming effects, in order to get us to behave in certain ways? Is this ethical?

2. Terror management theory, presented briefly in the Goldenberg article, is a very broad attempt to explain a vast array of human behavior. Do you agree that we are the only animal who can predict our own deaths, and that our attempts to cope with this unbearable knowledge motivate much of our behavior? If you disagree, saying "I rarely think about death" or "I'm not afraid of death," how can you prove that your disagreement isn't just a terror management strategy, or that it merely shows that your defenses are working?

This article has been reprinted as it originally appeared in *Current Directions in Psychological Science.* Citation information for this article as originally published appears above.

Section 4: Personal Emotion

Now we shift away from "motivation," to consider the topic of "emotion." In this section we consider *personal emotion*—the causes and consequences of particular emotions that we all feel in our conscious lives. Tracy and Robins describe new research on the emotion of *pride*. Pride is a very complex emotion because it involves self-evaluations and the motivation to impress both ourselves and others. This article first shows that everyone can recognize emotional expressions of pride, suggesting that pride is universal and has an evolved adaptive function—it reinforces our own accomplishments, making us want to accomplish more. But what if we are *too* proud? Tracy and Robins make an important distinction between authentic pride (based on confident accomplishment) and hubristic pride (based on arrogant self-conceit). Needless to say, the first form of pride is generally a good thing, and the second form is not! Silvia's article on the emotion of *interest* makes a good case that interest is also an evolved emotion, whose adaptive function is to promote knowledge acquisition. When people are interested their eyes widen and they tilt their heads— and they also learn and remember more, and understand more deeply. "Interest" could have gone in the personal motivation section, since interest is closely related to "intrinsic motivation" (not covered in this reader). However, I put it in this section because Silvia conceptualizes interest primarily as an emotion.

The third article in this section, by Cohen and Pressman, reviews the link between positive emotions and something we all hope to put off for as long as possible: Death! In fact, there are an increasing number of longitudinal studies suggesting that happier people live longer. For example, nuns who were happy in their 20s (according to coded diary entries) were more likely to be alive 60 years later. Such findings are important because they show that "positive psychology" really matters—positive emotions are not just nice, they also make a difference for this very "hard science" outcome. However, one caveat of Cohen and Pressman's review is that when one is seriously ill, being too happy may be risky! Finally, Salovey and Grewal summarize our current research knowledge concerning *emotional intelligence*. Emotional intelligence has been controversial in academic psychology—sure, the idea sells books, but is it a real thing that can be measured, in the way that cognitive intelligence is measured? This article claims that emotionally intelligent people can do four related things: accurately perceive emotions in others, use their emotions to achieve their goals, understand emotions and their causes, and regulate or change their own emotional states as necessary. Salovey and Grewal describe an interesting non-self-report way of measuring these four facets of emotional intelligence, showing that the four facets are independent from traditional intelligence and personality measures, and that they predict what you would expect them to predict. But can or should emotional intelligence be learned or taught? This interesting question concludes the article.

Emerging Insights Into the Nature and Function of Pride

Jessica L. Tracy[1]
University of British Columbia, Vancouver, British Columbia, Canada

Richard W. Robins
University of California, Davis

Abstract

Pride, a "self-conscious" emotion involving complex self-evaluative processes, is a fundamental human emotion. Recent research provides new insights into its nature and function. Like the "basic" emotions, pride is associated with a distinct, universally recognized, nonverbal expression, which is spontaneously displayed during pride experiences. Yet, pride differs from the basic emotions in its dependency on self-evaluations and in its complex structure, which is comprised of two theoretically and conceptually distinct facets that have divergent personality correlates and cognitive antecedents. In this article, we summarize findings from the growing body of research on pride and highlight the implications of this research for a broader understanding of emotions and social behavior.

Keywords

pride; authentic pride; hubristic pride; self-conscious emotion; nonverbal expression; emotion recognition

When it comes to motivating social behavior, pride may be the most important human emotion. Our most meaningful achievements, both everyday and life changing, are accompanied by feelings of pride. Students experience pride after receiving a good grade, children after succeeding at a new task, and adolescents after finding a mate. Adults feel pride in response to a promotion at work, a child's first steps, and once-in-a-lifetime accomplishments like winning the Nobel Prize. Conversely, wounded pride lies at the heart of many of society's largest problems, such as intergroup conflict and terrorism, as well as smaller interpersonal problems, such as an argument that destroys a friendship. Indeed, pride is a cornerstone emotion that fuels several fundamental human pursuits: the desire to achieve; to attain power and status; to meet a romantic partner with high mate value; to feel good about oneself and one's social group; and to raise successful, intelligent, and well-behaved children.

A COMPLEX EMOTION THAT IS "PLAINLY EXPRESSED"

One of the major findings in the social and behavioral sciences is the discovery that a small set of "basic" emotions (anger, disgust, happiness, fear, sadness, and surprise) have distinct, universally recognized, nonverbal expressions (Ekman & Friesen, 1971). This finding, which emerged from studies conducted across a wide range of cultures including highly isolated, preliterate groups, led many scientists to adopt a Darwinian perspective toward these emotions. In this framework, each emotion is assumed to be biologically based; shared with other animals; experienced across all cultures; and identifiable via a discrete, universal expression. The predominance of this perspective led to major advances in basic-emotion research but also to the neglect of more cognitively complex, "self-conscious" emotions, such as pride, which were assumed to be less evolutionarily basic.

In the decades following Ekman and Friesen's (1971) seminal work, researchers searched for but, with a few possible exceptions, failed to find additional universal emotion expressions. Long overlooked was Darwin's (1872/1998) suggestion that

Of all the . . . complex emotions, pride, perhaps, is the most plainly expressed . . . A proud man exhibits his superiority over others by holding his head and body erect. He . . . makes himself appear as large as possible; so that metaphorically he is said to be swollen or puffed up with pride. (pp. 262–263)

Building on Darwin's proposition, we conducted a series of studies testing whether pride has a distinct, recognizable nonverbal expression. We started by asking observers to identify the emotion conveyed in posed expressions, based on nonverbal behaviors documented in children following task success (Stipek, Recchia, & McClintic, 1992), as well as in our own work manipulating components of these expressions (e.g., posture, head tilt). We found that the best-recognized, or most prototypical, pride expression includes facial (low-intensity smile) and bodily components (expanded posture, slight head tilt, arms akimbo with hands on hips or raised above the head with hands in fists; see Fig. 1). This expression is reliably recognized and distinguished from similar emotions (e.g., happiness) by adults from several cultures and by children as young as 4 years old (Tracy & Robins, 2004; Tracy, Robins, & Lagattuta, 2005; see Fig. 2 on p. 104).

Perhaps the strongest evidence for Darwin's claim about pride is the recent finding that individuals from a highly isolated, preliterate tribe in Burkina Faso, West Africa, can reliably recognise the pride expression (Tracy & Robins, 2007a; Fig. 2). Given that these individuals are unlikely to have learned the pride expression through cross-cultural contact, such as exposure to Western media, their recognition suggests that the expression may be a human universal and not simply a culture-specific gesture like the "thumb's up" sign.

Other research confirms that the nonverbal display we identified is, in fact, expressed when individuals experience pride. Children tend show components of the expression, including head tilt and expanded posture, after success (e.g., Stipek et al., 1992). Athletes from a wide range of cultures were found to display several components of the pride expression (e.g., head tilt, expanded chest) after winning a match in the 2004 Olympic judo competition (Tracy & Matsumoto, 2007). However, future research should examine the extent to which the pride expression is displayed versus regulated in real-life contexts that are less emotionally intense or in which social norms prohibit pride displays. Moreover, studies should examine how pride-display rules might differ across (a) other aspects of the social context, such as being alone versus with others; (b) eliciting conditions, such as pride felt for a personal achievement versus an achievement

Expression A

Expression B

Fig. 1. Prototypical pride expressions. Expression A is slightly better recognized than Expression B, but both are reliably identified as pride. Reprinted from Tracy & Robins (2004).

involving the relational self (e.g., pride in one's child or spouse) or collective self (e.g., national or ethnic pride); and (c) cultures, such as those with individualistic as opposed to collectivistic orientations.

A TALE OF TWO PRIDES

The research we described demonstrates that the pride expression is cross-culturally recognized and spontaneously displayed in achievement contexts. However, these studies do not address the question of what, exactly, pride is. Writings

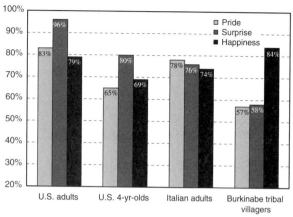

Fig. 2. Mean pride-recognition rates compared with recognition rates for two "basic" emotions, in four samples. All frequencies are significantly greater than chance. Ns = 56 (U.S. adults); 10 (U.S. 4-year-olds); 28 (Italian adults); 39 (Burkinabes). Full studies reported in Tracy and Robins (2004); Tracy and Robins (2007a); Tracy, Robins, and Lagattuta (2005).

by lay-people and scientists alike suggest that there may be more than a single emotion lurking beneath the term *pride*. Ancient Greek and biblical thought condemned excessive pride or *hubris*, yet in Western culture pride is widely viewed as a virtue to be sought and encouraged.

Reflecting these divergent views, pride has been linked to both adaptive and maladaptive outcomes. Although pride in one's successes promotes continued achievement-oriented behaviors, the "hubristic" pride associated with narcissism may contribute to aggression, hostility, and interpersonal problems. This paradox can be resolved by distinguishing between two facets of pride: authentic and hubristic.[2]

Several lines of research provide converging support for this two-facet account (Tracy & Robins, 2007b). First, when asked to think about and list words relevant to pride, participants consistently generate two very different categories of concepts, which empirically form two separate clusters of semantic meaning. The first cluster (authentic pride) includes words such as *accomplished* and *confident* and fits with the prosocial, achievement-oriented conceptualization. The second cluster (hubristic pride) includes words such as *arrogant* and *conceited* and fits with the self-aggrandizing side of pride. Second, when asked to rate their pride-related feelings during actual pride experiences, participants' ratings consistently form two relatively independent factors, which closely parallel the two semantic clusters. Third, when asked to rate their general dispositional tendency to feel each of a set of pride-related emotional states, participants' ratings again form the same two factors. Further analyses have demonstrated that the two pride factors are not statistical artifacts of the tendency to group together good versus bad, activated versus deactivated, or trait versus state words. Given that these factors are largely (though not entirely) independent, in any single pride experience the facets may co-occur, or may not.

To further explore the psychological meaning of the facets, we developed brief, reliable self-report measures of each (Tracy & Robins, 2007b). Using these scales, we found that authentic and hubristic pride have highly divergent personality correlates, such that authentic pride is positively associated with adaptive traits like extraversion, agreeableness, conscientiousness, and genuine self-esteem, whereas hubristic pride is negatively related to these traits but positively associated with self-aggrandizing narcissism and shame-proneness. This pattern suggests that authentic pride is the more prosocial, achievement-oriented, and socially desirable facet of the emotion.

A final piece of evidence supporting the two-facet account of pride is the finding that the facets have distinct cognitive antecedents. In correlational and experimental studies, we found that attributing positive events to internal, unstable, controllable causes (e.g., effort) tends to promote authentic pride, whereas attributing the same events to internal, stable, uncontrollable causes (e.g., ability) is more likely to promote hubristic pride. Importantly, the facets are not distinguished by the kinds of events that elicit them; both occur after success in a range of domains (e.g., academics, romantic relationships). Rather, it is the causes to which success is attributed that play a role in determining which facet of pride will emerge.

One question for future research is whether the two facets are, in fact, distinct emotions. In contrast to their divergent cognitive antecedents and personality correlates, the evidence collected to date indicates that both facets are reliably associated with the same nonverbal expression, suggesting that, at least based on this criterion, there is only one form of pride.

THE FUNCTION OF PRIDE

Emotions are likely to have evolved to serve two primary functions: promoting the attainment of survival and reproductive goals and promoting the attainment of social goals more indirectly related to survival. Whereas basic emotions clearly serve both survival and social functions, self-conscious emotions seem more narrowly tailored toward social functions. Specifically, pride might have evolved to provide information about an individual's current level of social status and acceptance (e.g., "I feel proud; I must have accomplished something that will make others like and respect me"). Self-esteem may be an important part of this process. After successes, individuals feel pride, and over time these feelings may promote positive feelings and thoughts about the global self (i.e., high self-esteem), which inform individuals of their social value. In fact, the development of pride may be closely linked to the development of self-esteem. Children first experience pride early in the course of development (at approximately 2.5 years), can recognize the pride expression by age 4, and reach an understanding of pride between the ages of 7 and 9 (see Lagattuta & Thompson, 2007, for a review). Future research should examine how the cognitive processes that underlie these transitions might be linked to the development of global self-esteem, which emerges around the age of 7.

Pride feelings also function to reinforce and motivate the socially valued behaviors that help maintain a positive self-concept and others' respect. We strive to achieve, to be a "good person," or to treat others well because doing so makes us proud of ourselves. Although we know cognitively that we should help others in need, it often takes the psychological force of an emotion like pride to make us act in altruistic ways, and individuals who perform such socially valued acts are, in turn, rewarded with social status and acceptance (Hardy & Van Vugt, 2006). At an interpersonal level, proud individuals ensure these benefits by directly informing others of their accomplishments; the two most frequent behavioral responses to a pride experience are "making contact with others" (reported by 47% of individuals experiencing pride) and "seeking out others" (39%; Noftle & Robins, 2006). At an intrapsychic level, the rewards of pride are experienced as pleasurable pride feelings, which motivate future pride-eliciting behaviors. Experiencing pride after task completion promotes improved performance at subsequent tasks (Herrald & Tomaka, 2002), and experiencing pride in one's altruistic activities promotes more time spent volunteering (Hart & Matsuba, 2007).

The nonverbal expression of pride may serve a similar adaptive function as the experience: alerting one's social group that the proud individual merits increased status and acceptance. The cross-cultural generalizability of the expression is consistent with its being an evolved response, as is the fact that similar "dominance" displays (e.g., expanded posture, erect gait) have been observed in some nonhuman primates—animals who show precursors of self-awareness (Hart & Karmel, 1996). The finding that the pride expression is associated with success across cultures also supports this functionalist account (Tracy & Matsumoto, 2007).

However, the functionalist account of pride also raises a perplexing question: Why does pride have a dark (i.e., hubristic) side? One possibility is that the two facets solve unique adaptive problems regarding the acquisition of status. Authentic pride might motivate behaviors geared toward long-term status attainment, whereas hubristic pride provides a "short cut" solution, promoting status that is more immediate but fleeting and, in some cases, unwarranted. A related possibility is that the second facet (hubristic pride) evolved as a "cheater" attempt to convince others of one's success by showing the same expression when no achievement has occurred. This view is supported by our failure to find distinct nonverbal expressions for authentic and hubristic pride, but future studies should examine whether both facets have the same impact on actual and perceived status and acceptance.

At a more distal level of analysis, perhaps the most important question about the adaptive nature of pride is this: Given our evolutionary history, how did humans come to experience and express pride in the ways we do? Humans and (possibly) the great apes seem to be the only animals that experience pride, perhaps because it requires self-awareness and the capacity to form stable self-representations. Previous studies on the ontological development of self have used the pride expression as a proxy for early signs of self (e.g., Stipek et al., 1992); similar methods could be used to address questions about the phylogenetic development of self. Given that pride is one of the only self-conscious emotions that seems to have a reliably recognized, universal expression, the ability to assess pride through observable behaviors across cultures and perhaps even species may prove useful for addressing long-standing questions about the evolution of self.

CONCLUSION

Over a century ago, Darwin (1872/1998) included pride within his functionalist model of emotions and emotion expressions. New findings support Darwin's view and demonstrate the significance of pride to research in social, personality, clinical, cultural, developmental, and biological psychology. We hope these findings provide the groundwork for future research on pride, an emotion that is central to the human need for status and acceptance. By coding pride from nonverbal behaviors and assessing its distinct facets using our self-report scales, researchers may gain new insights into the affective core of a wide range of psychological phenomena—from dominance, aggression, and narcissism to achievement, caretaking, and altruism.

Recommended Reading

Ekman, P. (1992). An argument for basic emotions. *Cognition and Emotion, 6,* 169–200.
Lewis, M. (2000). Self-conscious emotions: Embarrassment, pride, shame, and guilt. In M. Lewis & J.M. Haviland-Jones (Eds.), *Handbook of emotions* (2nd ed., pp. 623–636). New York: Guilford.
Tracy, J.L., & Robins, R.W. (2004). (See References)
Tracy, J.L., & Robins, R.W. (2007b). (See References)
Tracy, J.L., Robins, R.W., & Tangney, J.P. (in press). *The self-conscious emotions: Theory and research.* New York: Guilford.

Notes

1. Address correspondence to Jessica L. Tracy, Department of Psychology, University of British Columbia, 2136 West Mall, Vancouver, British Columbia V6T 1Z4, Canada; e-mail: jltracy@psych.ubc.ca.

2. We labeled the first facet "authentic" to emphasize that it is based on actual accomplishments and is likely accompanied by genuine feelings of self-worth. Although we do not view hubristic pride as an inauthentic emotional experience, its elicitors may be more loosely tied to actual accomplishments and may involve a self-evaluative process that reflects a less authentic sense of self (e.g., self-aggrandized self-views).

References

Darwin, C. (1998). *The expression of the emotions in man and animals* (3rd ed.). New York: Oxford University Press. (Original work published 1872)
Ekman, P., & Friesen, W.V. (1971). Constants across cultures in the face and emotion. *Journal of Personality and Social Psychology, 17,* 124–129.
Hardy, C.L., & Van Vugt, M. (2006). Nice guys finish first: The competitive altruism hypothesis. *Personality and Social Psychology Bulletin, 32,* 1402–1413.
Hart, D., & Karmel, M.P. (1996). Self-awareness and self-knowledge in humans, apes, and monkeys. In A.E. Russon, K.A. Bard, & S.T. Parker (Eds.), *Reaching into thought: The minds of the great apes* (pp. 325–347). Cambridge, England: Cambridge University Press.
Hart, D., & Matsuba, M.K. (2007). The development of pride in moral life. In J.L. Tracy, R.W. Robins, & J.P. Tangney (Eds.), *The self-conscious emotions: Theory and research* (pp. 114–133). New York: Guilford.
Herrald, M.M., & Tomaka, J. (2002). Patterns of emotion-specific appraisal, coping, and cardiovascular reactivity during an ongoing emotional episode. *Journal of Personality and Social Psychology, 83,* 434–450.

Lagattuta, K.H., & Thompson, R.A. (2007). The development of self-conscious emotions: Cognitive processes and social influences. In J.L. Tracy, R.W. Robins, & J.P. Tangney (Eds.), *The self-conscious emotions: Theory and research* (pp. 91–113). New York: Guilford.

Noftle, E.E., & Robins, R.W. (2006). *How are actions and inhibited actions related to discrete emotions? A functionalist perspective*. Manuscript submitted for publication.

Stipek, D., Recchia, S., & McClintic, S. (1992). Self-evaluation in young children. *Monographs of the Society for Research in Child Development, 57*(1, Serial No. 226).

Tracy, J.L., & Matsumoto, D. (2007). *More than a thrill: Cross-cultural evidence for spontaneous displays of pride in response to athletic success*. Manuscript submitted for publication.

Tracy, J.L., & Robins, R.W. (2004). Show your pride: Evidence for a discrete emotion expression. *Psychological Science, 15,* 194–197.

Tracy, J.L., & Robins, R.W. (2007a). *The nonverbal expression of pride: Evidence for cross-cultural recognition*. Manuscript submitted for publication.

Tracy, J.L., & Robins, R.W. (2007b). The psychological structure of pride: A tale of two facets. *Journal of Personality and Social Psychology, 92,* 506–525.

Tracy, J.L., Robins, R.W., & Lagattuta, K.H. (2005). Can children recognize the pride expression? *Emotion, 5,* 251–257.

Interest—The Curious Emotion

Paul J. Silvia[1]

University of North Carolina at Greensboro

Abstract

Despite their interest in why people do what they do, psychologists typically overlook interest itself as a facet of human motivation and emotion. In recent years, however, researchers from diverse areas of psychology have turned their attention to the role of interest in learning, motivation, and development. This article reviews the emerging body of work on the psychology of interest, with an emphasis on what contemporary emotion research has learned about the subject. After considering four central questions—Is interest like other emotions? What functions does interest serve? What makes something interesting? Is interest merely another label for happiness?—the article considers unanswered questions and fruitful applications. Given interest's central role in cultivating knowledge and expertise, psychologists should apply research on interest to practical problems of learning, education, and motivation.

Keywords

interest; curiosity; exploration; emotion; learning

Humans are curious creatures: They devote a lot of effort and brainpower to the things that interest them. How much money would it take to persuade an indifferent person to memorize a team's baseball statistics, compile a four-volume encyclopedia of Danish furniture, learn to play the banjo, or spend a career studying an obscure academic topic? As a source of intrinsic motivation, interest plays a powerful role in the growth of knowledge and expertise (Kashdan, 2004; Sansone & Thoman, 2005). The psychology of interest dates to the 1800s, and it has flourished in the last 10 years. Researchers who study emotion, personality, aesthetics, education, vocations, motivation, and development have taken a new look at what interest is, what it does, and how it works (Silvia, 2006). In this article, I'll review what emotion psychology has learned about interest, the curious emotion.

IS INTEREST AN EMOTION?

Interest is an eccentric emotion. Many theories don't include interest in their lists of major emotions, and a few theories reject interest as an emotion altogether. Nevertheless, interest has a proud history in emotion psychology. In his landmark book on emotional expression, Charles Darwin (1872/1998) described emotions related to learning, thinking, and exploring. Darwin's terms—*abstracted meditation, perplexed reflection,* and *stupefied amazement*—seem quaint to modern readers, but his ideas remain ahead of their time. Many decades later, modern emotion psychology doesn't know much about what I'll call *knowledge emotions*: states such as *interest, confusion, surprise,* and *awe.*

A good case can be made for viewing interest as an emotion. Modern theories of emotion propose that emotions are defined by a cluster of components.

Typical emotional components are physiological changes, facial and vocal expressions, patterns of cognitive appraisal, a subjective feeling, and an adaptive role across the lifespan (Lazarus, 1991). Interest appears to have these components: It has a stable pattern of cognitive appraisals (Silvia, 2005b), a subjective quality (Izard, 1977), and adaptive functions (Sansone & Smith, 2000). Interest's physiological and expressive components, not surprisingly, are associated with orientation, activation, concentration, and approach-oriented action (Libby, Lacey, & Lacey, 1973). Interest lacks the smiling and eye-crinkling expressions of happiness. Instead, interest involves movements of muscles in the forehead and eyes that are typical of attention and concentration (Langsdorf, Izard, Rayias, & Hembree, 1983; Libby et al., 1973; Reeve, 1993). When interested, people often still and tilt the head, which aids in tracking objects and sounds (Reeve, 1993). Interest's vocal expression involves a faster rate of speech and greater range in vocal frequency (Banse & Scherer, 1996). Taken together, interest appears to have the features typical of emotions.

WHAT DOES INTEREST DO?

According to functional approaches to emotion, emotions help people manage fundamental goals (Lazarus, 1991). Interest's function is to motivate learning and exploration. By motivating people to learn for its own sake, interest ensures that people will develop a broad set of knowledge, skills, and experience. The need for learning is pressing in infancy. Baby humans are cute but ignorant—they have a lot to learn. Early research on infancy found that exploration, play, and diverse experience enhanced motor and perceptual learning (e.g., Fiske & Maddi, 1961). Beyond infancy, interest is a source of intrinsic motivation for learning. When interested, students persist longer at learning tasks, spend more time studying, read more deeply, remember more of what they read, and get better grades in their classes (see Silvia, 2006). People seem to understand that interest enhances their motivation and performance. When faced with a boring task, people will use strategies to make it more interesting, such as working with a friend or making the task more complex (Sansone & Thoman, 2005).

Interest attracts people to new, unfamiliar things, and many of these things will turn out to be trivial, capricious, dangerous, or disturbing. Some people—such as researchers who study why people experiment with unsafe behaviors—might understandably see this as a dark side of interest. Nevertheless, it is because unfamiliar things can be harmful that people need a mechanism that motivates them to try new things. One never knows when some new piece of knowledge, new experience, or new friendship may be helpful. Interest is thus a counterweight to feelings of uncertainty and anxiety (Kashdan, 2004). Interest won't—and shouldn't—always win the tug-of-war between approach and avoidance, but, over the long haul, interest will motivate people to encounter new things.

WHAT IS INTERESTING?

What makes something interesting? This deceptively simple question has proved to be hard to answer. Any theory of what makes something interesting runs into two problems. First, people differ in whether they find something interesting: One

110

person's dissertation is another person's indifferent shrug. Consider a chair designed by Kaare Klint, a legendary Danish furniture designer. This chair will absorb a few people, but for most people it is merely another boring chair. Second, the same person will differ in interest over time. A once-interesting book can become boring, confusing, frustrating, or aversive. These two problems—the problems of between-person and within-person variability—confound theories that attribute interest to objective features of objects. For example, classic theories proposed that objective stimulus features—particularly novelty, complexity, uncertainty, and conflict (Berlyne, 1960)—evoked feelings of interest. Even some modern theories assume that some things (e.g., themes of sexuality and death) are inherently interesting to nearly everyone, an assumption that is probably wrong (see Silvia, 2006).

Modern emotion psychology offers a new way of thinking about what makes something interesting. Appraisal theories of emotion propose that emotions come from subjective evaluations of events: People appraise an event's meaning, and these appraisals bring about emotions (Lazarus, 1991). Emotions are thus caused by how people appraise what is happening, not by what is actually happening. Because people will interpret a situation differently, they will have different emotions in response to the situation (see Silvia, 2008). Visitors to a museum, for example, will make different appraisals of Andres Serrano's photograph *Piss Christ*. Many people—but not everyone—will appraise the photograph as violating their values and thus feel angry or disgusted (Silvia & Brown, 2007).

If emotions come from appraisals, what are the appraisals that cause interest? In my research, I have suggested that interest comes from two appraisals (Silvia, 2005b; Silvia, 2006). The first appraisal is an evaluation of an event's *novelty–complexity*, which refers to evaluating an event as new, unexpected, complex, hard to process, surprising, mysterious, or obscure. This appraisal isn't surprising: Intuition and decades of research (Berlyne, 1960) show that new, complex, and unexpected events can cause interest. The second, less obvious appraisal is an evaluation of an event's *comprehensibility*. Appraisal theories would label this appraisal a *coping-potential* appraisal because it involves people considering whether they have the skills, knowledge, and resources to deal with an event (Lazarus, 1991). In the case of interest, people are "dealing with" an unexpected and complex event—they are trying to understand it. In short, if people appraise an event as new and as comprehensible, then they will find it interesting.

Consider, for example, a group of college students meandering through the campus art museum. Some of the students find the modern-art gallery interesting: The works strike them as new, different, and unusual, and—thanks to a few classes in art history—they feel able to get what the artists are trying to express. But most of the students, such as the students forced to attend as part of a class assignment, do not find the modern-art gallery interesting. The works strike them as unusual but also meaningless and incomprehensible: They do not know enough about this art to find it interesting. Finding something understandable is the hinge between interest and confusion—a related knowledge emotion. New and comprehensible works are interesting; new and incomprehensible things are confusing.

Many studies suggest that these two appraisals cause interest. Most of these experiments have used real-world stimuli, such as abstract art, classical paintings, contemporary poetry, and brief essays. Experiments that manipulate participants' appraisals find that people are more interested when stimuli are made both more complex and more understandable. For example, people found an abstract poem more interesting when they received a hint that enabled them to understand it (Silvia, 2005b, Study 2), and they spent more time viewing complex polygons than they did viewing simple polygons (Silvia, 2005b, Study 4). Within-person correlational studies show that appraisals of complexity and understandability predict the experience of interest (Silvia, 2008; Turner & Silvia, 2006). People viewed a diverse set of art works and rated each picture for interest and for appraisals. The more novel and more comprehensible people rated a picture, the more they rated it as interesting. In one study, 100% of the within-person correlations were positive, indicating that the appraisals predicted interest for each person in the sample (Silvia, 2005a).

The appraisal approach to interest builds upon past theories of interest. In his landmark work, Berlyne (1960) proposed that curiosity is a way of managing arousal. Because stimuli high in novelty, complexity, uncertainty, and conflict enhance arousal, people seek novelty and complexity when they are understimulated (cf. Fiske & Maddi, 1961). In theories of optimal experience, feelings of absorption, concentration, and interest come from tasks in which a person's skills match the task's level of challenge (Csikszentmihalyi, 1990). The appraisal approach borrows from both traditions: Interest stems from events that are new, complex, and unfamiliar (Berlyne, 1960), provided that people feel able to comprehend them and master the challenges that they pose (Csikszentmihalyi, 1990).

Interest motivates learning about something new and complex; once people understand the thing, it is not interesting anymore. The new knowledge, in turn, enables more things to be interesting. For appraisals of novelty–complexity, knowledge about an area enables people to see subtle differences and contrasting perspectives that aren't apparent to novices. It is common for experts to feel that the more they learn, the more complex and mysterious their field becomes. (Many psychologists may agree that human behavior seemed simpler before we studied psychology.) For appraisals of comprehension, knowledge enables people to understand increasingly complex ideas and events. Concepts confusing to novices can be interesting to experts because experts feel able to understand them. In a sense, interest is self-propelling: It motivates people to learn, thereby giving them the knowledge needed to be interested.

What does this research mean for everyday practice? If interest comes from seeing something as new and comprehensible, then people who want to evoke interest should try to enhance both complexity and comprehension. College textbooks are an intriguing example. The typical textbook wants to engage students' interest, so it sprinkles each chapter with irrelevant quotes, cartoons, contrived stock photos, and random stories from the authors' distant childhoods. But diverting attention from the text's main points isn't the same thing as making the text's main points interesting. According to educational research (Sadoski, 2001; Silvia, 2006), the largest predictors of a text's interestingness are (a) a cluster of novelty–complexity variables (the material's novelty, vividness, complexity, and surprisingness) and (b) a cluster of comprehension variables (coherence, concreteness, and ease of processing). Intuition tells us that we can make writing interesting by "spicing it up"; research reminds us that clarity, structure, and coherence enhance a reader's interest, too.

WHAT ABOUT HAPPINESS?

Interest is often lumped together with happiness, but interest and happiness diverge in three ways. First, they serve different functions. Interest motivates people to try new things, places, and experiences; happiness cultivates attachments to things, places, and experiences that have proved rewarding in the past. Because they motivate different actions, interest and happiness can conflict. Imagine choosing between your favorite Thai restaurant and a new Thai restaurant. Happiness motivates sticking with the restaurant that has always been tasty; interest motivates trying the new place that might be tasty but could be abysmal. Without interest, people would stubbornly stick with what they like instead of trying new things. Without happiness, people would capriciously flit from new thing to new thing instead of returning to proven sources of enjoyment. Second, interest and happiness connect to different abstract dimensions of personality. Interest connects to *openness to experience*, a broad trait associated with curiosity, unconventionality, and creativity (McCrae & Costa, 1999). Happiness, in contrast, connects to *extraversion*, a broad trait associated with positive emotions and gregariousness (McCrae & Costa, 1999).

Finally, interest and happiness stem from different appraisals. In a recent experiment (Turner & Silvia, 2006), we asked people to view a set of paintings. Some of the paintings—such as landscapes by Claude Lorraine and Claude Monet—were soothing and relaxing. Other paintings—such as works by Francis Bacon and Francisco Goya—were twisted and disturbing. People rated their interest and enjoyment for each painting, and they appraised each painting on a wide range of appraisal dimensions. Our results showed that interest and enjoyment had contrasting within-person relationships with appraisals of the paintings. Paintings rated as interesting were appraised as complex, unfamiliar, negative, and disturbing; paintings rated as enjoyable were appraised as simple, positive, and calming.

WHAT NEXT?

The psychology of interest is enjoying a renaissance: Researchers across psychology are studying how interest relates to their area's important issues. Like many emerging areas, the study of interest risks splintering into many small literatures, such as interest and the arts, interest and education, interest and vocations, and interest and personality. One task for future research is to bring these diverse bodies of thought together. Can the study of momentary feelings of interest inform why some people are generally more curious than others? What role does interest play across the lifespan? How do enduring interests, hobbies, and avocations develop? A second task for future research is to put our knowledge to good use. If we know what makes art interesting, how can we cultivate engagement with challenging and controversial art? If we know how interest enhances learning, how can we teach better classes, write better books, and be better mentors? Based on research so far, psychology can expect some interesting answers.

Recommended Reading

Berlyne, D.E. (1960). (See References). A landmark work on the psychology of curiosity; it includes an insightful analysis of the nature of novelty, complexity, uncertainty, and conflict.

Kashdan, T.B. (2004). (See References). A contemporary review of curiosity research, with an emphasis on motivation and individual differences.

Renninger, K.A., Hidi, S., & Krapp, A. (Eds.). (1992). *The role of interest in learning and development*. Hillsdale, NJ: Erlbaum. An edited volume devoted to educational and developmental research on interest.

Sansone, C., & Thoman, D.B. (2005). (See References). A recent review of the role of interest in motivation and self-regulation.

Silvia, P.J. (2006). (See References). A wide-ranging review of research on what makes things interesting and how enduring interests develop.

Note

1. Address correspondence to Paul J. Silvia, Department of Psychology, P.O. Box 26170, University of North Carolina at Greensboro, Greensboro, NC, 27402-6170; e-mail: p_silvia@uncg.edu.

References

Banse, R., & Scherer, K.R. (1996). Acoustic profiles in vocal emotion expressions. *Journal of Personality and Social Psychology, 70,* 614–636.

Berlyne, D.E. (1960). *Conflict, arousal, and curiosity*. New York: McGraw-Hill.

Csikszentmihalyi, M. (1990). *Flow: The psychology of optimal experience*. New York: Harper & Row.

Darwin, C. (1998). *The expression of the emotions in man and animals* (3rd ed.). New York: Oxford University Press. (Original work published 1872).

Fiske, D.W., & Maddi, S.R. (Eds.). (1961). *Functions of varied experience*. Homewood, IL: Dorsey.

Izard, C.E. (1977). *Human emotions*. New York: Plenum.

Kashdan, T.B. (2004). Curiosity. In C. Peterson & M.E.P. Seligman (Eds.), *Character strengths and virtues* (pp. 125–141). New York: Oxford University Press.

Langsdorf, P., Izard, C.E., Rayias, M., & Hembree, E.A. (1983). Interest expression, visual fixation, and heart rate changes in 2- to 8-month old infants. *Developmental Psychology, 19,* 375–386.

Lazarus, R.S. (1991). *Emotion and adaptation*. New York: Oxford University Press.

Libby, L., Jr., Lacey, B.C., & Lacey, J.L. (1973). Pupillary and cardiac activity during visual attention. *Psychophysiology, 10,* 270–294.

McCrae, R.R., & Costa, T., Jr. (1999). A five-factor theory of personality. In L.A. Pervin & O.P. John (Eds.), *Handbook of personality* (2nd ed., pp. 139–153). New York: Guilford.

Reeve, J. (1993). The face of interest. *Motivation and Emotion, 17,* 353–375.

Sadoski, M. (2001). Resolving the effects of concreteness on interest, comprehension, and learning important ideas from text. *Educational Psychology Review, 13,* 263–281.

Sansone, C., & Smith, J.L. (2000). Interest and self-regulation: The relation between having to and wanting to. In C. Sansone & J.M. Harackiewicz (Eds.), *Intrinsic and extrinsic motivation* (pp. 341–372). San Diego, CA: Academic Press.

Sansone, C., & Thoman, D.B. (2005). Interest as the missing motivator in self-regulation. *European Psychologist, 10,* 175–186.

Silvia, P.J. (2005a). Cognitive appraisals and interest in visual art: Exploring an appraisal theory of aesthetic emotions. *Empirical Studies of the Arts, 23,* 119–133.

Silvia, P.J. (2005b). What is interesting? Exploring the appraisal structure of interest. *Emotion, 5,* 89–102.

Silvia, P.J. (2006). *Exploring the psychology of interest*. New York: Oxford University Press.

Silvia, P.J. (2008). Appraisal components and emotion traits: Examining the appraisal basis of trait curiosity. *Cognition and Emotion, 22,* 94–113.

Silvia, P.J., & Brown, E.M. (2007). Anger, disgust, and the negative aesthetic emotions: Expanding an appraisal model of aesthetic experience. *Psychology of Aesthetics, Creativity, and the Arts, 1,* 100–106.

Turner, A., Jr., & Silvia, P.J. (2006). Must interesting things be pleasant? A test of competing appraisal structures. *Emotion, 6,* 670–674.

Positive Affect and Health

Sheldon Cohen[1] and Sarah D. Pressman
Carnegie Mellon University

Abstract

Negative affective styles such as anxiety, depression, and hostility have long been accepted as predictors of increased risk for illness and mortality. In contrast, positive affective styles have been relatively ignored in the health literature. Here we highlight consistent patterns of research associating trait positive affect (PA) and physical health. The evidence we review suggests an association of trait PA and lower morbidity and decreased symptoms and pain. PA is also associated with increased longevity among community-dwelling elderly. The association of PA and survival among those with serious illness is less clear and suggests the possibility that PA may be harmful in some situations. We conclude by raising conceptual and methodological reservations about this literature and suggesting directions for future research.

Keywords

positive emotion; positive affect; morbidity; mortality; health; symptoms

The role of emotions in physical health has been a central topic in health psychology for some time. Emotions are thought to represent the principal pathway linking psychological stress to disease, and enduring affective styles such as anxiety and depression have been found to be associated with greater morbidity and mortality. However, when health psychologists have referred to the roles of emotions and affect in health, they have typically meant negative emotions such as anger, depression, and anxiety. Only recently has there been any serious discussion of the potential effect of positive affect (PA).

One challenge in making sense of the literature on PA and health is that there is little agreement on what is meant by PA. We define positive emotion or affect as feelings that reflect a level of pleasurable engagement with the environment, such as happiness, joy, excitement, enthusiasm, and contentment (Clark, Watson, & Leeka, 1989). These can be brief, longer lasting, or more stable trait-like feelings. Importantly, the lack of positive engagement does not necessarily imply negative affect such as anger, anxiety, and depression.

REVIEW

The strongest links between positive emotions and health are found in studies that examine trait affective style, which reflects a person's typical emotional experience, rather than state affect, which reflects momentary responses to events. Here we provide short descriptions of the associations between trait PA and mortality (longevity), morbidity (illness onset), survival from life-threatening disease, and reports of symptoms and pain. (For a comprehensive review of this literature see Pressman & Cohen, 2005.) The studies we review use prospective designs that help to eliminate the explanation that being sick resulted in lower PA. This

116

is done by measuring PA and health at study onset (baseline) and assessing whether PA predicts changes in health over the follow-up period. Because the measure of PA is given before the change in health, it cannot have been caused by that change. Many, but not all, of the studies also include controls for spurious (third) factors such as age, sex, socioeconomic status, and race/ethnicity. Overall, the literature reviewed here is provocative, although it suffers from a range of methodological and conceptual limitations. It does however allow us to highlight both consistencies in results as well as the issues that need to be addressed to ultimately determine if a positive affective style is an important predictor of good health.

Mortality

A study that has received considerable attention evaluated PA by coding autobiographical writing samples collected from a group of nuns when they were in their early twenties (Danner, Snowdon, & Friesen, 2001). The greater the number of positive emotion words and sentences, the greater was the probability (adjusting for age and education) of being alive 60 years later. In contrast, the number of negative emotions reported was not associated with mortality.

However, the overall evidence on PA and mortality is more complex. Most (seven) of these studies have been done in elderly persons (average age over 60) living either on their own or with their families. These studies are virtually unanimous in linking positive emotional dispositions to longer life. But positive emotions are not generally associated with increased longevity in studies of other populations. For example, two studies suggest that institutionalized elderly with high PA are at increased risk of mortality (Janoff-Bulman & Marshall, 1982; Stones, Dornan, & Kozma, 1989) and an analysis of a sample of gifted children found that PA during childhood was associated with greater risk for death 65 years later (Friedman et al., 1993).

Illness Onset

In a study from our own laboratory (Cohen, Doyle, Turner, Alper, & Skoner, 2003), 334 adult volunteers were phone interviewed seven times over a 3-week period. For each interview, participants rated how accurately each of nine positive and nine negative adjectives described how they felt over the last day. Examples of PA items included *lively, energetic, happy, cheerful, at ease*, and *calm*. Examples of negative-affect (NA) items included *sad, depressed, nervous,* and *hostile*. Daily mood scores were calculated and averaged across the 7 days to create summary measures of trait PA and NA. Subsequently, subjects were exposed to one of two viruses that cause a common cold and were monitored for 5 days for the development of clinical illness. Colds were defined by objective markers of illness, including infection, mucus production (assessed by weighing tissues), and congestion (assessed by the amount of time it took for a dye put into the nostrils to reach the back of the throat). Those with high levels of PA were less likely to develop a cold when exposed to a virus (see Fig. 1). This relationship remained after controlling for age, sex, immunity (baseline antibody to the experimental virus), education, and NA.

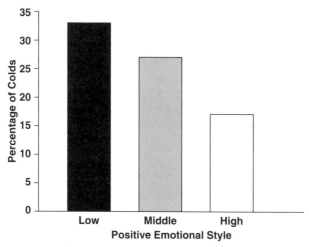

Fig. 1. The association between trait positive emotional style and the incidence of the common cold as diagnosed through objectively assessed markers of disease (infection, mucus weights, and congestion). Adapted from data reported in Cohen, Doyle, Turner, Alper, & Skoner (2003).

In other morbidity studies, trait PA has been associated with lower rates of stroke among noninstitutionalized elderly (Ostir, Markides, Peek, & Goodwin, 2001), lower rates of rehospitalization for coronary problems (Middleton & Byrd, 1996), fewer injuries (e.g., Koivumaa-Honkanen et al., 2000) and improved pregnancy outcomes among women undergoing assisted fertilization (Klonoff-Cohen, Chu, Natarajan, & Sieber, 2001). These studies are often limited by a lack of control for factors such as NA, optimism, and personal control that may influence both PA and disease susceptibility, and many do not rule out the possibility that PA itself (e.g., endorsing of items such as *energetic, full-of-pep,* and *vigorous*) is merely a marker of subclinical disease processes.

Survival

A popular hypothesis is that trait PA increases longevity of persons suffering from life-threatening disease. However, comparatively few studies have examined whether PA predicts survival among people with chronic diseases, and available findings are at best mixed. A pattern of results does however suggest a hypothesis. Individuals with diseases that have decent prospects for long-term survival, such as early-stage breast cancer, coronary heart disease, and AIDS, may benefit from PA. However, high levels of trait PA may be detrimental to the health of individuals who have advanced diseases with poor and short-term prognoses—e.g., patients with melanoma, metastatic breast cancer, and end-stage renal disease—possibly as a consequence of underreporting of symptoms resulting in inadequate care, or of a lack of adherence to treatment (Pressman & Cohen, 2005).

Symptoms and Pain

There is considerable evidence linking PA to reports of fewer symptoms, less pain, and better health. These outcomes have practical importance, but there is reason to think that this association may be driven primarily by PA influences on how people perceive their bodies rather than by affect-elicited changes in physiological processes (e.g., Pennebaker, 1983).

For example, a study from our own lab suggests that trait PA is associated with less symptom reporting when objective disease is held constant (Cohen et al., 2003). As described earlier, PA and NA were assessed by averaging responses across seven nightly interviews. Volunteers were then exposed to a virus that causes the common cold and monitored for objective signs of illness. To test whether trait affect could influence symptom reporting, we predicted self-reported cold symptoms (collected for 5 days following viral exposure) from trait affect, controlling for the objective markers of disease mentioned earlier. When objective signs of illness were held constant, those higher in trait PA reported less severe symptoms, and those higher in trait NA reported more severe ones. Figure 2 presents the residual scores derived from the PA analysis. These scores represent the extent to which one reports more (+ scores) or fewer (− scores) symptoms than would be predicted from the objective markers of disease. Interestingly, when both PA and NA were entered in the same regression equation, only PA continued to predict symptom reporting, suggesting that low PA (not high NA) may be the driving force in the reporting of unfound symptoms.

Other prospective evidence also reveals that trait PA predicts better self-reported health, fewer symptoms in the elderly, and less pain among rheumatoid arthritis and fibromyalgia patients. Interestingly, experimental evidence suggests that inducing state PA in both healthy and mildly ill individuals results in more

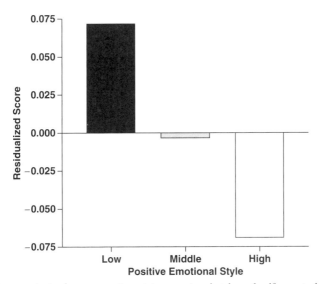

Fig. 2. The association between trait positive emotional style and self-reported symptoms, controlling for objective markers of disease (infection, mucus weights, and congestion). Residualized score represents the extent to which one reports more or fewer symptoms than is predicted by objective signs of illness. Scores above 0 indicate more symptoms than expected and those below 0 indicate fewer symptoms than expected. Adapted from data reported in Cohen, Doyle, Turner, Alper, & Skoner (2003).

favorable self-evaluations of health as compared to individuals induced to feel NA and a neutral control condition (e.g., Salovey & Birnbaum, 1989).

Although these data are provocative, many of these studies also found that NA was associated with greater symptom reporting and poorer self-reported health, begging the question of whether NA or PA is responsible for the effects found. However, there are several studies, like the one described at the beginning of this section, that provide evidence that PA effects on self-reported health are independent of, and often stronger than, those of NA.

LIMITATIONS OF THE EXISTING LITERATURE

Overall, there is provocative evidence that trait PA may influence health and well-being. Strong inferences are not yet possible, however. One problem in interpreting this literature is that in many cases it is difficult to distinguish between the effects of positive and negative emotions. For example, do community-residing elderly live longer because they are happy or because they are not sad? Interestingly, people's experiences of positive and negative emotions are partly independent in some circumstances (e.g., Diener & Emmons, 1985). For instance, in looking back over the last year of one's life (a typical trait PA measure), one can reasonably report having been both happy and sad. A definitive answer to whether positive or negative emotions are making independent contributions to a health outcome can only come from studies that measure both types of emotions separately. Surprisingly, studies that have focused on the effects of negative emotions on health have similarly failed to control for positive emotions. Consequently, it is difficult to conclude from the existing literature whether sadness results in a less healthy, shorter life or whether happiness leads to a healthier and longer one.

There is also concern that some measures of positive emotions may themselves be markers of associated cognitive and social dispositions such as extraversion, self-esteem, personal control, and optimism. In general, these factors have moderate associations with trait PA, but few existing studies control for the possibility that they, and not PA, are responsible for any associations with health that are found. A further issue with PA measurement is that some types of PA may themselves be direct indicators of physical health. For example, endorsing adjectives such as *energetic, full-of-pep,* and *vigorous* may reflect a positive mood, but may also reflect how healthy one feels. Self-rated health has been found to predict illness and longevity above and beyond objective health measures such as physician ratings. Consequently, it is important for future work to include standard measures of self-rated health to help exclude the possibility that we are merely predicting good objective health from good perceived health masquerading as positive emotions.

Another issue is the potential importance of differentiating activated (e.g., enthusiastic, joyful) and nonactivated (e.g., calm, content) affect. Health researchers consider physiological arousal to be a primary pathway through which emotions may influence health. It is thus likely that the arousing nature of an emotion, not only its valence, plays into its potential influences on health outcomes. This is especially relevant given that most measures of PA assess primarily activated emotions.

It is also unclear whether it is important to distinguish among the various subcomponents of PA, such as happiness, elation, and joy, or whether these affects cluster together in experience or in the manner by which they influence health. Few studies explicitly compare different positive emotions or compare individual emotions to a PA aggregate. Finally, there is evidence that the expression of PA varies across cultures, even Western cultures. Consequently, it is difficult to know to what extent this work would apply outside of the United States.

HOW COULD PA IMPROVE HEALTH?

Higher trait PA has been associated with better health practices such as improved sleep quality, more exercise, and more intake of dietary zinc, as well as with lower levels of the stress hormones epinephrine, norepinephrine, and cortisol (Pressman & Cohen, 2005). PA has also been hypothesized to be associated with other health-relevant hormones, including increases in oxytocin and growth hormone and secretion of endogenous opioids. Induced PA in the laboratory has been shown to alter various aspects of immune function, although the direction of changes are not entirely consistent and seem to be dependent on details of the manipulation and the degree of arousal produced via the induction (see Pressman & Cohen, 2005). PA may also influence health by altering social interactions. Persons who report more PA socialize more often and maintain more and higher-quality social ties. PA may result in more and closer social contacts because it facilitates approach behavior and because others are drawn to form attachments with pleasant individuals. More diverse and closer social ties have been associated with lower risk for both morbidity and premature mortality. Finally, health care providers may be more attentive to persons with more pleasant affect.

As an alternative to the arguments above, which assume that PA directly affects health, PA may influence health primarily through its ability to ameliorate the potentially pathogenic influences of stressful life events. For example, Fredrickson (1998) suggests that positive emotions encourage exploration and creativity and result in the building of social, intellectual, and physical resources. Similarly, Salovey, Rothman, Detweiler, and Steward (2000) suggest that positive emotions generate psychological resources by promoting resilience, endurance, and optimism.

WHERE DO WE GO FROM HERE?

Some key strategies to move this literature forward include (a) using more sophisticated measures of PA to differentiate between dimensions of affect (e.g., activated vs. unactivated; discrete positive emotions); (b) including both PA and NA in studies in order to assess whether they have independent associations with health outcomes; (c) including social and cognitive factors that correlate with PA, such as extraversion, personal control, purpose, self-esteem, and optimism, in order to assess whether these factors are responsible for associations attributed to PA; (d) including measures of self-reported health to exclude it as an alternative explanation; and (e) assessing alternative pathways through which PA could influence health.

Overall, we consider the literature associating trait PA with health provocative but not definitive. Nonetheless, the current findings should encourage those interested in affect and health to include PA as a potential predictor and to test the potential pathways that may link PA to health.

Recommended Reading

Lyubomirsky, S., King, L., & Diener, E. (2005). The benefits of frequent positive affect: Does happiness lead to success? *Psychological Bulletin, 131,* 803–855.
Pressman, S.D., & Cohen, S. (2005). (See References)
Salovey, P., Rothman, A.J., Detweiler, J.B., & Steward, W.T. (2000). (See References)

Acknowledgments—Preparation of this article was facilitated by support from Pittsburgh NIH Mind-Body Center (Grants HL65111 & HL65112), the John D. and Catherine T. MacArthur Foundation Network on Socioeconomic Status and Health, and a Postgraduate Scholarship from the Natural Science & Engineering Research Council of Canada.

Note

1. Address correspondence to Sheldon Cohen, Department of Psychology, Carnegie Mellon University, Pittsburgh, PA 15213; e-mail: scohen@cmu.edu.

References

Clark, L.A., Watson, D., & Leeka, J. (1989). Diurnal variation in the positive affects. *Motivation and Emotion, 13,* 205–234.
Cohen, S., Doyle, W.J., Turner, R.B., Alper, C.M., & Skoner, D.P. (2003). Emotional style and susceptibility to the common cold. *Psychosomatic Medicine, 65,* 652–657.
Danner, D.D., Snowdon, D.A., & Friesen, W.V. (2001). Positive emotions in early life and longevity: Findings from the nun study. *Journal of Personality & Social Psychology, 80,* 804–813.
Diener, E., & Emmons, R.A. (1985). The independence of positive and negative affect. *Journal of Personality and Social Psychology, 47,* 1105–1117.
Fredrickson, B.L. (1998). What good are positive emotions? *Review of General Psychology, 2,* 300–319.
Friedman, H.S., Tucker, J.S., Tomlinson-Keasey, C., Schwartz, J.E., Wingard, D.L., & Criqui, M.H. (1993). Does childhood personality predict longevity? *Journal of Personality & Social Psychology, 65,* 176–185.
Janoff-Bulman, R., & Marshall, G. (1982). Mortality, well-being, and control: A study of a population of institutionalized aged. *Personality & Social Psychology Bulletin, 8,* 691–698.
Klonoff-Cohen, H., Chu, E., Natarajan, L., & Sieber, W. (2001). A prospective study of stress among women undergoing in vitro fertilization or gamete intrafallopian transfer. *Fertility & Sterility, 76,* 675–687.
Koivumaa-Honkanen, H., Honkanen, R., Viinamaki, H., Heikkila, K., Kaprio, J., & Koskenvuo, M. (2000). Self-reported life satisfaction and 20-year mortality in healthy Finnish adults. *American Journal of Epidemiology, 152,* 983–991.
Middleton, R.A., & Byrd, E.K. (1996). Psychosocial factors and hospital readmission status of older persons with cardiovascular disease. *Journal of Applied Rehabilitation Counseling, 27,* 3–10.
Ostir, G.V., Markides, K.S., Peek, M.K., & Goodwin, J.S. (2001). The association between emotional well-being and the incidence of stroke in older adults. *Psychosomatic Medicine, 63,* 210–215.
Pennebaker, J.W. (1983). *The psychology of physical symptoms.* New York: Springer-Verlag.
Pressman, S.D., & Cohen, S. (2005). Does positive affect influence health? *Psychological Bulletin, 131,* 925–971.

Salovey, P., & Birnbaum, D. (1989). Influence of mood on health-relevant cognitions. *Journal of Personality & Social Psychology, 57,* 539–551.

Salovey, P., Rothman, A.J., Detweiler, J.B., & Steward, W.T. (2000). Emotional states and physical health. *American Psychologist, 55,* 110–121.

Stones, M.J., Dornan, B., & Kozma, A. (1989). The prediction of mortality in elderly institution residents. *Journals of Gerontology, 44,* P72–P79.

This article has been reprinted as it originally appeared in *Current Directions in Psychological Science*. Citation information for this article as originally published appears above.

The Science of Emotional Intelligence

Peter Salovey[1] and Daisy Grewal

Yale University

Abstract

This article provides an overview of current research on emotional intelligence. Although it has been defined in many ways, we focus on the four-branch model by Mayer and Salovey (1997), which characterizes emotional intelligence as a set of four related abilities: perceiving, using, understanding, and managing emotions. The theory provides a useful framework for studying individual differences in abilities related to processing emotional information. Despite measurement obstacles, the evidence in favor of emotional intelligence is accumulating. Emotional intelligence predicts success in important domains, among them personal and work relationships.

Keywords

emotional intelligence; emotions; social interaction

In the past decade, emotional intelligence has generated an enormous amount of interest both within and outside the field of psychology. The concept has received considerable media attention, and many readers of this article may have already encountered one or more definitions of emotional intelligence. The present discussion, however, focuses on the scientific study of emotional intelligence rather than on popularizations of the concept.

Mayer and Salovey (1997; see also Salovey & Mayer, 1990) proposed a model of emotional intelligence to address a growing need in psychology for a framework to organize the study of individual differences in abilities related to emotion. This theoretical model motivated the creation of the first ability-based tests of emotional intelligence. Although findings remain preliminary, emotional intelligence has been shown to have an effect on important life outcomes such as forming satisfying personal relationships and achieving success at work. Perhaps most importantly, ability-based tests of emotional intelligence reliably measure skills that are relatively distinct from commonly assessed aspects of personality.

THE FOUR-BRANCH MODEL OF EMOTIONAL INTELLIGENCE

Emotional intelligence brings together the fields of emotions and intelligence by viewing emotions as useful sources of information that help one to make sense of and navigate the social environment. Salovey and Mayer (1990, p. 189) proposed a formal definition of emotional intelligence as "The ability to monitor one's own and others' feelings, to discriminate among them, and to use this information to guide one's thinking and action." Later this definition was refined and broken down into four proposed abilites that are distinct yet related: perceiving, using, understanding, and managing emotions (Mayer & Salovey, 1997).

The first branch of emotional intelligence, *perceiving emotions,* is the ability to detect and decipher emotions in faces, pictures, voices, and cultural artifacts. It also includes the ability to identify one's own emotions. Perceiving emotions may represent the most basic aspect of emotional intelligence, as it makes all other processing of emotional information possible.

The second branch of emotional intelligence, *using emotions,* is the ability to harness emotions to facilitate various cognitive activities, such as thinking and problem solving. We can illustrate the skills in this branch through a hypothetical scenario. Imagine that you have to complete a difficult and tedious assignment requiring deductive reasoning and attention to detail in a short amount of time; would it be better, as far as completing the task goes, to be in a good mood or in a sad mood? Being in a slightly sad mood helps people conduct careful, methodical work. Conversely, a happy mood can stimulate creative and innovative thinking (e.g., Isen, Johnson, Mertz, & Robinson, 1985). The emotionally intelligent person can capitalize fully upon his or her changing moods in order to best fit the task at hand.

The third branch of emotional intelligence, *understanding emotions,* is the ability to comprehend emotion language and to appreciate complicated relationships among emotions. For example, understanding emotions encompasses the ability to be sensitive to slight variations between emotions, such as the difference between happy and ecstatic. Furthermore, it includes the ability to recognize and describe how emotions evolve over time, such as how shock can turn into grief.

The fourth branch of emotional intelligence, *managing emotions,* consists of the ability to regulate emotions in both ourselves and in others. Everyone is familiar with times in their lives when they have temporarily, and sometimes embarrassingly, lost control of their emotions. The fourth branch also includes the ability to manage the emotions of others. For example, an emotionally intelligent politician might increase her own anger and use it to deliver a powerful speech in order to arouse righteous anger in others. Therefore, the emotionally intelligent person can harness emotions, even negative ones, and manage them to achieve intended goals.

EMOTIONAL INTELLIGENCE IN CONTEXT

Intrinsic to the four-branch model of emotional intelligence is the idea that these skills cannot exist outside of the social context in which they operate. In order to use these skills, one must be aware of what is considered appropriate behavior by the people with whom one interacts. This point is central to our discussion of how to measure emotional intelligence.

We consider the role of emotional intelligence in personality to be similar to that played by traditional, analytic intelligence. Specifically, emotional intelligence is a set of interrelated skills that allows people to process emotionally relevant information efficiently and accurately (Mayer, Caruso, & Salovey, 1999). Although emotional intelligence correlates to some extent with tests that measure verbal abilities, it overlaps only modestly with standard measures of personality such as those organized by the Big Five personality traits: openess to experience, conscientiousness, extroversion, agreeableness, and neuroticism. Our conceptualization therefore defines emotional intelligence as a set of skills or competenencies rather than personality traits. Whether these skills as a whole operate similarly in every social context is a question requiring further research. It is possible that people may differ in emotional intelligence for different kinds of emotions or that some individuals are better able to harness their emotional intelligence in social or other situations. These sorts of contextual questions require much more investigation.

As noted earlier, one of the primary purposes in proposing a model of emotional intelligence was to provide a framework for investigators exploring individual differences in the processing of emotion-relevant information. In recent years, a number of researchers have made important discoveries suggesting places to look for such differences. For example, positive emotions can temporarily broaden a person's repertoire of thoughts, leading to creative problem solving (Frederickson, 1998). People vary in their abilities to differentiate their emotions; that is, some people can recognize fine-grained distinctions in what they are feeling (e.g., "I feel angry and guilty, and a little bit sad too"), whereas other people can only recognize their feelings in a vague way (e.g., "I feel bad"; Barrett, Gross, Christensen, & Benvenuto, 2001). In addition, sharing traumatic personal experiences can often help people achieve emotional closure, leading to better long-term emotional and physical health (Pennebaker, 1997).

Based on the four-branch model of emotional intelligence, we can interpret Frederickson's work as important to branch two, using emotions. Furthermore, Barrett et al.'s (2001) research on emotional differentiation relates to the third branch of emotional intelligence, understanding emotions. Pennebaker's (1997) findings tie in nicely with the fourth branch, managing emotions. Emotional intelligence provides an organizing heuristic that helps us to understand the relationships among reported findings and guides directions for future research.

MEASURING EMOTIONAL INTELLIGENCE

The first tests of emotional intelligence consisted of self-report scales, which ask people to rate themselves on a number of characteristics (e.g. displaying patience, having good relationships, tolerating stress well) that the authors of such tests believe represent emotional intelligence. However, scores on self-report tests of emotional intelligence such as these are highly correlated with standard personality constructs such as extroversion and neuroticism (Brackett & Mayer, 2003). Such tests raise two difficult questions: whether people are sufficiently aware of their own emotional abilities to report upon them accurately, and whether people answer the questions truthfully instead of reporting in a socially desirable manner. To address these problems, ability-based tests such as the Mayer-Salovey-Caruso Emotional Intelligence Test (MSCEIT) were constructed (Mayer, Salovey, & Caruso, 2002).

The MSCEIT is a 40-minute battery that may be completed either on paper or computer. By testing a person's abilities on each of the four branches of emotional intelligence, it generates scores for each of the branches as well as a total score (see Figs. 1–4 for items similar to those on the MSCEIT for each of the

Fig. 1. Example item similar to those from the *perceiving emotions* branch of the Mayer-Salovey-Caruso Emotional Intelligence Test (MSCEIT).

What mood(s) might be helpful to feel when meeting in-laws for the very first time?

	Not Useful			Useful	
a) Tension	1	2	3	4	5
b) Surprise	1	2	3	4	5
c) Joy	1	2	3	4	5

Fig. 2. Example item similar to those from the *using emotions* branch of the Mayer-Salovey-Caruso Emotional Intelligence Test (MSCEIT).

Tom felt anxious, and became a bit stressed when he thought about all the work he needed to do. When his supervisor brought him an additional project, he felt ____.

a) Overwhelmed

b) Depressed

c) Ashamed

d) Self Conscious

e) Jittery

Fig. 3. Example item similar to those from the *understanding emotions* branch of the Mayer-Salovey-Caruso Emotional Intelligence Test (MSCEIT).

four branches). Central to the four-branch model is the idea that emotional intelligence requires attunement to social norms. Therefore, the MSCEIT is scored in a consensus fashion, with higher scores indicating higher overlap between an individual's answers and those provided by a worldwide sample of thousands of respondents. In addition, the MSCEIT can be expert scored, so that the amount of overlap is calculated between an individual's answers and those provided by a group of 21 emotion researchers. Importantly, both methods are reliable and

1. Debbie just came back from vacation. She was feeling peaceful and content. How well would each action preserve her mood?

Action 1: She started to make a list of things at home that she needed to do.

Very Ineffective..1.....2.....3.....4.....5..Very Effective

Action 2: She began thinking about where and when she would go on her next vacation.

Very Ineffective..1.....2.....3.....4.....5..Very Effective

Action 3: She decided it was best to ignore the feeling since it wouldn't last anyway.

Very Ineffective..1.....2.....3.....4.....5..Very Effective

Fig. 4. Example item similar to those from the *managing emotions* branch of the Mayer-Salovey-Caruso Emotional Intelligence Test (MSCEIT).

yield similar scores, indicating that both laypeople and experts possess shared social knowledge about emotions (Mayer, Salovey, Caruso, & Sitarenios, 2003).

Creating an assessment battery that successfully tests a construct as broad as emotional intelligence is challenging, but it appears that the MSCEIT is an appropriate starting point. Scores on each of the four branches (perceiving, using, understanding, managing) correlate modestly with one another, and the branch and overall scores are reliable (Mayer et al., 2003). Lopes, Salovey, and Straus (2003) found small positive correlations between scores on the MSCEIT and the Big Five traits of agreeableness and conscientiousness. However, not only does the MSCEIT appear to test emotional abilities rather than personality traits, it also does not correlate with scales that measure a person's likelihood to respond in socially desirable ways.

FINDINGS USING THE MSCEIT

Since the concept first became popular, eager advocates of emotional intelligence have claimed that emotional skills matter in almost all areas of life—from career success to being liked by others. Although many of these claims await empirical test, research using the MSCEIT has corroborated a few of them and has offered some new insights. We have explored the importance of how these skills operate within interpersonal interaction, and clinical researchers have speculated about using the MSCEIT in the assessment of psychopathology. We begin with a study looking at the relationship between emotional intelligence and antisocial behavior.

Emotional intelligence is negatively associated with deviant behavior in male adolescents (Brackett, Mayer, & Warner, 2004). College-aged students were asked to take the MSCEIT, a Big Five personality test, and an array of measures that assessed the frequency of engaging in various behaviors. Males who scored lower on the MSCEIT reported engaging in more recreational drug use and consuming more alcohol. In addition, these participants reported having more unsatisfying relationships with their friends. Even when controlling for the effects of participants' personality and for analytic intelligence, the findings involving emotional intelligence remained significant (this is true also for the other MSCEIT studies discussed in this article).

Lopes et al. (2003) administered the MSCEIT to a sample of college students, along with questionnaires that assessed self-reported satisfaction with social relationships. Participants who scored higher on the MSCEIT were more likely to report having positive relationships with others, including greater perceived support from their parents and fewer negative interactions with their close friends.

A limitation of the two studies described above is that they used the MSCEIT to predict the self-reported quality of social relationships. Lopes et al. (2004), however, examined the relationship between individuals' emotional intelligence and reports of their attributes by their peers. American college students took the MSCEIT and were asked to have two of their close friends rate their personal qualities. The students who scored higher on the MSCEIT received more positive ratings from their friends. The friends also reported that students high in emotional intelligence were more likely to provide them with emotional support in times of need. Emotionally intelligent people may have the capacity to increase favorable reciprocity within a relationship.

In another study, German students were asked to keep diaries of their daily social interactions (Lopes et al., 2004). Those students who scored higher on the MSCEIT reported greater success in their social interactions with members of the opposite sex. For example, they were more likely to report that they had come across in a competent or attractive manner and that their opposite-sex partner perceived them as having desirable qualities, such as intelligence and friendliness.

Emotional intelligence may also help people in relationships with their partners and spouses. One study examined the emotional intelligence of 180 college-age couples (Brackett, Cox, Gaines, & Salovey, 2005). They completed the MSCEIT and then answered questions about the quality of their relationships. The couples were classified by how matched they were in emotional intelligence. The couples in which both individuals scored low on the MSCEIT reported the greatest unhappiness with their relationship, as compared to the happiness ratings of the other two groups. The couples in which both partners were emotionally intelligent were very happy. Furthermore, couples in which only one partner had high emotional intelligence tended to fall between the other groups in happiness.

Emotional intelligence also may matter at work. A sample of employees of a Fortune 500 insurance company, who worked in small teams each headed by a supervisor, completed the MSCEIT. All employees were asked to rate each other on the qualities they displayed at work, such as handling stress and conflict well and displaying leadership potential. Supervisors were also asked to rate their employees. Employees with higher scores on the MSCEIT were rated by their colleagues as easier to deal with and as more responsible for creating a positive work environment. Their supervisors rated them as more interpersonally sensitive, more tolerant of stress, more sociable, and having greater potential for leadership. Moreover, higher scores on the MSCEIT were related to higher salary and more promotions. Despite its small sample, the study shows exciting new evidence that emotional intelligence may in fact play an important role in career success (Lopes, Grewal, Kadis, Gall, & Salovey, in press).

FUTURE DIRECTIONS

We have discussed the four-branch model of emotional intelligence and its utility as a guiding framework for research on emotions. In addition, we have described a recently developed ability-based test of emotional intelligence, the MSCEIT, and its value as a tool with which to assess a person's emotion-related abilities. We view the MSCEIT as an early step in the assessment of emotional intelligence. New interactive technologies should lead to innovative and valid ways of assessing people's abilities, especially fluid emotional intelligence in online situations.

This area of research also can benefit from a focus on several theoretical challenges. We lack a thorough understanding of the underlying mechanisms by which emotion-related abilities affect relationships. Research is needed to understand the motivational underpinnings of using certain skills depending on the particular interpersonal context. One of the biggest challenges is figuring out how to examine the influence of such contextual factors on the application and functionality of these skills. It seems likely that individual differences in temperament, which affect levels of arousal, might influence the application of emotion-related skills. Furthermore, some have argued that much emotion-related knowledge and subsequent behavior operate outside of conscious awareness, an idea that has yet to receive much exploration.

Finally, future researchers will need to address more fully the potential impact—positive and negative—of instituting emotional-intelligence training programs. Although such programs appear to offer the possibilities of tackling major social problems, from obesity to school violence, we must caution researchers that the same problems that face any application of basic science to real-world settings also apply to emotional intelligence. The curricula of programs aimed at increasing emotional intelligence should be empirically-based. Rather than a panacea for all human problems, emotional intelligence is a set of abilities that can be applied in prosocial or antisocial ways. Simply developing the skills of emotional intelligence may not prove fruitful unless we also implement interventions that address the contextual and motivational factors affecting the use of these skills. A careful application of the scientific basis of emotional intelligence holds promise in affecting the lives of schoolchildren, workers, and family members.

Recommended Reading

Barrett, L.F., & Salovey, P. (Eds.). (2002). *The wisdom in feeling: Psychological processes in emotional intelligence*. New York: Guilford Press.
Grewal, D., & Salovey, P. (2005). Feeling smart: The science of emotional intelligence. *American Scientist, 93*, 330–339.

Note

1. Address correspondence to Peter Salovey, Department of Psychology, Yale University, PO Box 208205, New Haven, CT 06520-8205; e-mail: peter.salovey@yale.edu.

References

Barrett, L.F., Gross, J., Christensen, T., & Benvenuto, M. (2001). Knowing what you're feeling and knowing what to do about it: Mapping the relation between emotion differentiation and emotion regulation. *Cognition and Emotion, 15*, 713–724.

Brackett, M.A., Cox, A., Gaines, S.O., & Salovey, P. (2005). *Emotional intelligence and relationship quality among heterosexual couples.* Manuscript submitted for publication.

Brackett, M.A., & Mayer, J.D. (2003). Convergent, discriminant, and incremental validity of competing measures of emotional intelligence. *Personality and Social Psychology Bulletin, 29*, 1147–1158.

Brackett, M.A., Mayer, J.D., & Warner, R.M. (2004). Emotional intelligence and the prediction of behavior. *Personality and Individual Differences, 36*, 1387–1402.

Frederickson, B.L. (1998). What good are positive emotions? *Review of General Psychology, 2*, 300–319.

Isen, A.M., Johnson, M.M., Mertz, E., & Robinson, G.F. (1985). The influence of positive affect on the unusualness of word associations. *Journal of Personality and Social Psychology, 48*, 1413–1426.

Lopes, P.N., Brackett, M.A., Nezlek, J.B., Schütz, A., Sellin, I., & Salovey, P. (2004). Emotional intelligence and social interaction. *Personality and Social Psychology Bulletin, 30*, 1018–1034.

Lopes, P.N., Grewal, D., Kadis, J., Gall, M., & Salovey, P. (in press). Evidence that emotional intelligence is related to job performance and affect and attitudes at work. *Psicothema.*

Lopes, P.N., Salovey, P., & Straus, R. (2003). Emotional intelligence, personality, and the perceived quality of social relationships. *Personality and Individual Differences, 35*, 641–658.

Mayer, J.D., Caruso, D., & Salovey, P. (1999). Emotional intelligence meets traditional standards for an intelligence. *Intelligence, 27*, 267–298.

Mayer, J.D., & Salovey, P. (1997). What is emotional intelligence? In P. Salovey & D. Sluyter (Eds.), *Emotional development and emotional intelligence: Educational implications* (pp. 3–31). New York: Basic Books.

Mayer, J.D., Salovey, P., & Caruso, D. (2002). *The Mayer-Salovey-Caruso Emotional Intelligence Test (MSCEIT).* Toronto, Ontario: Multi-Health Systems.

Mayer, J.D., Salovey, P., Caruso, D.R., & Sitarenios, G. (2003). Measuring emotional intelligence with the MSCEIT V 2.0. *Emotion, 3*, 97–105.

Pennebaker, J.W. (1997). *Opening up: The healing power of expressing emotion.* New York: Guilford Press.

Salovey, P., & Mayer, J.D. (1990). Emotional intelligence. *Imagination, Cognition, and Personality, 9*, 185–211.

Section 4: Critical Thinking Questions

1. Three of the articles in this section address positive emotions—a fairly new topic for emotion researchers, who have in the past focused mostly on negative emotions like anxiety, anger, and depression. Are you persuaded that positive emotions are just as important as negative emotions? Or, are positive emotions merely a luxury that are quickly forgotten "when the tiger comes?"

2. Is there such a distinct construct such as "emotional intelligence," or does emotional intelligence simply boil down to being an insightful and socially aware person? Regular IQ scores are sometimes used for selection purposes (e.g., to screen candidates for a job). Should emotional intelligence scores be used in the same way? Would this be fair—can we really summarize a person's emotional knowledge with just one (or just four) numbers?

This article has been reprinted as it originally appeared in *Current Directions in Psychological Science.* Citation information for this article as originally published appears above.

Section 5: Non-Conscious Influences on Emotion

Most of us think of emotions as things we definitely feel and know about—conscious by definition. This section deals with *non-conscious influences on emotion,* including the possibility that some emotions themselves are non-conscious. Winkielman and Berridge describe research showing that various emotions can be subliminally primed, and can then have effects even though the person does not know she is feeling them. Thirsty people will pay more for a drink, and consume more of the drink, after being subliminally primed with "happy" faces! The authors suggest that the brain systems underlying emotional responses evolved prior to the brain systems underlying conscious experiences, and thus that the two processes can be "de-coupled." Have you ever found yourself doing things that don't fit with how you think you feel? This article may help to explain this common experience. The second article addresses a different kind of non-conscious emotional response—*implicit attitudes.* Implicit attitudes are "hot" in contemporary psychology. It turns out that people take longer to respond to certain concepts when those concepts are paired with positive words. At a deep level, the concept and the emotion (i.e., "old" and "good") don't go together for us, and this slows us down. Tests to measure implicit attitudes have been used to predict automatic behavioral responses (i.e., avoiding a senior citizen) that people don't even know they are doing. Rudman considers a variety of possible sources of negative implicit attitudes, including developmental experiences, emotional conditioning, and cultural biases.

The third and fourth articles in this section deal, again, with evolution and emotion. Darwin himself proposed that emotions serve adaptive functions, and more recent evolutionary psychology research conceptualizes emotions as evolved "mental modules" that exist because they solved common problems in our evolutionary history. Öhman and Mineka discuss *snake-phobia* as an excellent case in point: Humans (like all primates) seem especially prepared to learn to be afraid of snakes, even if they are only perceived subliminally. This suggests that a part of our brain is "hard-wired" to respond to this dangerous stimulus from our ancestral past. It also raises the question of what else are we hard-wired to feel, and can we ever achieve conscious control over such feelings? In the fourth article, Elfenbein and Ambady consider the complex issue of how we perceive and recognize emotional expressions in others. Research by Ekman in the 1960s provided early support for evolutionary theories of emotion, showing that all people, even tribesmen in isolated cultures, could recognize and agree on basic emotional expressions (i.e., fear, sadness, joy). I.e., we have "emotion recognition" modules? This article shows that this view must be qualified: We are best at recognizing the expressions of those within our own culture, faces that are most familiar. Of course, we are typically unaware of both evolutionary and cultural influences upon our emotional lives, which is why this article has been placed in the "unconscious influences on emotion" section of the reader.

Unconscious Emotion

Piotr Winkielman[1]
University of California, San Diego
Kent C. Berridge
University of Michigan

Abstract

Conscious feelings have traditionally been viewed as a central and necessary ingredient of emotion. Here we argue that emotion also can be genuinely unconscious. We describe evidence that positive and negative reactions can be elicited subliminally and remain inaccessible to introspection. Despite the absence of subjective feelings in such cases, subliminally induced affective reactions still influence people's preference judgments and even the amount of beverage they consume. This evidence is consistent with evolutionary considerations suggesting that systems underlying basic affective reactions originated prior to systems for conscious awareness. The idea of unconscious emotion is also supported by evidence from affective neuroscience indicating that subcortical brain systems underlie basic "liking" reactions. More research is needed to clarify the relations and differences between conscious and unconscious emotion, and their underlying mechanisms. However, even under the current state of knowledge, it appears that processes underlying conscious feelings can become decoupled from processes underlying emotional reactions, resulting in genuinely unconscious emotion.

Keywords

affect; automaticity; consciousness; emotion; neuroscience

To say that people are conscious of their own emotions sounds like a truism. After all, emotions are feelings, so how could one have feelings that are not felt? Of course, people sometimes may be mistaken about the cause of their emotion or may not know why they feel a particular emotion, as when they feel anxious for what seems no particular reason. On occasion, people may even incorrectly construe their own emotional state, as when they angrily deny that they are angry. But many psychologists presume that the emotion itself is intrinsically conscious, and that with proper motivation and attention, it can be brought into the full light of awareness. So, at least, goes the traditional view.

Our view goes a bit further. We suggest that under some conditions an emotional process may remain entirely unconscious, even when the person is attentive and motivated to describe his or her feelings correctly (Berridge & Winkielman, 2003; Winkielman, Berridge, & Wilbarger, in press). Such an emotional process may nevertheless drive the person's behavior and physiological reactions, even while remaining inaccessible to conscious awareness. In short, we propose the existence of genuinely unconscious emotions.

THE TRADITIONAL VIEW: EMOTION
AS A CONSCIOUS EXPERIENCE

The assumption that emotions are always conscious has been shared by some of the most influential psychologists in history. In his famous article "What Is an Emotion," James (1884) proposed that emotion is a perception of bodily changes. This perception forms a conscious feeling, which is a necessary ingredient of both simple affective states, such as pleasure and pain, and more complex emotions, such as love or pride. Conscious feeling is exactly what distinguishes emotion from other mental states. Without it, "we find that we have nothing left behind, no 'mind-stuff' out of which the emotion can be constituted . . ." (p. 193). For Freud (1950), too, emotions themselves were always conscious, even if their underlying causes sometimes were not: "It is surely of the essence of an emotion that we should feel it, i.e. that it should enter consciousness" (pp. 109–110).

The assumption that affective reactions are conscious is widely shared in the contemporary literature on emotion. Explaining how most researchers use the term "affect," Frijda (1999) said that the term "primarily refers to hedonic experience, the experience of pleasure and pain" (p. 194). Clore (1994) unequivocally titled one of his essays "Why Emotions Are Never Unconscious" and argued that subjective feeling is a necessary (although not a sufficient) condition for emotion. In short, psychologists past and present generally have agreed that a conscious feeling is a primary or even a necessary ingredient of affect and emotion.

IMPLICIT EMOTION AND UNCONSCIOUS AFFECT

By contrast, it is now widely accepted that cognitive processes and states can be unconscious (occurring below awareness) or implicit (occurring without attention or intention). So, it may not require much of a leap to consider the possibility of unconscious or implicit emotion. As Kihlstrom (1999) put it,

> Paralleling the usage of these descriptors in the cognitive unconscious, "explicit emotion" refers to the person's conscious awareness of an emotion, feeling, or mood state; "implicit emotion", by contrast, refers to changes in experience, thought, or action that are attributable to one's emotional state, independent of his or her conscious awareness of that state. (p. 432)

Unconscious Elicitation of Conscious Affective Reactions

Research advances in the past few years challenge the traditional view by demonstrating "unconscious emotion," at least in a limited sense of unconscious causation. Several studies have shown that stimuli presented below awareness can elicit an affective reaction that is itself consciously felt. An example is subliminal induction of the mere-exposure effect, that is, a positive response to repeatedly presented items. In one study, some participants were first subliminally exposed to several repeated neutral stimuli consisting of random visual patterns. Later, those participants reported being in a better mood—a conscious feeling state—than participants who had been subliminally exposed to neutral stimuli that had not been repeatedly presented (Monahan, Murphy, & Zajonc, 2000). In other studies, changes in self-reported mood have been elicited by subliminal presentation

136

of positive or negative images, such as pictures of snakes and spiders presented to phobic individuals (Öhman, Flykt, & Lundqvist, 2000).

But asserting that subliminal stimuli may cause emotion is different from asserting that emotional reactions themselves can ever be unconscious (Berridge & Winkielman, 2003; Kihlstrom, 1999). The research we just mentioned still fits into the conventional view that once emotions are caused, they are always conscious. In fact, these studies relied on introspective reports of conscious feelings to demonstrate the presence of emotion once it was unconsciously caused.

So the question remains: Can one be unconscious not only of the causes of emotion, but also of one's own emotional reaction itself—even if that emotional reaction is intense enough to alter one's behavior? Studies from our lab suggest that the answer is yes. Under some conditions, people can have subliminally triggered emotional reactions that drive judgment and behavior, even in the absence of any conscious feelings accompanying these reactions.

Uncorrected and Unremembered Emotional Reactions

In an initial attempt to demonstrate unconscious emotion, a series of studies examined participants' ratings of neutral stimuli, such as Chinese ideographs, preceded by subliminally presented happy or angry faces (Winkielman, Zajonc, & Schwarz, 1997). Some participants in those studies were asked to monitor changes in their conscious feelings, and told not to use their feelings as a source of their preference ratings. Specifically, experimental instructions informed those participants that their feelings might be "contaminated" by irrelevant factors, such as hidden pictures (Study 1) or music playing in the background (Study 2). Typically, such instructions eliminate the influence of conscious feelings on evaluative judgments (Clore, 1994). However, even for participants told to disregard their feelings, the subliminally presented happy faces increased and subliminally presented angry faces decreased preference ratings of the neutral stimuli. This failure to correct for invalid feelings indicates that participants might not have experienced any conscious reactions in the first place. Indeed, after the experiment, participants did not remember experiencing any mood changes when asked about what they had felt during the rating task. Still, memory is not infallible. A skeptic could argue that participants had conscious feelings immediately after subliminal exposure to emotional faces, but simply failed to remember the feelings later. Thus, it is open to debate whether these studies demonstrate unconscious emotion.

Unconscious Emotional Reactions Strong Enough to Change Behavior

We agreed that stronger evidence was needed. Proof of unconscious emotion requires showing that participants are unable to report a conscious feeling at the same time their behavior reveals the presence of an emotional reaction. Ideally, the emotional reaction should be strong enough to change behavior with some consequences for the individual. To obtain such evidence, we assessed participants' pouring and drinking of a novel beverage after they were subliminally exposed to several emotional facial expressions (Berridge & Winkielman, 2003;

Winkielman et al., in press). The general procedure of these experiments can be seen in Figure 1. Participants were first asked if they were thirsty. Next, they were subliminally exposed to several emotional expressions (happy, neutral, or angry) embedded in a cognitive task requiring participants to classify a clearly visible neutral face as male or female. Immediately afterward, some participants rated their feelings on scales assessing emotional experience and then were given a novel lemon-lime beverage to consume and evaluate. Other participants consumed and evaluated the beverage before rating their feelings. Specifically, in Study 1, participants were asked to pour themselves a cup of the beverage from a pitcher and then drink from the cup, whereas in Study 2, participants were asked to take a small sip of the beverage from a prepared cup and then rate it on various dimensions, including monetary value.

In both studies, conscious feelings were not influenced by subliminal presentation of emotional faces, regardless of whether participants rated their feelings on a simple scale from positive to negative mood or from high to low arousal, or on a multi-item scale asking about specific emotions, such as contentment or irritation. That is, participants did not feel more positive after subliminally presented happy expressions than after subliminally presented neutral expressions. Nor did they feel more negative after angry expressions than after neutral expressions. Yet participants' consumption and ratings of the drink were influenced by those subliminal stimuli—especially when participants were thirsty. Specifically, thirsty participants poured significantly more drink from the pitcher and drank more from their cup after happy faces than after angry faces (Study 1). Thirsty participants were also willing to pay about twice as much for the drink after happy than after angry expressions (Study 2). The modulating role of thirst indicates

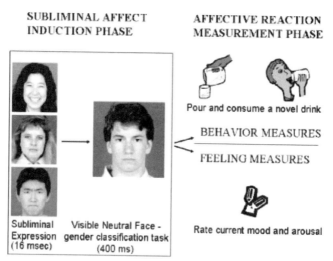

Fig. 1. Sequence of events in research investigating the impact of subliminally presented emotional facial expressions. First, participants are subliminally exposed to several expressions of the same valence (happy, neutral, or angry). The expressions are hidden by a visible neutral face that participants classify as male or female. Second, participants pour and drink a beverage and report their conscious feelings (in counter-balanced order).

that unconscious emotional reactions acted through basic biopsychological mechanisms that determine reactions to incentives, such as a drink, rather than through cognitive mechanisms influencing interpretation of the stimulus (Berridge & Winkielman, 2003; Winkielman et al., 2002).

In summary, the studies just described show that subliminally presented emotional faces can cause affective reactions that alter consumption behavior, without eliciting conscious feelings at the moment the affective reactions are caused. Because the influence of emotional faces on consumption behavior was observed also for those participants who rated their feelings immediately after the subliminal presentation of the faces, these results cannot be explained by failures of memory. Thus, we propose that these results demonstrate unconscious affect in the strong sense of the term—affect that is powerful enough to alter behavior, but that people are simply not aware of, even when attending to their feelings.

Support From Evolution and Neuroscience

From the standpoint of evolution and neuroscience, there are good reasons to suppose that at least some forms of emotional reaction can exist independently of subjective correlates. Evolutionarily speaking, the ability to have conscious feelings is probably a late achievement compared with the ability to have behavioral affective reactions to emotional stimuli (LeDoux, 1996). Basic affective reactions are widely shared by animals, including reptiles and fish, and at least in some species may not involve conscious awareness comparable to that in humans. The original function of emotion was to allow the organism to react appropriately to positive or negative events, and conscious feelings might not always have been required.

The neurocircuitry needed for basic affective responses, such as a "liking" reaction[2] to a pleasant sensation or a fear reaction to a threatening stimulus, is largely contained in emotional brain structures that lie below the cortex, such as the nucleus accumbens, amygdala, hypothalamus, and even lower brain stem (Berridge, 2003; LeDoux, 1996). These subcortical structures evolved early and may carry out limited operations that are essentially preconscious, compared with the elaborate human cortex at the top of the brain, which is more involved in conscious emotional feelings. Yet even limited subcortical structures on their own are capable of some basic affective reactions. A dramatic demonstration of this point comes from affective neuroscience studies with anencephalic human infants. The brain of such infants is congenitally malformed, possessing only a brain stem, and lacking nearly all structures at the top or front of the brain, including the entire cortex. Yet sweet tastes of sugar still elicit positive facial expressions of liking from anencephalic infants, whereas bitter tastes elicit negative facial expressions of disgust (Steiner, 1973).

Even in normal brains, the most effective "brain tweaks" so far discovered for enhancing liking and related affective reactions all involve deep brain structures below the cortex. Thus, animal studies have shown that liking for sweetness increases after a drug that activates opioid receptors is injected into the nucleus accumbens (a reward-related structure at the base of the front of the brain). Liking reactions to sugar can even be enhanced by injecting a drug that activates other receptors into the brain stem, which is perhaps the most basic component of the brain. Such examples reflect the persisting importance of early-evolved neurocircuitry in generating behavioral emotional reactions in modern mammalian brains (Berridge, 2003; LeDoux, 1996). In short, evidence from affective neuroscience suggests that basic affective reactions are mediated largely by brain structures deep below the cortex, raising the possibility that these reactions might not be intrinsically accessible to conscious awareness.

KEY QUESTIONS FOR FUTURE RESEARCH

As we have argued, there are good theoretical reasons why some emotional reactions might be unconscious, and we suggest that our recent empirical evidence actually provides an example. However, several critical issues need to be addressed by future research.

The studies discussed here focused only on basic liking-disliking, so it is possible that the crucial property of unconscious emotion is simply positive-negative valence, rather than qualitative distinctions associated with categorical emotion (fear, anger, disgust, joy, etc.). However, evidence suggests that subcortical circuitry may be capable of some qualitative differentiation. For example, human neuroimaging studies reveal differential activation of the amygdala in response to consciously presented facial expressions of fear versus anger (Whalen, 1998). If future research shows that subliminally presented expressions of fear, anger, disgust, and sadness can create qualitatively different physiological and behavioral reactions, all without conscious experience, then there may indeed exist implicit affective processes deserving the label "unconscious emotion" in its strongest sense. Studies that simultaneously measure psychophysiology, behavior, and self-reports of emotion could be particularly useful to address such issues (Winkielman, Berntson, & Cacioppo, 2001).

The studies discussed here employed basic affective stimuli, such as subliminally presented facial expressions, to influence emotional behavior without eliciting conscious feelings. Future studies might address whether more complex stimuli that derive their positive or negative value from a person's cultural environment can also influence emotional behavior without eliciting any accompanying feelings. A related question concerns whether stimuli presented above the threshold of awareness can also change emotional behavior and physiology without influencing feelings.

The studies described here suggest that under some conditions emotional reactions are genuinely unconscious. But obviously many emotional states are conscious, even when elicited with subliminal stimuli (Monahan et al., 2000; Öhman et al., 2000). What determines when a basic emotional reaction is accompanied by conscious feelings? Is it possible for even a strong emotional reaction to be unconscious? What are the neural mechanisms by which emotion is made conscious? How do behavioral consequences of conscious and unconscious reactions differ?

Finally, a question of practical importance to many emotion researchers, as well as clinicians, concerns the meaning of people's reports of their own emotions.

The existence of verifiable but unconscious emotional reactions does not mean that subjective feelings are merely "icing on the emotional cake." At least, that is not our view. We believe that self-reports of feelings have a major place in emotion research and treatment. However, it is also clear that psychologists should not limit themselves to subjective experiences. A combination of approaches and techniques, from psychology and human and animal affective neuroscience, will best lead to understanding the relation between conscious and unconscious emotions.

Recommended Reading

Bargh, J.A., & Ferguson, M.L. (2000). Beyond behaviorism: On the automaticity of higher mental processes. *Psychological Bulletin, 126,* 925–945.
Berridge, K.C., & Winkielman, P. (2003). (See References)
Damasio, A.R. (1999). *The feeling of what happens: Body and emotion in the making of consciousness.* New York: Harcourt Brace.
Wilson, T.D. (2002). *Strangers to ourselves: Discovering the adaptive unconscious.* Cambridge, MA: Harvard University Press.
Zajonc, R.B. (2000). Feeling and thinking: Closing the debate over the independence of affect. In J.P. Forgas (Ed.), *Feeling and thinking: The role of affect in social cognition* (pp. 31–58). New York: Cambridge University Press.

Notes

1. Address correspondence to Piotr Winkielman, Department of Psychology, University of California, San Diego, 9500 Gilman Dr., La Jolla, CA 92093-0109, e-mail: pwinkiel@ucsd.edu, or to Kent Berridge, Department of Psychology, University of Michigan, 525 East University, Ann Arbor, MI 48109-1109, e-mail: berridge@umich.edu.

2. We use the term "liking" to indicate an unconscious reaction, not a conscious feeling of pleasure.

References

Berridge, K.C. (2003). Pleasures of the brain. *Brain and Cognition, 52,* 106–128.
Berridge, K.C., & Winkielman, P. (2003). What is an unconscious emotion: The case for unconscious 'liking.' *Cognition and Emotion, 17,* 181–211.
Clore, G.L. (1994). Why emotions are never unconscious. In P. Ekman & R.J. Davidson (Eds.), *The nature of emotion: Fundamental questions* (pp. 285–290). New York: Oxford University Press.
Freud, S. (1950). *Collected papers, Vol. 4* (J. Riviere, Trans.). London: Hogarth Press and Institute of Psychoanalysis.
Frijda, N.H. (1999). Emotions and hedonic experience. In D. Kahneman, E. Diener, & N. Schwarz (Eds.), *Well-being: The foundations of hedonic psychology* (pp. 190–210). New York: Russell Sage Foundation.
James, W. (1884). What is an emotion. *Mind, 9,* 188–205.
Kihlstrom, J.F. (1999). The psychological unconscious. In L.A. Pervin & O.P. John (Eds.), *Handbook of personality: Theory and research* (2nd ed., pp. 424–442). New York: Guilford Press.
LeDoux, J. (1996). *The emotional brain: The mysterious underpinnings of emotional life.* New York: Simon & Schuster.
Monahan, J.L., Murphy, S.T., & Zajonc, R.B. (2000). Subliminal mere exposure: Specific, general, and diffuse effects. *Psychological Science, 11,* 462–466.
Öhman, A., Flykt, A., & Lundqvist, D. (2000). Unconscious emotion: Evolutionary perspectives, psychophysiological data and neuropsychological mechanisms. In R.D. Lane, L. Nadel, & G. Ahern (Eds.), *Cognitive neuroscience of emotion* (pp. 296–327). New York: Oxford University Press.

Steiner, J.E. (1973). The gustofacial response: Observation on normal and anencephalic newborn infants. *Symposium on Oral Sensation and Perception, 4*, 254–278.

Whalen, P.J. (1998). Fear, vigilance, and ambiguity: Initial neuroimaging studies of the human amygdala. *Current Directions in Psychological Science, 7*, 177–188.

Winkielman, P., Berntson, G.G., & Cacioppo, J.T. (2001). The psychophysiological perspective on the social mind. In A. Tesser & N. Schwarz (Eds.), *Blackwell handbook of social psychology: Intraindividual processes* (pp. 89–108). Oxford, England: Blackwell.

Winkielman, P., Berridge, K.C., & Wilbarger, J. (in press). Unconscious affective reactions to masked happy versus angry faces influence consumption behavior and judgments of value. *Personality and Social Psychology Bulletin.*

Winkielman, P., Zajonc, R.B., & Schwarz, N. (1997). Subliminal affective priming resists attributional interventions. *Cognition and Emotion, 11*, 433–465.

This article has been reprinted as it originally appeared in *Current Directions in Psychological Science*. Citation information for this article as originally published appears above.

Sources of Implicit Attitudes

Laurie A. Rudman[1]
Rutgers University

Abstract

Response latency measures have yielded an explosion of interest in implicit attitudes. Less forthcoming have been theoretical explanations for why they often differ from explicit (self-reported) attitudes. Theorized differences in the sources of implicit and explicit attitudes are discussed, and evidence consistent with each theory is presented. The hypothesized causal influences on attitudes include early (even preverbal) experiences, affective experiences, cultural biases, and cognitive consistency principles. Each may influence implicit attitudes more than explicit attitudes, underscoring their conceptual distinction.

Keywords

implicit attitudes; implicit social cognition; response latency measures

Attitude researchers have long been wary of taking people's reports of their own attitudes at face value, particularly when the topics being considered impinge on people's morality. Prejudice and attitudes toward immoral (e.g., cheating) or illegal (e.g., substance abuse) behaviors are but a few examples of such topics. Response latency measures, which yield evaluations that are unlikely to be controlled, have been heralded because they override the obvious problem of distortion. This is because they are taken from reaction time tasks that measure people's attitudes or beliefs indirectly (i.e., without asking people how they feel or think). That is, people's attention is focused not on the attitude object, but on performing an objective task, and attitudes are then inferred from systematic variations in task performance. For example, in the Implicit Association Test, automatic pro-White bias is indicated when people show faster performance categorizing pleasant words and Whites (and unpleasant words and Blacks) together, compared with categorizing unpleasant words and Whites (and pleasant words and Blacks) together. Thus, implicit attitudes can be characterized as the automatic association people have between an object and evaluation (whether it is good or bad). By contrast, explicit attitudes may reflect more thoughtful or deliberative responding.

More substantively, response latency measures have also led to increased interest in potential theoretical differences between implicit and explicit attitudes. Although there have been no formal frameworks (cf. Fazio & Olson, 2003), there have been a few attempts to conceptually distinguish what is being measured when people report their attitudes from what is measured by response latency. In this review, I discuss four factors that have been theorized to influence implicit more than explicit attitudes. Although preliminary, the evidence suggests that automatic and controlled evaluations stem from different sources and, therefore, should be conceptualized as distinct constructs.

EARLY EXPERIENCES

A prominent conception is that implicit attitudes stem from past (and largely forgotten) experiences, whereas explicit attitudes reflect more recent or accessible events (Greenwald & Banaji, 1995). In a study supporting this hypothesis (Rudman & Heppen, 2001), smokers' implicit attitudes toward their habit covaried with their earliest experiences with smoking, which were mainly unpleasant (e.g., aversion to tobacco smoke and nausea from their first cigarettes). Thus, automatic attitudes were negative if early experiences were unpleasant. By contrast, smokers' explicit attitudes covaried with their recent experiences toward smoking, which were mainly positive (e.g., drinking coffee and smoking with friends). Thus, self-reported attitudes were negative if recent experiences were unpleasant. Differences in the underlying sources of smokers' implicit and explicit attitudes helps to explain why they were only weakly related.

A logical extension of Greenwald and Banaji's (1995) argument is that developmental events may inform implicit more than explicit attitudes. Much of what is learned early in life is preverbal and taught indirectly. These lessons form the foundation on which later learning is built and may also serve as a nonconscious source for related evaluations and actions. Goodwin and I obtained results consistent with this possibility when we investigated whether early (even preverbal) attachment to maternal caregivers was associated with people's gender-related attitudes (Rudman & Goodwin, 2003). First, people raised primarily by their mothers implicitly preferred women to men. Second, people implicitly favored women if they automatically preferred their mothers to their fathers. By contrast, explicit attitudes toward parents and gender were not related.

Finally, in three experiments (Rudman & Heppen, 2003), women who possessed an automatic association between romantic partners and chivalric roles (e.g., White Knight, Prince Charming) reported less interest in personal power, including economic and educational achievement, than woman who did not have this automatic association. By contrast, explicit romantic fantasies did not covary with explicit power-related variables. Because women are socialized early and often to view men as their heroes and rescuers (e.g., through romantic fairy tales), these findings indirectly support the hypothesis that developmental events can inform automatic mental habits.

AFFECTIVE EXPERIENCES

It is also possible that implicit attitudes are more sensitive to affective experiences than are explicit attitudes. For example, Phelps et al. (2000) found that estimates of implicit (but not explicit) prejudice positively covaried with activation in a brain structure called the amygdala in Whites exposed to photos of Blacks. Because the amygdala is implicated in the control of affective responses, these results suggest that implicit attitudes may stem from automatic emotional reactions to stimuli, whereas explicit attitudes may be "cooler" (more cognitively controlled).

In addition, my colleagues and I found that Whites who volunteered for diversity education showed reduced anti-Black attitudes, both implicit and explicit, at the end of the course. However, changes in the two kinds of attitudes were only weakly associated. Further examination revealed that reductions in implicit attitudes were linked to emotion-based predictors, including reduced fear of Blacks, increased friendships with Blacks, and liking for the African American professor who taught the course. By contrast, reductions in explicit attitudes covaried with students' increased awareness of bias and their desire to overcome their own prejudice (i.e., "trying hard" to change). These findings suggest that changes in implicit attitudes may depend on emotional reconditioning, whereas changes in explicit attitudes may depend on more cognitive and motivational factors (Rudman, Ashmore, & Gary, 2001).

Finally, the sensitivity of implicit attitudes to priming effects (i.e., to the influence of contextual factors) has now been well established (Blair, 2002). Because priming manipulations are recent events, at first blush such findings appear to conflict with the hypothesis that early experiences impact implicit more than explicit attitudes. However, the two views can be reconciled if affect comes into play during the priming manipulation. Learning about admired Blacks and criminal Whites, mentally imagining heroic women, and listening to rap music have all been shown to modify implicit associations. It is possible that these effects were due, at least in part, to the feelings aroused by the stimuli. Likewise, it is conceivable that the studies that found past events influenced implicit attitudes more than explicit attitudes obtained these results precisely because the events were emotional (e.g., aversive experiences with smoking, maternal bonding, and romantic fantasies). Although speculative, the possibility that affect accounts for the influence of both recent and past experiences on implicit attitudes seems worthy of pursuit.

CULTURAL BIASES

The third possibility is that implicit attitudes are more influenced by one's cultural milieu than explicit attitudes are (Devine, 1989). For example, Greenwald, McGhee, and Schwartz (1998, Experiment 2) found that Korean and Japanese American students showed greater automatic in-group bias to the extent they were immersed in their ancestors' culture (e.g., spoke the language). The linkage between attitudes and culture was less evident using a self-report measure of attitudes.

Further, it has been shown repeatedly that Blacks and Whites alike possess more anti-Black bias on implicit measures, compared with self-reports (e.g., Nosek, Banaji, & Greenwald, 2002). Although the pattern for Blacks is provocative, it is consistent with system-justification theory's argument that minorities nonconsciously rationalize their lower status by internalizing society's negative view of their group (Jost & Banaji, 1994). My colleagues and I (Rudman, Feinberg, & Fairchild, 2002) tested this hypothesis using minority groups whose relative status (based on explicit ratings from an independent sample) ranged from low (poor, overweight) to high (Asians, Jews). The results supported system-justification theory. First, the lower their cultural status, the more minorities implicitly favored the dominant out-group. In fact, poor and overweight participants showed significant preference for rich and slim out-group members, respectively. Second, participants were asked to report their group's relative status, and these ratings also covaried with their implicit attitudes. For example, Jews who ranked Christians as higher in status than Jews tended to automatically associate Christians with positive attributes and Jews with negative attributes. In contrast to these results, minorities showed robust explicit in-group bias, which was unrelated to their status.

More dramatically, Livingston (2002) found that social standing had opposite influences on Blacks' automatic and self-reported in-group bias. Specifically, Blacks who perceived that Whites disliked their group showed stronger automatic pro-White bias, but at the same time, stronger pro-Black bias in their self-reports, compared with Blacks who perceived that Whites liked their group. When the same variable pulls implicit attitudes in one direction and explicit attitudes in another, their conceptual distinction is strongly supported.

Finally, high-status groups (e.g., Whites, Christians, slim people, rich people) routinely show stronger implicit in-group bias than do low-status groups, but again, this is a function of their relative status (whereas explicit in-group bias is not; Rudman et al., 2002). Thus, for members of dominant and minority groups alike, societal evaluations appear to have an assimilative effect on automatic (but not controlled) attitudes, suggesting that cultural biases inform implicit attitudes more than explicit attitudes. Because learning about one's place in the world is likely to occur early (and often) in life, and is likely to be emotionally charged, the influence of cultural biases on implicit attitudes may be reconcilable with the influence of early and affective experiences.

COGNITIVE CONSISTENCY PRINCIPLES

A venerable principle in social psychology is that people prefer consonant (as opposed to dissonant) evaluations of related attitude objects. For example, according to this principle, if I like myself and I am female, then I should also like women. This prediction means that cognitive consistency should be observed among the variables of self-esteem, gender identity, and gender attitude. In a compelling demonstration suggesting that automatic and controlled evaluations stem from different causes, implicit attitudes, identity, self-esteem, stereotypes, and self-concept conformed to cognitive consistency principles, whereas self-reports of these same constructs did not (an observation that led the development of the unified theory of implicit social cognition; Greenwald et al., 2002). The general pattern of results the unified theory predicts for implicit measures can be characterized as "If I am Y and I am X, then X is also Y," where Y represents evaluation and X represents group membership. In five experiments, this pattern of results was obtained using the Implicit Association Test. For example, Whites who showed high self-esteem and who identified with their ethnicity also preferred Whites to Blacks. Thus, the logic underlying implicit attitudes was "If I am good and I am X, then X is also good." A similar pattern emerged when implicit stereotypes and self-concept were measured, rather than attitudes and self-esteem. For example, men and women who associated themselves with warmth (or power) also associated warmth (or power) with their own gender, provided they identified with their gender; self-report measures did not conform to this pattern.

Identical findings were found using an academic (math-arts) gender stereotype, but again, only with implicit estimates of self-concept, stereotypes, and gender identity. By uncovering cognitive balance at the automatic level, research that supports the unified theory underscores important differences in the sources of implicit and explicit constructs.

The unified theory may be reconciled with other theories that distinguish sources of implicit and explicit attitudes. First, the theory converges with the hypothesis that cultural milieu biases implicit attitudes. Societal evaluations clearly influence implicit in-group appraisal, which contributes to self-appraisal when in-group identification is strong. Second, affect may inform the unified model by means of evaluative links that involve the self. Given that people likely do not view themselves impartially, emotional self-appraisals may spill over into automatic (more than self-reported) evaluations. For example, early and affective lessons learned about the self may shape one's implicit appraisals of other objects that are (or are not) connected to the self. Interestingly, the resulting implicit structure can be counterstereotypical (e.g., "If I am warm and I am male, then men are warmer than women"). In this way, automatic self-appraisals may counter the influence of culture on implicit associations.

FUTURE DIRECTIONS

In sum, the preliminary evidence indicates that early and affective experiences may influence automatic evaluations more than explicit attitudes. In addition, there is growing evidence that systemic, culturally held appraisals can bias people's automatic evaluations irrespective of their personal opinion. Finally, only implicit (not explicit) evaluations appear to be sensitive to cognitive consistency principles. By better understanding disparities in the underlying causes of implicit and explicit attitudes, psychologists can begin to formulate more sophisticated frameworks for conceptualizing them. At the very least, the observation that they stem from different sources suggests they should be viewed as theoretically distinct.

The argument that implicit and explicit attitudes are conceptually distinct can help to explain why the two types of attitudes are often dissociated, and why response latency measures (sometimes) predict behaviors better than self-reports. Although the untrustworthiness of self-reports is often blamed for these findings, the picture is more complex than that. For one thing, implicit and explicit attitudes sometimes correlate well. This is particularly true when attitude objects are noncontroversial (e.g., politicians, academic subjects, and vegetarianism), but even measures of implicit and explicit prejudice sometimes converge. Moreover, implicit and explicit attitudes can be dissociated even for noncontroversial objects (e.g., flowers, insects, apples, candy bars). Thus, a challenge for future research is to uncover the variables that determine when implicit and explicit attitudes converge. To meet this challenge, researchers should go beyond the controllability of self-reports as an explanation for the weak convergence between implicit and explicit attitudes because this explanation assumes that the underlying evaluation is the same for both types of attitudes (and people are either unable or unwilling to report their "true" attitude). If automatic and controlled evaluations stem from different sources, their underlying valence may dramatically differ. That is, implicit attitudes may be unfavorable despite favorable explicit attitudes, and vice versa. Attending to source differences provides a rationale for deeming both kinds of evaluations as genuine, albeit limited in their ability to encompass the range of human responses to attitude objects.

Future work should also focus on the conditions under which implicit attitudes predict behavior better than explicit attitudes. It has been proposed that automatic and controlled evaluations best predict spontaneous and deliberative actions, respectively. Although there is some evidence that implicit attitudes are linked to involuntary behaviors (e.g., eye blinking), the larger picture is more complicated. First, implicit attitudes often influence deliberative actions, including choosing which consumer products to purchase, volunteering for leadership roles, using condoms, and discriminating against job applicants who are minority-group members. Second, there is substantial evidence, some of it presented here, that controlled responses covary with implicit attitudes (e.g., reports of early experiences covaried with implicit attitudes toward smoking, explicit predictions of status predicted implicit in-group bias, and self-reported interest in power correlated with implicit romantic fantasies). And finally, as already noted, implicit and explicit attitudes sometimes converge. Thus, although implicit attitudes might be the best predictor of spontaneous actions, they are also capable of predicting a large array of controlled behaviors. As opposed to taking a purely "process-matching" approach to predicting behavior, researchers should consider additional factors, including the extent to which the situation increases the salience of implicit attitudes and their relevance to the behavior or judgment at hand (see also Fazio & Olson, 2003).

Focusing on the automatic versus controlled nature of implicit and explicit attitudes has been fruitful, but may mask other ways in which they differ, including their underlying causes. I have presented four factors known to influence implicit attitudes more than explicit attitudes, and suggested how they might overlap. Attending to differences in sources should promote integrative theoretical frameworks that differentiate the two kinds of attitudes. It should also aid in identifying factors that modify each, variables that determine when implicit and explicit attitudes converge, and conditions that promote their utility in predicting behavior.

Recommended Reading

Banaji, M.R. (2001). Implicit attitudes can be measured. In H.L. Roediger & J.S. Nairne (Eds.), *The nature of remembering: Essays in honor of Robert G. Crowder* (pp. 117–150). Washington, DC: American Psychological Association.

Greenwald, A.G., Banaji, M.R., Rudman, L.A., Farnham, S.D., Nosek, B.A., & Mellott, D.S. (2002). (See References)

Wilson, T.D., Lindsey, S., & Schooler, T.Y. (2000). A model of dual attitudes. *Psychological Review, 107*, 101–126.

Acknowledgments—National Science Foundation Grant BCS-0109997 and the Fetzer Institute supported my research reported in this article. I thank Richard Ashmore and Tony Greenwald for their helpful comments on an earlier draft.

Note

1. Address correspondence to Laurie A. Rudman, Department of Psychology, Tillett Hall, Rutgers University, 53 Avenue E, Piscataway, NJ 08854-8040; e-mail: rudman@rci.rutgers.edu.

References

Blair, I.V. (2002). The malleability of automatic stereotypes and prejudice. *Personality and Social Psychology Review, 6,* 242–261.

Devine, P.G. (1989). Stereotypes and prejudice: Their automatic and controlled components. *Journal of Personality and Social Psychology, 56,* 5–18.

Fazio, R.H., & Olson, M.A. (2003). Implicit measures in social cognition research: Their meaning and use. *Annual Review of Psychology, 54,* 297–327.

Greenwald, A.G., & Banaji, M.R. (1995). Implicit social cognition: Attitudes, self-esteem, and stereotypes. *Psychological Review, 102,* 4–27.

Greenwald, A.G., Banaji, M.R., Rudman, L.A., Farnham, S.D., Nosek, B.A., & Mellott, D.S. (2002). A unified theory of implicit attitudes, stereotypes, self-esteem, and self-concept. *Psychological Review, 109,* 3–25.

Greenwald, A.G., McGhee, D.E., & Schwartz, J.L.K. (1998). Measuring individual differences in implicit cognition: The Implicit Association Test. *Journal of Personality and Social Psychology, 74,* 1464–1480.

Jost, J.T., & Banaji, M.R. (1994). The role of stereotyping in system-justification and the production of false-consciousness. *British Journal of Social Psychology, 33,* 1–27.

Livingston, R.W. (2002). The role of perceived negativity in the moderation of African Americans' implicit and explicit racial attitudes. *Journal of Experimental Social Psychology, 38,* 405–413.

Nosek, B.A., Banaji, M.R., & Greenwald, A.G. (2002). Harvesting implicit group attitudes and beliefs from a demonstration web site. *Group Dynamics: Theory, Research, and Practice, 6,* 101–115.

Phelps, E.A., O'Connor, K.J., Cunningham, W.A., Gatenby, J.C., Funayama, E.S., Gore, J.C., & Banaji, M.R. (2000). Amygdala activation predicts performance on indirect measures of racial bias. *Journal of Cognitive Neuroscience, 12,* 729–738.

Rudman, L.A., Ashmore, R.D., & Gary, M.L. (2001). "Unlearning" automatic biases: The malleability of implicit stereotypes and prejudice. *Journal of Personality and Social Psychology, 81,* 856–868.

Rudman, L.A., Feinberg, J.M., & Fairchild, K. (2002). Minority members' implicit attitudes: Ingroup bias as a function of group status. *Social Cognition, 20,* 294–320.

Rudman, L.A., & Goodwin, S.A. (2003). *Gender differences in automatic in-group bias: Why do women like women more than men like men?* Manuscript submitted for publication.

Rudman, L.A., & Heppen, J. (2001). *The smoking gun: Implicit and explicit attitudes toward smoking.* Manuscript submitted for publication.

Rudman, L.A., & Heppen, J. (2003). Implicit romantic fantasies and women's interest in personal power: A glass slipper effect? *Personality and Social Psychology Bulletin, 29,* 1357–1370.

This article has been reprinted as it originally appeared in *Current Directions in Psychological Science*. Citation information for this article as originally published appears above.

The Malicious Serpent: Snakes as a Prototypical Stimulus for an Evolved Module of Fear

Arne Öhman[1] and Susan Mineka

Department of Clinical Neuroscience, Karolinska Institute, Stockholm, Sweden (A.Ö.), and Department of Psychology, Northwestern University, Evanston, Illinois (S.M.)

Abstract

As reptiles, snakes may have signified deadly threats in the environment of early mammals. We review findings suggesting that snakes remain special stimuli for humans. Intense snake fear is prevalent in both humans and other primates. Humans and monkeys learn snake fear more easily than fear of most other stimuli through direct or vicarious conditioning. Neither the elicitation nor the conditioning of snake fear in humans requires that snakes be consciously perceived; rather, both processes can occur with masked stimuli. Humans tend to perceive illusory correlations between snakes and aversive stimuli, and their attention is automatically captured by snakes in complex visual displays. Together, these and other findings delineate an evolved fear module in the brain. This module is selectively and automatically activated by once-threatening stimuli, is relatively encapsulated from cognition, and derives from specialized neural circuitry.

Keywords

evolution; snake fear; fear module

Snakes are commonly regarded as slimy, slithering creatures worthy of fear and disgust. If one were to believe the Book of Genesis, humans' dislike for snakes resulted from a divine intervention: To avenge the snake's luring of Eve to taste the fruit of knowledge, God instituted eternal enmity between their descendants. Alternatively, the human dislike of snakes and the common appearances of reptiles as the embodiment of evil in myths and art might reflect an evolutionary heritage. Indeed, Sagan (1977) speculated that human fear of snakes and other reptiles may be a distant effect of the conditions under which early mammals evolved. In the world they inhabited, the animal kingdom was dominated by awesome reptiles, the dinosaurs, and so a prerequisite for early mammals to deliver genes to future generations was to avoid getting caught in the fangs of Tyrannosaurus rex and its relatives. Thus, fear and respect for reptiles is a likely core mammalian heritage. From this perspective, snakes and other reptiles may continue to have a special psychological significance even for humans, and considerable evidence suggests this is indeed true. Furthermore, the pattern of findings appears consistent with the evolutionary premise.

THE PREVALENCE OF SNAKE FEARS IN PRIMATES

Snakes are obviously fearsome creatures to many humans. Agras, Sylvester, and Oliveau (1969) interviewed a sample of New Englanders about fears, and found snakes to be clearly the most prevalent object of intense fear, reported by 38% of females and 12% of males.

Fear of snakes is also common among other primates. According to an exhaustive review of field data (King, 1997), 11 genera of primates showed fear-related responses (alarm calls, avoidance, mobbing) in virtually all instances in which they were observed confronting large snakes. For studies of captive primates, King did not find consistent evidence of snake fear. However, in direct comparisons, rhesus (and squirrel) monkeys reared in the wild were far more likely than lab-reared monkeys to show strong phobiclike fear responses to snakes (e.g., Mineka, Keir, & Price, 1980). That this fear is adaptive in the wild is further supported by independent field reports of large snakes attacking primates (M. Cook & Mineka, 1991).

This high prevalence of snake fear in humans as well as in our primate relatives suggests that it is a result of an ancient evolutionary history. Genetic variability might explain why not all individuals show fear of snakes. Alternatively, the variability could stem from differences in how easily individuals learn to fear reptilian stimuli when they are encountered in aversive contexts. This latter possibility would be consistent with the differences in snake fear between wild- and lab-reared monkeys.

LEARNING TO FEAR SNAKES

Experiments with lab-reared monkeys have shown that they can acquire a fear of snakes vicariously, that is, by observing other monkeys expressing fear of snakes. When nonfearful lab-reared monkeys were given the opportunity to observe a wild-reared "model" monkey displaying fear of live and toy snakes, they were rapidly conditioned to fear snakes, and this conditioning was strong and persistent. The fear response was learned even when the fearful model monkey was shown on videotape (M. Cook & Mineka, 1990).

When videos were spliced so that identical displays of fear were modeled in response to toy snakes and flowers, or to toy crocodiles and rabbits (M. Cook & Mineka, 1991), the lab-reared monkeys showed substantial conditioning to toy snakes and crocodiles, but not to flowers and toy rabbits. Toy snakes and flowers served equally well as signals for food rewards (M. Cook & Mineka, 1990), so the selective effect of snakes appears to be restricted to aversive contexts. Because these monkeys had never seen any of the stimuli used prior to these experiments, the results provide strong support for an evolutionary basis to the selective learning.

A series of studies published in the 1970s (see Öhman & Mineka, 2001) tested the hypothesis that humans are predisposed to easily learn to fear snakes. These studies used a discriminative Pavlovian conditioning procedure in which various pictures served as conditioned stimuli (CSs) that predicted the presence and absence of mildly aversive shock, the unconditioned stimulus (US). Participants for whom snakes (or spiders) consistently signaled shocks showed stronger and more lasting conditioned skin conductance responses (SCRs; palmar sweat responses that index emotional activation) than control participants for whom flowers or mushrooms signaled shocks. When a nonaversive US was used, however, this difference disappeared. E.W. Cook, Hodes, and Lang (1986) demonstrated that qualitatively different responses were conditioned to snakes (heart rate acceleration, indexing fear) than to flowers and mushrooms (heart rate deceleration, indexing attention to the eliciting stimulus). They also reported superior conditioning to snakes than to gun stimuli paired with loud noises. Such results suggest that the selective association between snakes and aversive USs reflects evolutionary history rather than cultural conditioning.

NONCONSCIOUS CONTROL OF RESPONSES TO SNAKES

If the prevalence and ease of learning snake fear represents a core mammalian heritage, its neural machinery must be found in brain structures that evolved in early mammals. Accordingly, the fear circuit of the mammalian brain relies heavily on limbic structures such as the amygdala, a collection of neural nuclei in the anterior temporal lobe. Limbic structures emerged in the evolutionary transition from reptiles to mammals and use preexisting structures in the "reptilian brain" to control emotional output such as flight/fight behavior and cardiovascular changes (see Öhman & Mineka, 2001).

From this neuroevolutionary perspective, one would expect the limbically controlled fear of snakes to be relatively independent of the most recently evolved control level in the brain, the neocortex, which is the site of advanced cognition. This hypothesis is consistent with the often strikingly irrational quality of snake phobia. For example, phobias may be activated by seeing mere pictures of snakes. Backward masking is a promising methodology for examining whether phobic responses can be activated without involvement of the cortex. In this method, a brief visual stimulus is blanked from conscious perception by an immediately following masking stimulus. Because backward masking disrupts visual processing in the primary visual cortex, responses to backward-masked stimuli reflect activation of pathways in the brain that may access the fear circuit without involving cortical areas mediating visual awareness of the stimulus.

In one study (Öhman & Soares, 1994), pictures of snakes, spiders, flowers, and mushrooms were presented very briefly (30 ms), each time immediately followed by a masking stimulus (a randomly cut and reassembled picture). Although the participants could not recognize the intact pictures, participants who were afraid of snakes showed enhanced SCRs only to masked snakes, whereas participants who were afraid of spiders responded only to spiders. Similar results were obtained (Öhman & Soares, 1993) when nonfearful participants, who had been conditioned to unmasked snake pictures by shock USs, were exposed to masked pictures without the US. Thus, responses to conditioned snake pictures survived backward masking; in contrast, masking eliminated conditioning effects in another group of participants conditioned to neutral stimuli such as flowers or mushrooms.

Furthermore, subsequent experiments (Öhman & Soares, 1998) also demonstrated conditioning to masked stimuli when masked snakes or spiders (but not masked flowers or mushrooms) were used as CSs followed by shock USs. Thus, these masking studies show that fear responses (as indexed by SCRs) can be learned and elicited when backward masking prevents visually presented snake stimuli from accessing cortical processing. This is consistent with the notion that responses to snakes are organized by a specifically evolved primitive neural circuit that emerged with the first mammals long before the evolution of neocortex.

ILLUSORY CORRELATIONS BETWEEN SNAKES AND AVERSIVE STIMULI

If expression and learning of snake fear do not require cortical processing, are people's cognitions about snakes and their relationships to other events biased and irrational? One example of such biased processing occurred in experiments on illusory correlations: Participants (especially those who were afraid of snakes) were more likely to perceive that slides of fear-relevant stimuli (such as snakes) were paired with shock than to perceive that slides of control stimuli (flowers and mushrooms) were paired with shock. This occurred even though there were no such relationships in the extensive random sequence of slide stimuli and aversive and nonaversive outcomes (tones or nothing) participants had experienced (Tomarken, Sutton, & Mineka, 1995).

Similar illusory correlations were not observed for pictures of damaged electrical equipment and shock even though they were rated as belonging together better than snakes and shock (Tomarken et al., 1995). In another experiment, participants showed exaggerated expectancies for shock to follow both snakes and damaged electrical equipment before the experiment began (Kennedy, Rapee, & Mazurski, 1997), but reported only the illusory correlation between snakes and shock after experiencing the random stimulus series. Thus, it appears that snakes have a cognitive affinity with aversiveness and danger that is resistant to modification by experience.

AUTOMATIC CAPTURE OF ATTENTION BY SNAKE STIMULI

People who encounter snakes in the wild may report that they first froze in fear, only a split second later realizing that they were about to step on a snake. Thus, snakes may automatically capture attention. A study supporting this hypothesis (Öhman, Flykt, & Esteves, 2001) demonstrated shorter detection latencies for a discrepant snake picture among an array of many neutral distractor stimuli (e.g., flower pictures) than vice versa. Furthermore, "finding the snake in the grass" was not affected by the number of distractor stimuli, whereas it took longer to detect discrepant flowers and mushrooms among many than among few snakes when the latter served as distractor stimuli. This suggests that snakes, but not flowers and mushrooms, were located by an automatic perceptual routine that effortlessly found target stimuli that appeared to "pop out" from the matrix independently of the number of distractor stimuli. Participants who were highly fearful of snakes showed even superior performance in detecting snakes. Thus, when snakes elicited fear in participants, this fear state sensitized the perceptual apparatus to detect snakes even more efficiently.

THE CONCEPT OF A FEAR MODULE

The evidence we have reviewed shows that snake stimuli are strongly and widely associated with fear in humans and other primates and that fear of snakes is relatively independent of conscious cognition. We have proposed the concept of an evolved fear module to explain these and many related findings (Öhman & Mineka, 2001). The fear module is a relatively independent behavioral, mental, and neural system that has evolved to assist mammals in defending against threats such as snakes. The module is selectively sensitive to, and automatically activated by, stimuli related to recurrent survival threats, it is relatively encapsulated from more advanced human cognition, and it relies on specialized neural circuitry.

This specialized behavioral module did not evolve primarily from survival threats provided by snakes during human evolution, but rather from the threat that reptiles have provided through mammalian evolution. Because reptiles have been associated with danger throughout evolution, it is likely that snakes represent a prototypical stimulus for activating the fear module. However, we are not arguing that the human brain has a specialized module for automatically generating fear of snakes. Rather, we propose that the blueprint for the fear module was built around the deadly threat that ancestors of snakes provided to our distant ancestors, the early mammals. During further mammalian evolution, this blueprint was modified, elaborated, and specialized for the ecological niches occupied by different species. Some mammals may even prey on snakes, and new stimuli and stimulus features have been added to reptiles as preferential activators of the module. For example, facial threat is similar to snakes when it comes to activating the fear module in social primates (Öhman & Mineka, 2001). Through Pavlovian conditioning, the fear module may come under the control of a very wide range of stimuli signaling pain and danger. Nevertheless, evolutionarily derived constraints have afforded stimuli once related to recurrent survival threats easier access for gaining control of the module through fear conditioning (Öhman & Mineka, 2001).

ISSUES FOR FURTHER RESEARCH

The claim that the fear module can be conditioned without awareness is a bold one given that there is a relative consensus in the field of human conditioning that awareness of the CS-US contingency is required for acquiring conditioned responses. However, as we have extensively argued elsewhere (Öhman & Mineka, 2001; Wiens & Öhman, 2002), there is good evidence that conditioning to nonconsciously presented CSs is possible if they are evolutionarily fear relevant. Other factors that might promote such nonconscious learning include intense USs, short CS-US intervals, and perhaps temporal overlap between the CS and the US. However, little research on these factors has been reported, and there is a pressing need to elaborate their relative effectiveness in promoting conditioning of the fear module outside of awareness.

One of the appeals of the fear module concept is that it is consistent with the current understanding of the neurobiology of fear conditioning, which gives a central role to the amygdala (e.g., Öhman & Mineka, 2001). However, this understanding is primarily based on animal data. Even though the emerging brain-imaging literature on human fear conditioning is consistent with this database, systematic efforts are needed in order to tie the fear module more convincingly to human brain mechanisms. For example, a conspicuous gap in knowledge concerns whether the amygdala is indeed specially tuned to conditioning contingencies involving evolutionarily fear-relevant CSs such as snakes.

An interesting question that can be addressed both at a psychological and at a neurobiological level concerns the perceptual mechanisms that give snake stimuli privileged access to the fear module. For example, are snakes detected at a lower perceptual threshold relative to non-fear-relevant objects? Are they identified faster than other objects once detected? Are they quicker to activate the fear module and attract attention once identified? Regardless of the locus of perceptual privilege, what visual features of snakes make them such powerful fear elicitors and attention captors? Because the visual processing in pathways preceding the cortical level is crude, the hypothesis that masked presentations of snakes directly access the amygdala implies that the effect is mediated by simple features of snakes rather than by the complex configuration of features defining a snake. Delineating these features would allow the construction of a "super fear stimulus." It could be argued that such a stimulus would depict "the archetypical evil" as represented in the human brain.

Recommended Reading

Mineka, S. (1992). Evolutionary memories, emotional processing, and the emotional disorders. *The Psychology of Learning and Motivation, 28,* 161–206.

Öhman, A., Dimberg, U., & Öst, L.-G. (1985). Animal and social phobias: Biological constraints on learned fear responses. In S. Reiss & R.R. Bootzin (Eds.), *Theoretical issues in behavior therapy* (pp. 123–178). New York: Academic Press.

Öhman, A., & Mineka, S. (2001). (See References)

Note

1. Address correspondence to Arne Öhman, Psychology Section, Department of Clinical Neuroscience, Karolinska Institute and Hospital, Z6:6, S-171 76 Stockholm, Sweden; e-mail: arne.ohman@cns.ki.se.

References

Agras, S., Sylvester, D., & Oliveau, D. (1969). The epidemiology of common fears and phobias. *Comprehensive Psychiatry, 10,* 151–156.

Cook, E.W., Hodes, R.L., & Lang, P.J. (1986). Preparedness and phobia: Effects of stimulus content on human visceral conditioning. *Journal of Abnormal Psychology, 95,* 195–207.

Cook, M., & Mineka, S. (1990). Selective associations in the observational conditioning of fear in rhesus monkeys. *Journal of Experimental Psychology: Animal Behavior Processes, 16,* 372–389.

Cook, M., & Mineka, S. (1991). Selective associations in the origins of phobic fears and their implications for behavior therapy. In P. Martin (Ed.), *Handbook of behavior therapy and psychological science: An integrative approach* (pp. 413–434). Oxford, England: Pergamon Press.

Kennedy, S.J., Rapee, R.M., & Mazurski, E.J. (1997). Covariation bias for phylogenetic versus ontogenetic fear-relevant stimuli. *Behaviour Research and Therapy, 35,* 415–422.

King, G.E. (1997, June). *The attentional basis for primate responses to snakes.* Paper presented at the annual meeting of the American Society of Primatologists, San Diego, CA.

Mineka, S., Keir, R., & Price, V. (1980). Fear of snakes in wild- and laboratory-reared rhesus monkeys (*Macaca mulatta*). *Animal Learning and Behavior, 8,* 653–663.

Öhman, A., Flykt, A., & Esteves, F. (2001). Emotion drives attention: Detecting the snake in the grass. *Journal of Experimental Psychology: General, 131,* 466–478.

Öhman, A., & Mineka, S. (2001). Fear, phobias and preparedness: Toward an evolved module of fear and fear learning. *Psychological Review, 108,* 483–522.

Öhman, A., & Soares, J.J.F. (1993). On the automatic nature of phobic fear: Conditioned electrodermal responses to masked fear-relevant stimuli. *Journal of Abnormal Psychology, 102,* 121–132.

Öhman, A., & Soares, J.J.F. (1994). "Unconscious anxiety": Phobic responses to masked stimuli. *Journal of Abnormal Psychology, 103,* 231–240.

Öhman, A., & Soares, J.J.F. (1998). Emotional conditioning to masked stimuli: Expectancies for aversive outcomes following nonrecognized fear-irrelevant stimuli. *Journal of Experimental Psychology: General, 127,* 69–82.

Sagan, C. (1977). *The dragons of Eden: Speculations on the evolution of human intelligence.* London: Hodder and Stoughton.

Tomarken, A.J., Sutton, S.K., & Mineka, S. (1995). Fear-relevant illusory correlations: What types of associations promote judgmental bias? *Journal of Abnormal Psychology, 104,* 312–326.

Wiens, S., & Öhman, A. (2002). Unawareness is more than a chance event: Comment on Lovibond and Shanks (2002). *Journal of Experimental Psychology: Animal Behavior Processes, 28,* 27–31.

This article has been reprinted as it originally appeared in *Current Directions in Psychological Science*. Citation information for this article as originally published appears above.

Universals and Cultural Differences in Recognizing Emotions

Hillary Anger Elfenbein[1] and Nalini Ambady
Haas School of Business, University of California at Berkeley, Berkeley, California (H.A.E.), and Department of Psychology, Harvard University, Cambridge, Massachusetts (N.A.)

Abstract

Moving beyond the earlier nature-versus-nurture debate, modern work on the communication of emotion has incorporated both universals and cultural differences. Classic research demonstrated that the intended emotions in posed expressions were recognized by members of many different cultural groups at rates better than predicted by random guessing. However, recent research has also documented evidence for an in-group advantage, meaning that people are generally more accurate at judging emotions when the emotions are expressed by members of their own cultural group rather than by members of a different cultural group. These new findings provide initial support for a dialect theory of emotion that has the potential to integrate both classic and recent findings. Further research in this area has the potential to improve cross-cultural communication.

Keywords

emotion; universality; cross-cultural differences

The scientific study of how people express emotion has been intertwined with the question of whether or not emotions are universal across cultures and species. Many psychology textbooks describe classic research from the 1960s demonstrating that participants around the world could judge the intended basic emotional states portrayed in posed photographs at rates better than would be expected from random guessing (Ekman, 1972; Izard, 1971). On the basis of these and related studies, many psychologists concluded that the recognition of emotion is largely universal, with the implication that this skill is not learned, but rather has an evolutionary and thus biological basis.

More recently, researchers have attempted to move beyond an either-or approach to the nature-versus-nurture debate, in order to explore how differences across cultures may affect the universal processes involved in expressing and understanding emotions. In this article, we contrast the ability of two theories to account for recent research findings.

EVIDENCE FOR BOTH UNIVERSALS AND CULTURAL DIFFERENCES IN COMMUNICATING EMOTION

The communication of emotion has a strong universal component. For example, people of different cultures can watch foreign films and understand much of their original feeling. Likewise, people can develop strong bonds with pets while

157

communicating largely through nonverbal displays of emotion. Thus, messages on an emotional level can cross the barrier of a cultural or species difference.

Still, although much of an emotional message is retained across these barriers, some of the message gets lost along the way. For example, when traveling or living abroad, or when working in multinational environments, many people develop an intuition that their basic communication signals tend to be misinterpreted more frequently when they interact with individuals from cultures foreign to them than when they interact with compatriots. Therefore, it is not a contradiction to say that the expression of emotion is largely universal but there are subtle differences across cultures that can create a challenge for effective communication.

New Interpretations of Classic Research

The early researchers who studied how people communicate emotion across cultures focused their efforts on establishing universality, and therefore did not pay as much attention to the cultural differences as to the cross-cultural similarities in their data (Matsumoto & Assar, 1992). For example, Table 1 lists the results from Ekman's (1972) five-culture study. Participants viewed photographs and for each one selected an emotion label from six possible choices, so that guessing entirely at random would yield one correct answer out of six, or 16.7% accuracy. Because all cultural groups' performance for all six emotional expressions was much higher than 16.7%, Ekman and his colleagues concluded that there is a *universal affect program,* a biologically programmed guide that governs the communication of emotion.

However, other researchers have noticed different patterns in these same data. For example, Matsumoto (1989) noted that U.S. participants outperformed the Japanese in the study. He argued that some cultures, such as Japanese culture, encourage the use of decoding rules (Buck, 1984), social norms that inhibit the understanding of emotion in cases when understanding may be disruptive to social harmony. Further, he argued that some languages, such as English, are superior to others in their emotion vocabulary (Matsumoto & Assar, 1992). Thus, he argued that Americans are generally more effective than most other cultural groups at understanding emotion.

Table 1. *Accuracy at recognizing American facial expressions (Ekman's 1972 five-culture study)*

	Participant group				
Expression	United States	Chile	Brazil	Argentina	Japan
Happiness	97	90	92	94	87
Fear	88	78	77	68	71
Disgust	84	85	86	79	82
Anger	68	76	82	72	63
Surprise	91	88	81	93	87
Sadness	87	91	82	88	80
Average	86	85	83	82	78

Note. All values listed are the percentage of participants who correctly judged the emotional expression indicated.

We noticed yet a different pattern in the data in Table 1: The group with the highest performance is also the same group from which the experimental stimuli originated (Elfenbein & Ambady, 2002b). All participants in the study viewed photographs of American facial expressions, so Americans were the only participants to view members of their own cultural group, or in-group. Everyone else in the study judged expressions from a foreign group, or out-group. We found it interesting that the South American participants were only slightly less accurate than U.S. participants, whereas the difference in performance was larger for the Japanese, who were the most culturally distant.

New Findings on In-Group Advantage

In explaining these cultural differences, earlier researchers tended to focus either on the attributes of the group expressing the emotions or on the attributes of the group perceiving the emotions. In contrast, we tried to think about both groups at the same time, in terms of the match between them. In other words, we considered whether observers were judging emotional expressions made by members of their own cultural in-group or made by members of a cultural out-group. In a meta-analysis (a statistical analysis that combines the results of multiple studies), we assembled the results of 97 studies, which involved 182 different samples representing more than 22,000 total participants (Elfenbein & Ambady, 2002a). These studies included the classic research of Ekman (1972) and Izard (1971), more recent work on the understanding of emotions across cultures, and unintentionally cross-cultural studies in which researchers borrowed testing materials that portrayed people who were not from the geographic location where they were conducting their research.

Our results strongly replicated the earlier finding that people can understand the intended emotional state in posed expressions from other cultures with accuracy greater than predicted by chance guessing. However, this observation alone does not necessarily mean that emotion recognition is governed entirely by universals (Russell, 1994). We also found evidence for an *in-group advantage* in the understanding of emotion: Participants were generally more accurate in recognizing emotions expressed by members of their own culture than in recognizing emotions expressed by members of a different cultural group. The in-group advantage was replicated across a range of experimental methods, positive and negative emotions, and different nonverbal channels of communicating emotion, such as facial expressions, tone of voice, and body language.

Even when the cultural differences in understanding emotion are small, they can still have important real-world consequences. If cross-cultural interactions are slightly less smooth than same-culture interactions, then misunderstandings can accumulate over time and make interpersonal relationships less satisfying. However, the findings of this and our other studies also provide a hopeful message regarding cross-cultural communication: The in-group advantage is lower when groups are nearer geographically or have greater cross-cultural contact with each other, and over time participants appear to learn how to understand the emotions of people from foreign cultures (Elfenbein & Ambady, 2002b, 2003a, 2003b).

The idea of an in-group advantage has been controversial (Elfenbein & Ambady, 2002a, Matsumoto, 2002), largely because of a theoretical disagreement about whether it is necessary to force members of different cultures to express their emotions using exactly the same style. Researchers have debated whether the studies that have not done this are a valid test of the in-group advantage. Understanding this controversy requires first understanding some theoretical perspectives on the communication of emotion.

A PRELIMINARY DIALECT THEORY

Researchers have attempted to weave together diverse strands of evidence to develop theory about how biology and culture influence the communication of emotion.

Ekman's Neurocultural Theory

The neurocultural theory of emotion (Ekman, 1972), based on Tomkins's earlier work (Tomkins & McCarter, 1964), posits the existence of a universal *facial affect program* that provides a one-to-one map between the emotion a person feels and the facial expression the person displays. According to this theory, the facial affect program is the same for all people in all cultures, and therefore everyone expresses emotion in the same manner in nonsocial settings. However, in social settings, people use conscious "management techniques" (Ekman, 1972, p. 225) called *display rules* to control and override the operation of the universal facial affect program. These display rules can vary across cultures, and they are norms that serve to intensify, diminish, neutralize, or mask emotional displays that would otherwise be produced automatically. Extending neurocultural theory from the expression to the perception of emotion, Matsumoto (1989) argued that all people in all cultures perceive emotional expressions in the same manner, but that there are culturally specific norms (i.e., decoding rules) about whether or not to acknowledge that one has understood.

Developing a Dialect Theory

Tomkins and McCarter (1964) articulated the metaphor that cultural differences in emotional expression are like "dialects" of the "more universal grammar of emotion" (p. 127): Just as dialects of a language (e.g., American vs. British English) can differ in accent, grammar, and vocabulary, the universal language of emotion may also have dialects that differ subtly from each other.

Expanding on these ideas, we developed the new dialect theory to account for the empirical evidence of an in-group advantage in understanding emotion. Earlier researchers who had noticed this effect referred to it as *bias* and argued that participants were more motivated and perhaps paid closer attention when judging in-group members than when judging out-group members. However, our evidence did not support this interpretation, because in many of the studies reviewed in our meta-analysis, participants could not have known that the emotional expressions were from a foreign culture (this was the case, e.g., in studies in which Caucasians judged facial expressions of Caucasians from other cultures and in studies in which filtered vocal tones served as stimuli). Translation difficulties (i.e., mismatches between the emotion words participants used to judge stimuli and experimenters used to instruct the posers who generated the stimuli) could have contributed to the in-group effect but could not fully explain it, given that the in-group advantage also existed across cultural groups speaking the same language. Thus, we had to find another explanation for the in-group advantage.

Two central observations inspired the dialect theory. The first observation was that any explanation of the in-group advantage must consider the cultural match between the expresser and the perceiver of an emotional display, rather than considering either group independently. This was a logical point because the definition of the in-group advantage is that perceivers' emotion judgments are more accurate with culturally matched than culturally mismatched materials. The second observation was that the cultural differences that cause the in-group advantage must be contained within the appearance of the emotional expressions themselves, because the in-group advantage was found when participants did not have any other cues about the cultural identity of the expresser. For example, Americans could have outperformed other Caucasian cultural groups when judging American facial expressions only if there was something particularly American about the expressions.

The dialect theory arose from these two observations. It begins with a universal affect program,[2] a guide for expressing emotions that is the same for all cultural groups. Because a person can express any single emotion in multiple ways, this program is not necessarily the one-to-one map of neurocultural theory.[3] Additionally, each cultural group has a *specific affect program* that incorporates some adjustments to the universal program. Acquired through social learning, these adjustments create subtle differences in the appearance of emotional expression across cultures. These stylistic differences do not necessarily have a specific purpose or meaning; thus, they differ from display and decoding rules, which are conscious management techniques for the benefit of social harmony. Figure 1, on p. 162 illustrates the relation between the universal affect program and specific affect programs from different cultures.

Figure 2, on p. 162 illustrates the dialect theory of how emotion is communicated and perceived. A key distinction between dialect theory and neurocultural theory is that dialect theory suggests that cultural differences in emotional expression can arise from two sources—the specific affect program and display rules—rather than from display rules alone. Similarly, dialect theory posits two different sources of cultural differences in perceiving emotion—the specific affect program and decoding rules—rather than decoding rules alone.

A second key distinction from neurocultural theory is that dialect theory suggests there is a direct link between the cultural differences that arise in the expression and perception of emotion. This link is the specific affect program, which governs the two complementary processes. After all, people tend to interpret another person's behavior in terms of what they would have intended if they had used the same expression. In contrast, neurocultural theory posits that cultural differences in emotional expression and perception emerge from two separate processes: display rules and decoding rules. Because these two sets of rules are not explicitly linked to each other, neurocultural theory does not account for

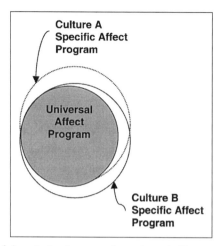

Fig. 1. Illustration of the relation between the universal affect program and the specific affect programs for two cultures. Copyright 2003 by Hillary Anger Elfenbein. Reprinted with permission of the author.

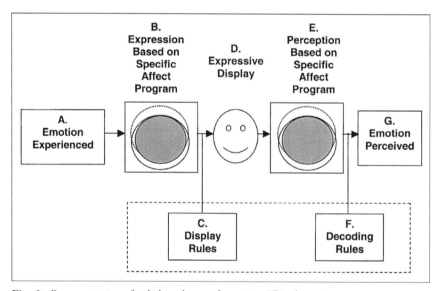

Fig. 2. Representation of a dialect theory of emotion. This theory incorporates processes described by Brunswick (1955), Buck (1984), and Ekman (1972). The universal affect program is represented by the gray circles, and specific affect programs of two different cultures are represented by the partially overlapping white circles (see Fig. 1). The dashed box shows the only sources of cultural differences in the communication of emotion according to Ekman (1972) and Matsumoto (1989). Copyright 2003 by Hillary Anger Elfenbein. Reprinted with permission of the author.

the empirical evidence of the in-group advantage. This is because, as we have noted, any explanation of the in-group advantage must consider the cultural match between the expresser and the perceiver of an emotional display, rather than either group independently.

Evidence for the In-Group Advantage

This background assists in clarifying the disagreement regarding whether the evidence supports the existence of an in-group advantage in emotion. Matsumoto (2002) argued that an in-group advantage in perceiving emotion should result only from differences across perceivers. This is because his theoretical perspective treats cultural differences in expressing and perceiving emotion as two unlinked processes, and he argued that they should be examined separately. Thus, he argued that a valid test of the in-group advantage in emotion recognition should remove all cultural differences in the appearance of emotional expressions in order to achieve "stimulus equivalence" (Matsumoto, 2002, p. 236). However, according to dialect theory, there are cultural differences in the appearance of emotional expressions resulting from the specific affect program. Therefore, forcibly eliminating all cultural differences in the appearance of facial expressions also would eliminate one of the two matched processes responsible for the in-group advantage, cultural differences in expression and perception that arise from the specific affect program. Thus, failures to demonstrate an in-group advantage under stimulus equivalence fit rather than disconfirm the predictions of dialect theory. Further, not only is eliminating cultural differences in the appearance of emotional expression an undesirable step for researchers according to dialect theory, but recent empirical evidence demonstrates that in practice it can be nearly impossible to do so—such differences are so robust that they can leak through processes designed specifically to neutralize them (Marsh, Elfenbein, & Ambady, 2003).

FUTURE DIRECTIONS

Universals and cultural differences in the communication of emotion have been hotly debated and will likely continue to be. Research studies that can help to tease apart the competing perspectives—while acknowledging the complex roles of both nature and nurture—would greatly benefit the field.

The dialect theory of emotion is still speculative and being developed primarily on the basis of recent empirical data. The theory requires direct testing. The most authoritative studies would uncover the particular aspects of emotional expression that vary across cultures—such as specific facial muscle movements, features of vocal tones, or body movements—and would map the use of these cues directly to cross-cultural differences in perceiving emotion. It is important to do this research in a context that limits alternative explanations for the in-group advantage, such as language differences and bias. Further research could determine how these cues are learned.

Although differences in emotion across cultures can create a barrier to effective communication, it is heartening to know that people can overcome these barriers. Further work in this field has the potential to help bridge intergroup differences by contributing to training and intervention programs that can help to improve cross-cultural communication.

Recommended Reading

Darwin, C. (1998). *The expression of the emotions in man and animals* (3rd ed.). New York: Oxford University Press. (Original work published 1872)
Ekman, P. (1993). Facial expression and emotion. *American Psychologist, 48,* 384–392.
Elfenbein, H.A., & Ambady, N. (2002b). (See References)
Russell, J.A. (1994). (See References)

Acknowledgments—We thank James Russell, Anita Williams Woolley, and Kevyn Yong for their helpful comments on the manuscript.

Notes

1. Address correspondence to Hillary Anger Elfenbein, Haas School of Business, University of California, Berkeley, CA 94720-1900; e-mail: hillary@post.harvard.edu.

2. We do not refer to the universal affect program as a facial affect program in order to emphasize that it includes additional nonverbal channels of communication, such as vocal tone and body movements.

3. We thank James Russell for this observation.

References

Brunswick, E. (1955). Representative design and probabilistic theory in a functional psychology. *Psychological Review, 62,* 193–217.
Buck, R. (1984). *The communication of emotion.* New York: Guilford Press.
Ekman, P. (1972). Universals and cultural differences in facial expressions of emotion. In J. Cole (Ed.), *Nebraska Symposium on Motivation, 1971* (Vol. 19, pp. 207–282). Lincoln: University of Nebraska Press.
Elfenbein, H.A., & Ambady, N. (2002a). Is there an in-group advantage in emotion? *Psychological Bulletin, 128,* 243–249.
Elfenbein, H.A., & Ambady, N. (2002b). On the universality and cultural specificity of emotion recognition: A meta-analysis. *Psychological Bulletin, 128,* 203–235.
Elfenbein, H.A., & Ambady, N. (2003a). Cultural similarity's consequences: A distance perspective on cross-cultural differences in emotion recognition. *Journal of Cross-Cultural Psychology, 34,* 92–110.
Elfenbein, H.A., & Ambady, N. (2003b). When familiarity breeds accuracy: Cultural exposure and facial emotion recognition. *Journal of Personality and Social Psychology, 85,* 276–290.
Izard, C.E. (1971). *The face of emotion.* New York: Appleton-Century-Crofts.
Marsh, A., Elfenbein, H.A., & Ambady, N. (2003). Nonverbal "accents": Cultural differences in facial expressions of emotion. *Psychological Science, 14,* 373–376.
Matsumoto, D. (1989). Cultural influences on the perception of emotion. *Journal of Cross-Cultural Psychology, 20,* 92–105.
Matsumoto, D. (2002). Methodological requirements to test a possible ingroup advantage in judging emotions across cultures: Comments on Elfenbein and Ambady and evidence. *Psychological Bulletin, 128,* 236–242.
Matsumoto, D., & Assar, M. (1992). The effects of language on judgments of universal facial expressions of emotion. *Journal of Nonverbal Behavior, 16,* 85–99.

Russell, J.A. (1994). Is there universal recognition of emotion from facial expression? A review of the cross-cultural studies. *Psychological Bulletin, 115,* 102–141.

Tomkins, S.S., & McCarter, R. (1964). What and where are the primary affects: Some evidence for a theory. *Perceptual and Motor Skills, 18,* 119–158.

Section 5: Critical Thinking Questions

1. Can an emotion be non-conscious, or does it have to be something you feel and know about? What about attitudes—do we have to know how we feel about some category (i.e., blacks, women, the elderly), or can we have non-conscious "implicit" attitudes that are the opposite of how we *think* we feel? Suppose conscious and non-conscious feelings or attitudes disagree. Which one is more true—the conscious or the non-conscious versions? Does the IAT offer a "window into the soul," or does it simply reveal subtle cultural conditioning that we routinely ignore or override?

2. Do you agree that we are more evolutionarily prepared to learn fear of some stimuli, compared to others? What else fits in this category besides snakes? Would the same process apply to positive stimuli, such that we are more prepared to like certain stimuli than others? To what extent is human nature like an non pre-programmed "blank slate" (at one extreme), versus "a large collection of pre-programmed mental mechanisms" (at the other extreme)?

This article has been reprinted as it originally appeared in *Current Directions in Psychological Science*. Citation information for this article as originally published appears above.

Section 6: Happiness and Well-Being

This final section addresses emotion from a somewhat different slant: What are the causes of positive emotion, and happiness more generally? These articles well represent the still-new movement of "positive psychology," which tries to understand the roots of human thriving. Of course, the bookstores are filled with "happiness self-help" books. Such books are usually not based on science, as are the articles in this section. The first article considers the important question of whether our happiness levels are genetically determined. Perhaps what goes up must come down, and there is no way to become permanently happier? Lucas considers the problem of "adaptation"—the fact that we get used to any positive change, so that it ceases to affect us and we return to where we started. He discusses new large-sample longitudinal data showing that certain major life-events (divorce, disability) can permanently change peoples' happiness levels. Although Lucas puts a positive spin on these findings, astute readers will notice that subjects only changed for the worse, in his data. Thus, it is still an open question whether people can "escape the set-point" in a positive direction, i.e., become permanently happier than their inherited temperament dictates. The second article, by Ekman, Ricard, Davidson, and Wallace, is unusual because it draws from the religious/philosophical tradition of Buddhism—asking whether what we now know about happiness is consistent or inconsistent with the Buddhist account of what makes people happy. The answer to this question is complex, but to make a long story short, it appears that much contemporary positive psychology research is converging upon ancient Buddhist insights concerning the problematic effects of attachment, craving, and hostility. Furthermore, Buddhist practices involving mindful attention, cognitive re-framing, and the quest for self-insight are now being shown, just as long claimed, to have positive effects upon peoples' functioning.

The third article in this section, by Wilson and Gilbert, addresses the question of whether we even know what will make us happy (or unhappy). Their research on *affective forecasting* has shown a variety of biases that impact our ability to predict our own future emotional states. This is a problem because if we don't know what choices will make us happy, then how can we make those choices, and might we instead find ourselves making the "wrong" choices? However, there is also an unexpected positive side to the affective forecasting message: We tend to overestimate how negatively we will react to the tragedies of life, and underestimate how quickly we will recover from them. This article also suggests that when good things happen to us, we shouldn't spend too much time thinking about them or trying to explain them. The final article in this section addresses a very different question from the first three: The surprising problems faced by the children of affluent parents. Although low-income children are typically considered to be at higher risk for developmental difficulties, high-income children may have their own problems—they use drugs at a higher rate, and do so in a seeming attempt to "self-medicate." This fits with other recent research showing that materialistic and consumerist values can create stresses and corrode relationships, and that this aspect of the "American dream" may actually be empty. So, think twice before being too envious of those who have more "stuff!"

Adaptation and the Set-Point Model of Subjective Well-Being: Does Happiness Change After Major Life Events?

Richard E. Lucas[1]
Michigan State University and German Institute for Economic Research, Berlin

Abstract

Hedonic adaptation refers to the process by which individuals return to baseline levels of happiness following a change in life circumstances. Dominant models of subjective well-being (SWB) suggest that people can adapt to almost any life event and that happiness levels fluctuate around a biologically determined set point that rarely changes. Recent evidence from large-scale panel studies challenges aspects of this conclusion. Although inborn factors certainly matter and some adaptation does occur, events such as divorce, death of a spouse, unemployment, and disability are associated with lasting changes in SWB. These recent studies also show that there are considerable individual differences in the extent to which people adapt. Thus, happiness levels do change, and adaptation is not inevitable.

Keywords

happiness; subjective well-being; adaptation; set-point theory

People's greatest hopes and fears often center on the possible occurrence of rare but important life events. People may dread the possibility of losing a loved one or becoming disabled, and they may go to great lengths to find true love or to increase their chances of winning the lottery. In many cases, people strive to attain or avoid these outcomes because of the outcomes' presumed effect on happiness. But do these major life events really affect long-term levels of subjective well-being (SWB)? Dominant models of SWB suggest that after experiencing major life events, people inevitably adapt. More specifically, set-point theorists posit that inborn personality factors cause an inevitable return to genetically determined happiness set points. However, recent evidence from large-scale longitudinal studies challenges some of the stronger conclusions from these models.

ADAPTATION RESEARCH AND THEORY

Although the thought that levels of happiness cannot change may distress some people, researchers believe that adaptation processes serve important functions (Frederick & Loewenstein, 1999). For one thing, these processes protect people from potentially dangerous psychological and physiological consequences of prolonged emotional states. In addition, because adaptation processes allow unchanging stimuli to fade into the attentional background, these processes ensure that change in the environment receives extra attention. Attention to environmental change is advantageous because threats that have existed for prolonged periods of time are likely to be less dangerous than novel threats. Similarly, because rewards that have persisted are less likely to disappear quickly than are novel rewards, it will often be advantageous to attend and react more strongly to these novel rewards. Finally, by reducing emotional reactions over time, adaptation processes allow individuals to disengage from goals that have little chance of success. Thus, adaptation can be beneficial, and some amount of adaptation to life circumstances surely occurs.

Yet many questions about the strength and ubiquity of adaptation effects remain, partly because of the types of evidence that have been used to support adaptation theories. In many cases, adaptation is not directly observed. Instead, it must be inferred from indirect evidence. For instance, psychologists often cite the low correlation between happiness and life circumstances as evidence for adaptation effects. Factors such as income, age, health, marital status, and number of friends account for only a small percentage of the variance in SWB (Diener, Suh, Lucas, & Smith, 1999). One explanation that has been offered for this counterintuitive finding is that these factors initially have an impact but that people adapt over time. However, the weak associations between life circumstances and SWB themselves provide only suggestive evidence for this explanation.

Additional indirect support for the set-point model comes from research that takes a personality perspective on SWB. Three pieces of evidence are relevant (Lucas, in press-b). First, SWB exhibits moderate stability even over very long periods of time and even in the face of changing life circumstances. Recent reviews suggest that approximately 30 to 40% of the variance in life-satisfaction measures is stable over periods as long as 20 years. Second, a number of studies have shown that well-being variables are about 40 to 50% heritable. These heritability estimates appear to be even higher (about 80%) for long-term levels of happiness (Lykken & Tellegen, 1996). Finally, personality variables like extroversion and neuroticism are relatively strong predictors of happiness, at least when compared to the predictive power of external factors. The explanation for this set of findings is that events can influence short-term levels of happiness, but personality-based adaptation processes inevitably move people back to their genetically determined set point after a relatively short period of time.

More direct evidence for hedonic adaptation comes from studies that examine the well-being of individuals who have experienced important life events. However, even these studies can be somewhat equivocal. For instance, one of the most famous studies is that of Brickman, Coates, and Janoff-Bulman (1978) comparing lottery winners and patients with spinal-cord injuries to people in a control group. Brickman et al. showed that lottery winners were not significantly happier than the control-group participants and that individuals with spinal-cord injuries "did not appear nearly as unhappy as might be expected" (p. 921). This study appears to show adaptation to even the most extreme events imaginable. What is often not mentioned, however, is that although the participants with spinal-cord injuries were above neutral on the happiness scale (which is what led Brickman et al. to conclude that they were happier than might be expected), they were significantly less happy than the people in the control group, and the difference between the groups was actually quite large. Individuals with spinal-cord injuries were more than three quarters of a standard deviation below the mean of the

170

control group. This means that the average participant from the control group was happier than approximately 78% of participants with spinal-cord injuries. This result has now been replicated quite often—most existing studies show relatively large differences between individuals with spinal-cord injuries and healthy participants in control groups (Dijkers, 1997).

In addition to problems that result from the interpretation of effect sizes, methodological limitations restrict the conclusions that can be drawn from many existing studies of adaptation. Most studies are not longitudinal, and even fewer are prospective (though there are some notable exceptions; see e.g., Bonanno, 2004; Caspi et al., 2003). Because participants' pre-event levels of SWB are not known, it is always possible that individuals who experienced an event were more or less happy than average before the event occurred. Certain people may be predisposed to experience life events, and these predisposing factors may be responsible for their happiness levels being lower than average. For instance, in a review of the literature examining the well-being of children who had lost limbs from various causes, Tyc (1992) suggested that those who lost limbs due to accidents tended to have higher levels of premorbid psychological disorders than did those who lost limbs due to disease. Thus, simply comparing the well-being of children who lost limbs to those who did not might overestimate the effect of the injury. Psychologists have demonstrated that level of happiness predicts the occurrence of a variety of events and outcomes (Lyubomirsky, King, & Diener, 2005), and therefore, studies that compare individuals who have experienced a particular event with those who have not but that do not take into account previous happiness level must be interpreted cautiously.

A second methodological concern relates to what are known as demand characteristics. When researchers recruit participants specifically because they have experienced a given life event, participants may over- or underreport SWB. These reports may occur because people believe the life event should have an impact, because they want to appear well-adjusted, or simply because the context of the study makes the event more salient. For instance, Smith, Schwarz, Roberts, and Ubel (2006) showed that patients with Parkinson's disease reported lower life satisfaction when the study instructions indicated that Parkinson's disease was a focus than when the instructions indicated that the study focused on the general population.

USING LARGE-SCALE PANEL STUDIES TO ASSESS ADAPTATION TO LIFE EVENTS

Recently, my colleagues and I have turned to archival data analysis using large, nationally representative panel studies to address questions about adaptation to life events. These studies have a number of advantages over alternative designs. First, they are prospective, which means that pre-event levels of SWB are known. Second, they are longitudinal, which means that change over time can be accurately modeled. Third, very large samples are often involved, which means that even rare events are sampled. Finally, because designers of these studies often recruit nationally representative samples, and because the questionnaires often focus on a variety of issues, demand characteristics are unlikely to have much of an effect.

We have used two such panel studies—the German Socioeconomic Panel Study (GSOEP) and the British Household Panel Study (BHPS)—to examine the amount of adaptation that occurs following major life events. The GSOEP includes almost 40,000 individuals living in Germany who have been assessed yearly for up to 21 years. The BHPS includes more than 27,000 individuals living in Great Britain who have been assessed yearly for up to 14 years. We have used these data sets to examine the extent to which people adapt to events such as marital transitions (Lucas, 2005; Lucas, Clark, Georgellis, & Diener, 2003), bouts of unemployment (Lucas, Clark, Georgellis, & Diener, 2004), and the onset of a disability (Lucas, in press-a). At least three important findings have emerged (see Diener, Lucas, & Scollon, 2006, for a more detailed review).

First, long-term levels of SWB do change, and adaptation is not inevitable. In fact, these studies show that there is no single answer to the question of whether people adapt to life events. Instead, the pattern of adaptation varies across different events. Figure 1 shows the average within-person trajectories for life satisfaction before and after various life events. These data show that although the average person adapts to marriage (and this adaptation tends to occur within just a couple of years; Lucas et al., 2003), adaptation to other events is often very slow or incomplete. Widows and widowers return very close (within about .15 points) to the level of life satisfaction that they reported before their spouse died, but this process of adaptation takes approximately 7 years (Lucas et al., 2003). Individuals who get divorced or experience unemployment report what appear to be permanent changes in life satisfaction following these events (Lucas, 2005; Lucas et al., 2004). Furthermore, these changes can sometimes be very large. Individuals who acquire a severe disability report life-satisfaction levels that are more than a full standard deviation below their baseline levels, and these levels do not appear to rebound over time (Lucas, in press-a).

A second important finding is that, for all events we have studied, there are large individual differences in the amount of adaptation that occurs. To demonstrate, it is possible to calculate the variability in within-person change that occurs before and after the event. In the case of marriage, very little change occurs on average. However, the standard deviation for the amount of change that occurs was approximately 1.0 (for responses derived from an 11-point scale). This means that approximately 30% of participants reported lasting changes in satisfaction of between a half and a full point, and an additional 32% reported lasting changes of more than a full point. These effects are quite large in relation to the amount of variance that exists in baseline levels of well-being. A participant who began the study with an average level of life satisfaction but experienced a change that was one standard deviation above the mean change would move to the 74th percentile overall in level of life satisfaction. Similarly, someone who experienced a change that was one standard deviation below the mean would move to the 26th percentile overall. These individual differences in reaction and adaptation likely result both from variability in the nature of the event (some marriages are better than others) and from variability in people's reactions to similar events. In either case, the average trajectory does not tell the whole story about the potential for life events to have a major impact on people's long-term levels of SWB.

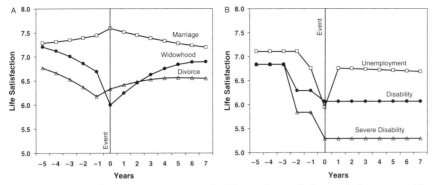

Fig. 1. Average within-person trajectories for life satisfaction before and after various life events. Panel A shows reaction and adaptation to marriage, death of a spouse, and divorce. Panel B shows reaction and adaptation to unemployment and the onset of varying degrees of disability. Adapted from Lucas (2005), Lucas (in press-a), Lucas, Clark, Georgellis, and Diener (2003), and Lucas, Clark, Georgellis, and Diener (2004).

A third major finding is that people who will eventually experience a major life event often differ from people who will not, even before the event occurs. Therefore prospective longitudinal studies are necessary to separate pre-existing differences from longitudinal change. For instance, cross-sectional studies have consistently shown that married people are happier than single, divorced, or widowed people; yet our studies showed that marriage was not associated with lasting increases in happiness. Instead, people who eventually married were happier than average (or at least happier than those who married and then divorced) even more than 5 years before the marriage (Lucas, 2005; Lucas et al., 2003). People who eventually divorced, on the other hand, started out with lower levels of well-being than those who did not divorce, and they reported lasting changes following this event. These findings are illustrated in Figure 2 (see p. 174), in which levels of life satisfaction before and after marriage are plotted for participants who eventually divorced and for those who stayed married. These results suggest that about half of the difference that is typically found between married and divorced individuals in cross-sectional studies is the result of selection effects, and half is the result of lasting changes that follow divorce.

FUTURE DIRECTIONS

Although large-scale, nationally representative panel studies are an important tool for answering questions about adaptation, they are not without limitations. The set of psychological variables that has been assessed thus far is relatively limited. This lack of information about psychological characteristics means that moderators and process variables cannot be examined. Future research on adaptation should focus on achieving the following three goals.

First, sophisticated methodologies to assess adaptation to a wide variety of events must be used, so that researchers can develop a clear picture of the events to which people can and cannot adapt. As these events are catalogued, hypotheses about the characteristics that distinguish these events can be formulated and

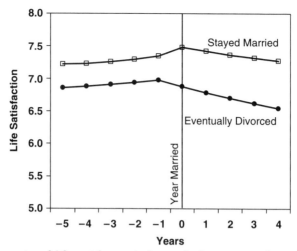

Fig. 2. Trajectories of life satisfaction before and after marriage for individuals who remain married and those who eventually divorce. Adapted from Lucas (2005).

tested. For instance, Frederick and Loewenstein (1999) suggested that people may be able to adapt to one-time events like the loss of a spouse or the onset of an unchanging medical condition but may be less able to adapt to conditions that change or worsen over time.

A second goal is that programmatic research should lead to greater insight into the processes that underlie hedonic adaptation. Adaptation may result from physiological processes that reduce emotional reactivity to constant stimuli, or it could result from psychological processes that change the way people think about events that have occurred in their lives. For instance, adaptation effects may emerge when people disengage from goals that have become unattainable and set new goals toward which they can strive, or it may occur as people develop strengths or acquire new skills that enable them to deal more effectively with less-than-ideal life circumstances.

A third research goal is to clarify the individual-level characteristics that promote or prevent adaptation. Our studies (Lucas, 2005, in press-a; Lucas et al., 2003, 2004) show that there are considerable individual differences in the amount of adaptation that occurs. One fruitful avenue for understanding these individual differences is to look for personality variables that moderate adaptation effects over time. For instance, Bonanno and colleagues have identified distinct trajectories of distress following major traumatic life events like the loss of a spouse or a child (Bonanno, 2004). Notably, characteristics including hardiness, self-enhancement, and positive emotions have been shown to be associated with the most resilient pattern of reactions. In addition, Caspi and colleagues have shown that interactions between stressful life events and specific genes predict the onset of depression (Caspi et al., 2003). It is possible that similar gene-by-environment interactions would also affect reaction and adaptation to life events. Future research must identify additional demographic, social, and personality factors that promote positive reactions to major life events.

IS THERE A HAPPINESS SET POINT?

The studies reviewed in this paper do not refute the set-point model of happiness. Instead, they put the empirical findings that have emerged from that model in a broader context. What does it mean to an individual that happiness is 50% or even 80% heritable? What does it mean that 35% of the variance in well-being is stable over time? Do these empirical facts mean that long-term levels of happiness do not change? The results reviewed in this paper show that the answer to this question is no. They confirm that although happiness levels are moderately stable over time, this stability does not preclude large and lasting changes. Happiness levels do change, adaptation is not inevitable, and life events do matter.

Recommended Reading

Bonanno, G. (2004). (See References)
Diener, E., Lucas, R.E., & Scollon, C.N. (2006). (See References)
Frederick, S., & Loewenstein, G. (1999). (See References)

Note

1. Address correspondence to Richard E. Lucas, Department of Psychology, Michigan State University, East Lansing, MI 48823; e-mail: lucasri@msu.edu.

References

Bonanno, G.A. (2004). Loss, trauma, and human resilience: Have we underestimated the human capacity to thrive after extremely aversive events? *American Psychologist, 59,* 20–28.
Brickman, P., Coates, D., & Janoff-Bulman, R. (1978). Lottery winners and accident victims: Is happiness relative? *Journal of Personality & Social Psychology, 36,* 917–927.
Caspi, A., Sugden, K., Moffitt, T.E., Taylor, A., Craig, I.W., Harrington, H., et al. (2003). Influence of life stress on depression: Moderation by a polymorphism in the 5-HTT gene. *Science, 301,* 386–389.
Diener, E., Lucas, R.E., & Scollon, C. (2006). Beyond the hedonic treadmill: Revising the adaptation theory of well-being. *American Psychologist, 61,* 305–314.
Diener, E., Suh, E.M., Lucas, R.E., & Smith, H.L. (1999). Subjective well-being: Three decades of progress. *Psychological Bulletin, 125,* 276–302.
Dijkers, M. (1997). Quality of life after spinal cord injury: A meta analysis of the effects of disablement components. *Spinal Cord, 35,* 829–840.
Frederick, S., & Loewenstein, G. (1999). Hedonic adaptation. In D. Kahneman, E. Diener, & N. Schwarz (Eds.), *Well-being: The foundations of hedonic psychology* (pp. 302–329). New York: Sage.
Lucas, R.E. (2005). Time does not heal all wounds: A longitudinal study of reaction and adaptation to divorce. *Psychological Science, 16,* 945–950.
Lucas, R.E. (in press-a). Long-term disability is associated with lasting changes in subjective well-being: Evidence from two nationally representative longitudinal studies. *Journal of Personality and Social Psychology.*
Lucas, R.E. (in press-b). Personality and subjective well-being. In M. Eid & R.J. Larsen (Eds.), *The science of subjective well-being.* New York: Guilford.
Lucas, R.E., Clark, A.E., Georgellis, Y., & Diener, E. (2003). Reexamining adaptation and the set point model of happiness: Reactions to changes in marital status. *Journal of Personality & Social Psychology, 84,* 527–539.
Lucas, R.E., Clark, A.E., Georgellis, Y., & Diener, E. (2004). Unemployment alters the set point for life satisfaction. *Psychological Science, 15,* 8–13.
Lykken, D., & Tellegen, A. (1996). Happiness is a stochastic phenomenon. *Psychological Science, 7,* 186–189.

Lyubomirsky, S., King, L., & Diener, E. (2005). The benefits of frequent positive affect: Does happiness lead to success? *Psychological Bulletin, 131,* 803–855.

Smith, D.M., Schwarz, N., Roberts, T.R., & Ubel, P.A. (2006). Why are you calling me? How study introductions change response patterns. *Quality of Life Research, 15,* 621–630.

Tyc, V.L. (1992). Psychosocial adaptation of children and adolescents with limb deficiencies: A review. *Clinical Psychology Review, 2,* 275–291.

This article has been reprinted as it originally appeared in *Current Directions in Psychological Science*. Citation information for this article as originally published appears above.

Buddhist and Psychological Perspectives on Emotions and Well-Being

Paul Ekman[1]
University of California, San Francisco

Richard J. Davidson
University of Wisconsin, Madison

Matthieu Ricard
Shechen Monastery, Katmandu, Nepal

B. Alan Wallace
Santa Barbara Institute for Consciousness Studies,
Santa Barbara, California

Abstract

Stimulated by a recent meeting between Western psychologists and the Dalai Lama on the topic of destructive emotions, we report on two issues: the achievement of enduring happiness, what Tibetan Buddhists call *sukha*, and the nature of afflictive and nonafflictive emotional states and traits. A Buddhist perspective on these issues is presented, along with discussion of the challenges the Buddhist view raises for empirical research and theory.

Keywords

Buddhism; consciousness

Buddhist thought, which arose more than 2,000 years ago in Asian cultures, holds assumptions that differ in important ways from modern psychology. The particular branch of Buddhist thinking we consider here is Indo-Tibetan, a tradition having roots in Indian thought and further developed by Tibetan theorists. It is a line of thinking that is more than 1,000 years old. Although different aspects of Buddhist thought have already influenced a number of psychologists, its challenges for research on emotion are not widely known. Some suggestive convergences between Buddhist thinking and, for example, findings in neurobiology, suggest the fruitfulness of integrating a Buddhist view into emotion research.

The traditional languages of Buddhism, such as Pali, Sanskrit, and Tibetan, have no word for "emotion" as such. Although discrepant from the modern psychological research tradition that has isolated emotion as a distinct mental process that can be studied apart from other processes, the fact that there is no term in Buddhism for emotion is quite consistent with what scientists have come to learn about the anatomy of the brain. Every region in the brain that has been identified with some aspect of emotion has also been identified with aspects of cognition (e.g., Davidson & Irwin, 1999). The circuitry that supports affect and the circuitry that supports cognition are completely intertwined—an anatomical arrangement consistent with the Buddhist view that these processes cannot be separated.

We have chosen two issues, the achievement of enduring happiness and the nature of afflictive emotions, to illustrate the usefulness of considering the Buddhist perspective in work on emotion. Given the space allowed, we present illustrative examples of possible areas for research, rather than a more complete discussion.

This report is a collaborative effort of Buddhists (Matthieu Ricard and B. Alan Wallace) and psychologists (Paul Ekman and Richard J. Davidson). Our report grew out of an extraordinary meeting with His Holiness the Dalai Lama, in Dharamsala, India, in March 2000, that focused on destructive emotions.[2] The Buddhist authors wrote the sections titled "The Buddhist View," and the psychologist authors wrote the sections on research directions and theory.

ACHIEVING ENDURING HAPPINESS

The Buddhist View

Buddhists and psychologists alike believe that emotions strongly influence people's thoughts, words, and actions and that, at times, they help people in their pursuit of transient pleasures and satisfaction. From a Buddhist perspective, however, some emotions are conducive to genuine and enduring happiness and others are not. A Buddhist term for such happiness is *sukha,* which may be defined in this context as a state of flourishing that arises from mental balance and insight into the nature of reality. Rather than a fleeting emotion or mood aroused by sensory and conceptual stimuli, *sukha* is an enduring trait that arises from a mind in a state of equilibrium and entails a conceptually unstructured and unfiltered awareness of the true nature of reality. Many Buddhist contemplatives claim to have experienced *sukha,* which increases as a result of sustained training.

Similarly, the Buddhist concept of *duhkha,* often translated as "suffering," is not simply an unpleasant feeling. Rather, it refers most deeply to a basic vulnerability to suffering and pain due to misapprehending the nature of reality. (The terms *sukha* and *duhkha* are from Sanskrit, one of the primary languages of Buddhist literature.)

How is *sukha* to be realized? Buddhists believe that the radical transformation of consciousness necessary to realize *sukha* can occur by sustained training in attention, emotional balance, and mindfulness, so that one can learn to distinguish between the way things are as they appear to the senses and the conceptual superimpositions one projects upon them. As a result of such training, one perceives what is presented to the senses, including one's own mental states, in a way that is closer to their true nature, undistorted by the projections people habitually mistake for reality.

Such training results not only in shifts in fleeting emotions but also leads to changes in one's moods and eventually even changes in one's temperament. For more than two millennia, Buddhist practitioners have developed and tested ways of gradually cultivating those emotions that are conductive to the pursuit of *sukha* and of freeing themselves from emotions that are detrimental to this pursuit. The ideal here is not simply to achieve one's own individual happiness in isolation from others, but to incorporate the recognition of one's deep kinship with all beings, who share the same yearning to be free of suffering and to find a lasting state of well-being.

Two Research Directions

We have begun to examine highly experienced Buddhist practitioners, who presumably have achieved *sukha,* to determine whether that trait manifests itself in their biological activity during emotional episodes (Lutz, Greischar, Rawlings, Ricard, & Davidson, in press) or increases their sensitivity to the emotions of other people, and to see how their interactive style may transform the nature of conflictual interactions. Such study of Buddhism's most expert practitioners may change psychology's conception of what at least some human beings are capable of achieving.

Another possible area of research concerns the reliability of self-report about mental states. Although much of the research on emotion has presumed that research subjects and our patients during psychotherapy can readily report on their subjective experience through questionnaires and interviews, findings to date show that most people report only the most recent or most intense of their emotional experiences (e.g., Kahneman, Fredrickson, Schreiber, & Redelmeier, 1993; Rosenberg & Ekman, 1994) and are subject to bias. Research could determine whether those schooled in Buddhist practices could offer a more refined and complete account of their immediately past emotional experience, exhibiting fewer judgmental biases. In a related vein, other research has demonstrated that most people are poor predictors of what will make them happy (e.g., Wilson & Gilbert, in press). It would be interesting to determine whether those who have engaged in Buddhist contemplative practices sufficiently to achieve *sukha* are more accurate in affective forecasting.

AFFLICTIVE MENTAL STATES

The Buddhist View

Buddhism does not distinguish between emotions and other mental processes. Instead, it is concerned with understanding which types of mental activity are truly conducive to one's own and others' well-being, and which ones are harmful, especially in the long run.

In Buddhism, a clear distinction is made between affective states that are directly aroused by the experience of pleasurable stimuli (sensory, as well as aesthetic and intellectual) and *sukha,* which arises from the attentional, emotional, and cognitive balance of the mind. (For a similar distinction, see Sheldon, Ryan, Deci, & Kasser, 2004.) The experience of pleasure is contingent upon specific times, places, and circumstances, and can easily change into a neutral or unpleasant feeling. When one disengages from the pleasant stimulus, the resultant pleasure vanishes, whether or not it is connected to any afflictive state.

The initial challenge of Buddhist meditative practice is not merely to suppress, let alone repress, destructive mental states, but instead to identify how they arise, how they are experienced, and how they influence oneself and others over the long run. In addition, one learns to transform and finally free oneself from all afflictive states. This requires cultivating and refining one's ability to introspectively monitor one's own mental activities, enabling one to distinguish disruptive from nondisruptive thoughts and emotions. In Buddhism, rigorous, sustained training in mindfulness and introspection is conjoined with the cultivation of attentional stability and vividness.

In contrast to Aristotelian ethics, Buddhism rejects the notion that all emotions are healthy as long as they are not excessive or inappropriate to the time and place. Rather, Buddhism maintains that some mental states are afflictive regardless of their degree or the context in which they arise. Here we focus on three mental processes that are considered to be fundamental toxins of the mind.

The first of these is craving. This mental process is based on an unrealistic, reified distinction between self and others—or between subject and object more generally—as being absolutely separate and unrelated. Craving is concerned with acquiring or maintaining some desirable object or situation for "me" and "mine," which may be threatened by "the other." One assumes that desirable qualities are inherent in the object desired and then exaggerates these qualities, while ignoring or deemphasizing that object's undesirable aspects. Craving is therefore an unrealistic way of engaging with the world, and it is harmful whenever one identifies with this afflictive mental process, regardless of how strong it is or the circumstances under which it arises. Craving is said to be afflictive, for it disrupts the balance of the mind, easily giving rise to anxiety, misery, fear, and anger; and it is unrealistic in the sense that it falsely displaces the source of one's well being from one's own mind to objects.

Hatred is the second of the fundamental afflictions of the mind and is a reverse reflection of craving. That is, hatred, or malevolence, is driven by the wish to harm or destroy anything that obstructs the selfish pursuit of desirable objects and situations for me and mine. Hatred exaggerates the undesirable qualities of objects and deemphasizes their positive qualities. When the mind is obsessed with resentment, it is trapped in the deluded impression that the source of its dissatisfaction belongs entirely to the external object (just as, in the case of craving, the mind locates the source of satisfaction in desirable objects). But even though the trigger of one's resentment may be the external object, the actual source of this and all other kinds of mental distress is in the mind alone.

The third, most fundamental affliction of the mind is the delusion of grasping onto one's own and others' reified personal identities as real and concrete. According to Buddhism, the self is constantly in a state of dynamic flux, arises in different ways, and is profoundly interdependent with other people and the environment. However, people habitually obscure the actual nature of the self by superimposing on reality the concepts of permanence, singularity, and autonomy. As a result of misapprehending the self as independent, there arises a strong sense of the absolute separation of self and other. Then, craving naturally arises for the "I" and for what is mine, and repulsion arises toward the other. The erroneous belief in the absolute distinction of self and other thus acts as the basis for the derivative mental afflictions of craving, hatred, jealousy, and arrogance. Such toxins of the mind are regarded, in Buddhism, as the sources of all mental suffering.

Theoretical Issues and Research Directions

Psychologists do not distinguish between beneficial and harmful emotions. Those who take an evolutionary view of emotion (e.g., Cosmides & Tooby, 2000; Ekman,

1992) have proposed that emotions were adaptive over the history of the species and remain adaptive today. Even those who categorize emotions as simply positive or negative (e.g., Watson, Clark, & Tellegen, 1988) do not propose that all of the negative emotions are harmful to oneself or to others. The goal in any psychologically informed attempt to improve one's emotional life is not to rid oneself of or transcend an emotion—not even hatred—but to regulate experience and action once an emotion is felt (Davidson, Jackson, & Kalin, 2000). (Note, however, that not all theorists consider hatred an emotion.)

One point of convergence between the Buddhist and psychological perspectives is that hostility, which is viewed in the West as a character or personality trait, is considered to be destructive to one's health. Impulsive chronic violence is also considered to be dysfunctional and is classified as pathological (Davidson, Putnam, & Larson, 2000). But neither of these is considered in psychology to be an emotion per se.

Rather than focusing on increasing consciousness of one's inner state, the emphasis in much of psychology is on learning how to reappraise situations (Lazarus, 1991) or how to control (regulate) emotional behavior and expressions (Gross, 1999; but see Ekman, 2003, for a psychological approach to enhancing awareness of emotions as they occur).

The growing literature based on self-report measures of well-being indicates that punctate events, even significant ones such as winning the lottery, phasically alter an individual's state of pleasure but do not change an individual's trait level of happiness. Buddhists agree that events such as winning the lottery would not alter an individual's dispositional level of happiness, but they do assert that happiness as a dispositional trait (*sukha*) can be cultivated through specific practices. Although the term trait positive affect as it has been used in the mood and temperament literature has some elements in common with *sukha*, it does not capture the essence of the Buddhist construct, which also includes a deep sense of well-being, a propensity toward compassion, reduced vulnerability to outer circumstances, and recognition of the interconnectedness with people and other living beings in one's environment. Moreover, *sukha* is a trait and not a state. It is a dispositional quality that permeates and pervades all experience and behavior.

Another important difference between Buddhism and psychological approaches is that the Buddhists provide a method for modifying affective traits and for cultivating *sukha* (Wallace, 2005), whereas in psychology the only methods for changing enduring affective traits are those that have been developed specifically to treat psychopathology. With a few notable exceptions (e.g., Seligman, 1998), no effort has been invested in cultivating positive attributes of mind in individuals who do not have mental disorders. Western approaches to changing enduring emotional states or traits do not involve the long-term persistent effort that is involved in all complex skill learning—for example, in becoming a chess master or learning to play a musical instrument. Typically, not even psychoanalysis or the most intensive forms of cognitive-behavior therapy involve the decades of training Buddhists consider necessary for the cultivation of *sukha*.

Buddhists, as we said, consider craving to be one of the primary toxins of the mind. Unlike psychologists, who restrict the idea of craving to states produced by substances of abuse or by strongly appetitive opportunities that offer the potential for abuse (e.g., gambling, sex), Buddhists use the term more generically to encompass the desire to acquire objects and situations for oneself. A growing body of neuroscientific literature has shown that activity of the neurotransmitter dopamine in a part of the brain called the nucleus accumbens is common to states of craving, including both pharmacologically induced addictions and activities such as gambling. Although activation of this system is highly reinforcing (i.e., it leads to the recurrence of behaviors associated with the system's activation), it is not associated with pleasure in the long run. Of course, what is not included in this neuroscientific framework is anything akin to the notion of *sukha*.

Buddhist contemplative practices are explicitly designed to counteract craving. It would thus be of great interest empirically to evaluate how effective these methods may be as interventions for addictive disorders, which are disorders of craving, and to determine if the brain systems associated with craving are altered by such training.

The Buddhist, but not Western, view considers hatred to be intrinsically harmful to people who experience it. This perspective suggests that it would be valuable to examine the different ways in which those who have been exposed to a major trauma react emotionally to the cause of their trauma—for example, how people whose children have been murdered react to the perpetrators once they are apprehended. In a study of such individuals, various biological, health, and social measures would provide information about the consequences of maintaining hatred or forgiveness toward the perpetrator.

JOINT CONCLUSION

Buddhist conceptions and practices that deal with emotional life make three very distinct contributions to psychology. Conceptually, they raise issues that have been ignored by many psychologists, calling on the field to make more finely nuanced distinctions in thinking about emotional experience. Methodologically, they offer practices that could help individuals report on their own internal experiences, and such practices might thereby provide crucial data that is much more detailed and comprehensive than that gathered by the techniques psychologists now use to study subjective emotional experience. Finally, Buddhist practices themselves offer a therapy, not just for the disturbed, but for all who seek to improve the quality of their lives. We hope what we have reported will serve to spark the interest of psychologists to learn more about this tradition.

Recommended Reading

Goleman, D. (2003). *Beyond destructive emotions: A scientific collaboration with the Dalai Lama*. New York: Bantam Books.
Teasdale, J.D., Segal, Z., & Williams, J.M. (1995). How does cognitive therapy prevent depressive relapse and why should attentional control (mindfulness) training help? *Behavior Research and Therapy, 33*, 25–39.
Wallace, B.A. (2005). (See References)

Acknowledgments—Paul Ekman's research was supported in part by a National Institute of Mental Health (NIMH) Senior Research Scientist Award, KO5-MH06092. Richard

Davidson's work described in this article has been supported by NIMH Grants MN43454, MH40747, P50-MH522354, and P50-MH61083; by NIMH Research Scientist Award KO5-MH00875; by grants from the Research Network on Mind-Body Interaction of the John D. and Catherine T. MacArthur Foundation; and by support from the University of Wisconsin. The authors are grateful to the many colleagues who read and gave helpful suggestions on earlier drafts of this article, but especially to Daniel Goleman.

Notes

1. Address correspondence to Paul Ekman, P.O. Box 5211, Berkeley CA 94705; e-mail: paul@paulekman.com.

2. The participants at this meeting, besides the Dalai Lama, were Richard Davidson, Paul Ekman, Owen Flannagen, Daniel Goleman, Mark Greenberg, Thupten Jinpa, Matthieu Ricard, Jeanne Tsai, Francisco Varela, and Alan Wallace. We thank the Mind and Life Institute of Boulder, Colorado for organizing the meeting in India and a subsequent meeting during which we wrote this article.

References

Cosmides, L., & Tooby, J. (2000). Evolutionary psychology and the emotions. In M.L. Lewis & J. Haviland-Jones (Eds.), *Handbook of emotions* (2nd ed., pp. 3–134). New York: Guilford Press.

Davidson, R.J., & Irwin, W. The functional neuroanatomy of emotion and affective style. *Trends in Cognitive Science, 3,* 11–21.

Davidson, R.J., Jackson, D.C., & Kalin, N.H. (2000). Emotion, plasticity, context and regulation: Perspectives from affective neuroscience. *Psychological Bulletin, 126,* 890–906.

Davidson, R.J., Putnam, K.M., & Larson, C.L. (2000). Dysfunction in the neural circuitry of emotion regulation—a possible prelude to violence. *Science, 289,* 591–594.

Ekman, P. (1992). An argument for basic emotions. *Cognition and Emotion, 6,* 169–200.

Ekman, P. (2003). *Emotions revealed: Recognizing faces and feelings to improve communication and emotional life.* New York. Times Books.

Gross, J.J. (1999). The emerging field of emotion regulation: An integrative review. *Review of General Psychology, 2,* 271–299.

Kahneman, D., Fredrickson, B.L., Schreiber, C.A., & Redelmeier, D.A. (1993). When more pain is preferred to less: Adding a better end. *Psychological Science, 4,* 401–405.

Lazarus, R. (1991). *Emotion and adaptation.* New York: Oxford University Press.

Lutz, A., Greischar, L.L., Rawlings, N.B., Ricard, M., & Davidson, R.J. (in press). Long-term meditators self-induce high-amplitude gamma synchrony during mental practice. *Proceedings of the National Academy of Sciences, USA.*

Rosenberg, E.L., & Ekman, P. (1994). Coherence between expressive and experiential systems in emotion. *Cognition and Emotion, 8,* 201–229.

Seligman, M.E.P. (1998). *Learned optimism.* New York: Pocket Books.

Sheldon, K.M., Ryan, R.M., Deci, E.L., & Kasser, T. (2004). The independent effects of goal contents and motives on well-being: It's both what you pursue and why you pursue it. *Personality and Social Psychology Bulletin, 30,* 475–486.

Wallace, B.A. (2005). *Genuine happiness: Meditation as the path to fulfillment.* Hoboken, NJ: John Wiley and Sons.

Watson, D., Clark, L.A., & Tellegen, A. (1988). Development and validation of brief measures of positive and negative affect: The PANAS scales. *Journal of Personality and Social Psychology, 54,* 1063–1070.

Wilson, T., & Gilbert, D. (in press). Affective forecasting: Knowing what to want. *Current Directions in Psychological Science.*

Affective Forecasting: Knowing What to Want

Timothy D. Wilson[1]
University of Virginia

Daniel T. Gilbert
Harvard University

Abstract

People base many decisions on affective forecasts, predictions about their emotional reactions to future events. They often display an impact bias, overestimating the intensity and duration of their emotional reactions to such events. One cause of the impact bias is focalism, the tendency to underestimate the extent to which other events will influence our thoughts and feelings. Another is people's failure to anticipate how quickly they will make sense of things that happen to them in a way that speeds emotional recovery. This is especially true when predicting reactions to negative events: People fail to anticipate how quickly they will cope psychologically with such events in ways that speed their recovery from them. Several implications are discussed, such as the tendency for people to attribute their unexpected resilience to external agents.

Keywords

affective forecasting; prediction; emotion; sense making

Many cultures have myths in which people can make their wishes come true. The story of Aladdin and his lamp is best known to readers of the *Arabian Nights* (and to Disney fans); in Irish legends, it is leprechauns who make wishes come true; whereas in a Chinese fable it is an obliging dragon that has the head of a camel, the eyes of a hare, the neck of a snake, the claws of an eagle, and the ears of a buffalo (McNeil, 2003).

Common to these myths is the notion that if people (perhaps with the help of a genie) could make their wishes come true, they would achieve everlasting happiness. Sometimes, however, people are disappointed by the very things they think they want. Research on *affective forecasting* has shown that people routinely mispredict how much pleasure or displeasure future events will bring and, as a result, sometimes work to bring about events that do not maximize their happiness.

These mispredictions can take a number of forms. People can be wrong about how positive or negative their reactions to future events will be, particularly if what unfolds is different from what they had imagined. Prospective dog owners might predict that Rover will bring nothing but joy because they picture a faithful companion who obediently fetches the newspaper each morning instead of an obstinate beast who chews shoes and demands 6:00-a.m. walks in the freezing rain. Generally, however, humans are adept at predicting whether events are likely to be pleasant or unpleasant. Even a rat can readily learn that pressing one bar will produce a food pellet and another an electric shock and will vote with its paws for the more pleasant option. People know that a root beer will be more pleasant than a root canal.

People are less adept at predicting the intensity and duration of their future emotional reactions. Occasionally they underestimate intensity and duration; this may happen, for example, when a person is in a "cold" emotional state at the time of prediction and is trying to imagine being in a "hot" emotional state in the future. Satiated shoppers underestimate how much they will want ice cream later in the week, and addicts who have just injected heroin underestimate how much they will crave the drug when they are deprived of it later (Gilbert, Gill, & Wilson, 2002; Loewenstein, O'Donoghue, & Rabin, 2003).

THE IMPACT BIAS

More common than underestimating future emotional reactions, however, is the *impact bias,* whereby people overestimate the intensity and duration of their emotional reactions to future events—even when they know what the future event is likely to entail and they are not in a particularly "hot" or "cold" emotional state at the time of making their forecast. This error has been found repeatedly in a variety of populations and contexts. College students overestimated how happy or unhappy they would be after being assigned to a desirable or undesirable dormitory (see Fig. 1), people overestimated how unhappy they would be 2 months after the dissolution of a romantic relationship, untenured college professors

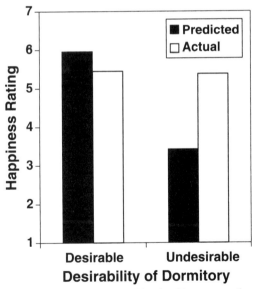

Fig. 1. College students' predicted and actual levels of happiness after dormitory assignments. Participants predicted what their overall level of happiness would be a year later if they were randomly assigned to a desirable or undesirable dormitory (on a 7-point scale, with 1 = *unhappy* and 7 = *happy*). Students predicted that their dormitory assignment would have a large positive or negative impact on their overall happiness (solid bars); but a year later, those living in undesirable and desirable dormitories were at nearly identical levels of happiness (open bars). Adapted from Dunn, Wilson, & Gilbert (2003).

overestimated how unhappy they would be 5 years after being denied tenure, women overestimated how unhappy they would be upon receiving unwanted results from a pregnancy test, and so on (see Loewenstein et al., 2003; Mellers & McGraw, 2001; Wilson & Gilbert, 2003). The impact bias is important because, when deciding what to work for, people need to predict not only the valence (positivity or negativity) of their emotional reactions ("Will I feel good or bad?"), but also the intensity and duration of these reactions (e.g., "Will I feel good for a few seconds or a few months?"). If consumers overestimate the intensity and duration of the pleasure they will get from purchasing a new car, for example, they may be better off spending their money in some other way.

One cause of the impact bias is *focalism,* the tendency to overestimate how much we will think about the event in the future and to underestimate the extent to which other events will influence our thoughts and feelings (Schkade & Kahneman, 1998; Wilson, Wheatley, Meyers, Gilbert, & Axsom, 2000). When football fans think about how they will feel after their favorite team wins an important game, for example, they are likely to focus exclusively on the game and neglect to think about the many other things—such as upcoming deadlines at work, the need to get the car fixed, or a visit from old family friends—that will influence their thoughts and feelings. Focalism is a straightforward and, we suspect, quite common source of the impact bias. It can be corrected, to some degree, by asking people to think carefully about the many other events that will demand their attention in the future; studies have found that this exercise tempers people's predictions about the impact of a victory or loss by their favorite football team on their happiness (Wilson et al., 2000).

SENSE MAKING AND PEOPLE'S IGNORANCE OF IT

Another cause of the impact bias is that forecasters fail to recognize how readily they will make sense of novel or unexpected events once they happen. Research across a variety of fields suggests that such events trigger four processes in sequence: attention, reaction, explanation, and adaptation.

- First, people are especially likely to attend to events that are self-relevant but poorly understood. For example, a student who unexpectedly receives an *A* on an important exam will initially think about little else.
- Second, people react emotionally to self-relevant, poorly understood events. The student who receives an unexpected *A* will initially feel overjoyed.
- Third, people attempt to explain or make sense of self-relevant, poorly understood events. For example, the overjoyed student will begin to search for reasons why she received a better-than-expected grade.
- Fourth, by making sense of events, people adapt emotionally to them. Once the student has explained the reasons for her grade, she will think about her achievement less and experience less happiness when she does think about it. The event will come to be seen as more normal and inevitable then it actually was, and hence it will lose some of the emotional power that it had when it still seemed extraordinary.

These four processes may seem relatively uncontroversial to psychologists, but research suggests that people neglect to take them into account when forecasting their future emotions. In particular, because the processes by which people explain or make sense of unexpected events are often quick and nonconscious, people do not recognize beforehand that such processes will occur; thus they do not consider how quickly their tendency to explain events will reduce the impact of those events. When a student tries to predict how she will feel if she receives an unexpected A, she has little trouble imagining herself feeling overjoyed but a lot of trouble imagining herself explaining the event in a way that makes it seem ordinary and predictable.

The Pleasure of Uncertainty About Positive Events

If making sense of positive events reduces the duration of the pleasure they cause, then inhibiting the sense-making process should prolong people's pleasure. In one study, for example, students who were studying in a library were unexpectedly given an index card with a dollar coin attached, and results showed that they were in a better mood 5 minutes later if the text on the card made it difficult rather than easy for them to explain why they had received the money. Yet people did not anticipate this effect; in fact, "forecaster" participants predicted that they would be happier if the card made explanation easy rather than difficult (Wilson, Centerbar, Kermer, & Gilbert, 2005). People do not realize how quickly they will make sense of unexpected positive events and how doing so will make their positive emotions dissipate.

A Pleasure Paradox

Most organisms avoid that which has previously caused them pain and approach that which has previously given them pleasure. Humans are better at this than most other animals because they do more than merely associate stimuli with their affective consequences. People are naive scientists who explain events to themselves, and the sophisticated causal theories people generate allow them to pursue pleasures and avoid pains with an unusual degree of success. But an ironic consequence of this inveterate sense making is that events tend to lose some of their hedonic impact as they become more sensible. People work to understand events so that they can repeat the good ones and avoid repeating the bad ones, but in understanding these events people may reduce their ability to be moved by them. True, some explanations of events make people feel better than other explanations do; taking credit for a major success is more pleasurable, for example, than attributing it to luck. Independent of the favorability of the explanation, however, sense making hastens emotional "recovery" from events. Things are rarely as good or bad as people expect them to be because people do not realize that by explaining the things that happen to them, they drain these things of the hedonic qualities that caused them to focus on the events in the first place.

NEGATIVE EVENTS: MOTIVATED SENSE MAKING

People are motivated to recover from negative emotional events, and the kind of sense making they engage in often involves coping, psychological defenses, and rationalization. Like the physiological immune system that fights threats to physical health, people have a psychological immune system that fights threats to emotional well-being. These defenses have been well documented by social and personality psychologists and include dissonance reduction, motivated reasoning, self-serving attributions, self-affirmation, and positive illusions.

A feature that all these defenses have in common is that they are largely unconscious, and in fact are more effective by operating behind the mental scenes. When trying to cope with a romantic breakup, for example, people usually will not be able deliberately and consciously to adopt a more negative view of their partner in order to make themselves feel better. Instead, the ex-partner will come to seem less suitable, with no awareness that one's own psychological immune system was responsible for this shift in view. Because people are generally unaware of the operation of these defenses, they tend not to take them into account when predicting their future emotional reactions—an oversight we have termed *immune neglect*.

In one study, for example, participants who failed to get a desirable job were less upset 10 minutes later when the failure was attributable to a single capricious interviewer (easy to rationalize: "The guy's a jerk") rather than to a team of interviewers (difficult to rationalize: "How could they all dislike me?"). In another study, participants were less upset when they received negative personality feedback from a computer (easy to rationalize: "Computers make mistakes") than from a clinician (difficult to rationalize: "How could I have scored so badly on the personality test?"). In both cases, people had stronger reactions when unexpected negative events were difficult to rationalize and explain, but in both cases they failed to anticipate that this would happen (Gilbert, Pinel, Wilson, Blumberg, & Wheatley, 1998).

Implications of Immune Neglect

People's failure to anticipate their natural tendency to make the best of bad outcomes has a number of consequences:

- Because people do not recognize that they have reduced the impact of negative events by explaining and rationalizing them, they sometimes attribute their unexpected resilience to the work of powerful, insightful, and benevolent external agents (Gilbert, Brown, Pinel, & Wilson, 2000). For example, employees who are transferred to undesirable locations might be surprised by how happy they are; by failing to recognize that they produced their own happiness with nonconscious coping and defensive processes, they might attribute their good fortune to the guiding hand of an external agent, such as God.
- When people make a decision that is difficult to reverse, such as buying a sweater from a store with a "no returns" policy, they are strongly motivated to rationalize the decision and make the best of it. When people can more easily undo a decision, such as buying a sweater they can return, they are less motivated to rationalize their choice, because they can always change their minds. Consequently people are often happier with irrevocable

choices because they do the psychological work necessary to rationalize what they can't undo. Because people do not realize in advance that they will work harder to rationalize irreversible decisions, however, they often avoid the binding commitments that would actually increase their satisfaction (Gilbert & Ebert, 2002). For example, many people pay more to purchase clothing from stores with a liberal return policy, when they would more satisfied with clothes they bought that they could not return.

- Not surprisingly, people believe that major traumas will have a more enduring emotional impact than minor ones will. Because people are more strongly motivated to make sense of major traumas than minor ones, however, the pain of minor traumas can sometimes last longer than more serious ones. It seems like it would be worse, for example, to be insulted by a close friend than a stranger. Because people are more motivated to cope with (and perhaps rationalize) the insult from the friend, however, they may recover from it more quickly (Gilbert, Lieberman, Morewedge, & Wilson, 2004).

- It is well-known that people weigh potential losses more heavily than corresponding gains, which often leads to economically illogical decisions. Kermer, Driver-Linn, Wilson, and Gilbert (2005), for example, found that most people refused a gamble in which they had a 50% of winning $5 and a 50% chance of losing only $3, demonstrating classic loss aversion. Loss aversion seems to involve a faulty affective forecast: Although participants predicted that losing a gamble would have a larger emotional impact than winning, they were wrong; the magnitude of unhappiness caused by losing was no greater than the magnitude of happiness caused by winning (Kermer et al., 2005).

SUMMARY AND FUTURE DIRECTIONS

Affective forecasts are important because people base many decisions on them. Decisions about who to marry, what career to pursue, and whether to donate money to the local homeless shelter are based, at least in part, on predictions about how these decisions will make one feel. To the extent that people's predictions about what will make them happy are flawed, people fail at maximizing their happiness.

One unanswered question is whether the impact bias is advantageous in some way. It could be argued that exaggerating the impact of emotional events serves as a motivator, making people work hard to obtain things that they predict will have large positive consequences and avoid things that they predict will have large negative consequences. It may be, however, that overestimating the impact of negative events creates unnecessary dread and anxiety about the future. And there are other costs to affective-forecasting errors. People suffering from debilitating digestive disorders who underestimate how quickly they will adapt to an ostomy bag might make less-than-optimal treatment decisions. People who overestimate the positive emotional impact of undergoing cosmetic surgery might be too willing to get an extreme makeover. Finding ways to increase the accuracy of affective forecasts is a worthy enterprise—though not, we suspect, a particularly easy one

(Ubel et al., 2001). It is difficult to place oneself in the future and imagine what it will be like to have made sense of an event that, in the present, seems extraordinary. Such mental time traveling, however, might ultimately lead to better decisions.

Recommended Reading

Gilbert, D.T., Driver-Linn, E., & Wilson, T.D. (2002). The trouble with Vronsky: Impact bias in the forecasting of future affective states. In L.F. Barrett & P. Salovey (Eds.), *The wisdom in feeling: Psychological processes in emotional intelligence* (pp. 114–143). New York: Guilford.
Loewenstein, G., O'Donoghue, T. and Rabin, M. (2003). (See References)
Mellers, B.A., & McGraw, A.P. (2001). (See References)
Wilson, T.D. (2002). *Strangers to ourselves: Discovering the adaptive unconscious.* Cambridge, MA: Harvard University Press.
Wilson, T.D., & Gilbert, D.T. (2003). (See References)

Acknowledgments—Much of the research discussed in this article was supported by research grant #RO1-MH56075 from the National Institute of Mental Health to the authors.

Note

1. Address correspondence to Timothy D. Wilson, P.O. Box 400400, 102 Gilmer Hall, University of Virginia, Charlottesville, VA 22904-4400, e-mail: twilson@virginia.edu, or to Daniel Gilbert, Department of Psychology, William James Hall, 33 Kirkland Street, Harvard University, Cambridge, MA, 02138, e-mail: gilbert@wjh.harvard.edu.

References

Dunn, E.W., Wilson, T.D., & Gilbert, D.T. (2003). Location, location, location: The misprediction of satisfaction in housing lotteries. *Personality and Social Psychology Bulletin, 29,* 1421–1432.
Gilbert, D.T., Brown, R.A., Pinel, E.C., & Wilson, T.D. (2000). The illusion of external agency. *Journal of Personality and Social Psychology, 79,* 690–700.
Gilbert, D.T., & Ebert, J.E. (2002). Decisions and revisions: The affective forecasting of changeable outcomes. *Journal of Personality and Social Psychology, 82,* 503–514.
Gilbert, D.T., Gill, M., & Wilson, T.D. (2002). The future is now: Temporal correction in affective forecasting. *Organizational Behavior and Human Decision Processes, 88,* 430–444.
Gilbert, D.T., Lieberman, M.D., Morewedge, C., & Wilson, T.D. (2004). The peculiar longevity of things not so bad. *Psychological Science, 15,* 14–19.
Gilbert, D.T., Pinel, E.C., Wilson, T.D., Blumberg, S.J., & Wheatley, T.P. (1998). Immune neglect: A source of durability bias in affective forecasting. *Journal of Personality and Social Psychology, 75,* 617–638.
Kermer, D.A., Driver-Linn, E., Wilson, T.D., & Gilbert, D.T. (2005). *Loss aversion applies to predictions more than experience.* Unpublished raw data, University of Virginia.
Loewenstein, G., O'Donoghue, T., & Rabin, M. (2003). Projection bias in predicting future utility. *Quarterly Journal of Economics, 118,* 1209–1248.
Mellers, B.A., & McGraw, A.P. (2001). Anticipated emotions as guides to choice. *Current Directions in Psychological Science, 10,* 210–214.
McNeil, D.G. Jr. (2003, April 29). Dragons, a brief history in long miles. *New York Times* (p. F2).
Schkade, D.A., & Kahneman, D. (1998). Does living in California make people happy? A focusing illusion in judgments of life satisfaction. *Psychological Science, 9,* 340–346.
Ubel, P.A., Loewenstein, G., Hershey, J., Baron, J., Mohr, T., Asch, D., & Jepson, C. (2001). Do non-patients underestimate the quality of life associated with chronic health conditions because of a focusing illusion? *Medical Decision Making, 21,* 190–199.

Wilson, T.D., Centerbar, D.B., Kermer, D.A., & Gilbert, D.T. (2005). The pleasures of uncertainty: Prolonging positive moods in ways people do not anticipate. *Journal of Personality and Social Psychology, 88*, 5–21.

Wilson, T.D., & Gilbert, D.T. (2003). Affective forecasting. In M.P. Zanna (Ed.), *Advances in experimental social psychology* (Vol. 35, pp. 345–411). San Diego, CA: Academic Press.

Wilson, T.D., Wheatley, T.P., Meyers, J.M., Gilbert, D.T., & Axsom, D. (2000). Focalism: A Source of durability bias in affective forecasting. *Journal of Personality and Social Psychology, 78*, 821–836.

This article has been reprinted as it originally appeared in *Current Directions in Psychological Science*. Citation information for this article as originally published appears above.

Children of the Affluent: Challenges to Well-Being

Suniya S. Luthar[1] and Shawn J. Latendresse
Teachers College, Columbia University

Abstract

Growing up in the culture of affluence can connote various psychosocial risks. Studies have shown that upper-class children can manifest elevated disturbance in several areas—such as substance use, anxiety, and depression—and that two sets of factors seem to be implicated, that is, excessive pressures to achieve and isolation from parents (both literal and emotional). Whereas stereotypically, affluent youth and poor youth are respectively thought of as being at "low risk" and "high risk," comparative studies have revealed more similarities than differences in their adjustment patterns and socialization processes. In the years ahead, psychologists must correct the long-standing neglect of a group of youngsters treated, thus far, as not needing their attention. Family wealth does not automatically confer either wisdom in parenting or equanimity of spirit; whereas children rendered atypical by virtue of their parents' wealth are undoubtedly privileged in many respects, there is also, clearly, the potential for some nontrivial threats to their psychological well-being.

Keywords

affluence; risk; contextual influences; socioeconomic status

Children of upper-class, highly educated parents are generally assumed to be at "low risk," but recent evidence suggests that they can face several unacknowledged pressures. In this article, we describe programmatic research relevant to this issue. We begin by characterizing the samples of youth we have studied across suburban communities in the Northeast. We then provide an overview of findings of problems in various spheres of adjustment and discuss associated implications for research, practice, and policy.

RESEARCH INVOLVING UPPER-CLASS SAMPLES

Since the late 1990s, our group has accumulated data on three cohorts of youth from high-income communities; characteristics of these cohorts are summarized in Table 1. The first, which we refer to as Cohort I, consisted of 264 tenth graders attending a suburban high school serving three contiguous towns.[2] These students were followed annually through their senior year, and as sophomores, we contrasted them with 224 tenth graders in an inner-city school.

Cohort II encompassed 302 middle school students from another high-income town, whom we studied when they were in the sixth and seventh grades (Luthar & Becker, 2002). Cohort III, subsequently recruited from the same community as Cohort II, incorporated all children attending the sixth grade during the 1998–1999 academic year, and these students were then followed annually (11th-grade assessments had been completed at the time of writing this

Table 1. *Characteristics of the samples*

Source and sample	N	Minority ethnicity in sample (%)	Eligible for free or reduced lunch in school (%)	Median annual family income in region (census)	Adults with graduate or professional degrees in region (%; census)
Luthar & D'Avanzo (1999)					
Suburban Cohort I: 10th graders followed through high school	264	18	1	$80,000–$102,000	24–37
Comparison sample: inner-city 10th graders	224	87	86	$35,000	5
Luthar & Becker (2002)					
Suburban Cohort II: 6th and 7th graders	302	8	3	$120,000	33
Luthar & Latendresse (in press)					
Suburban Cohort III: 6th graders followed annually through high school (ongoing)	314	7	3	$125,000	33
Comparison sample: inner-city 6th graders followed through 8th grade	300	80	79	$27,000	6

report). In parallel, we obtained annual assessments of an inner-city middle school sample, enabling further comparisons of youngsters from widely disparate socio-demographic settings.

EVIDENCE OF ADJUSTMENT DISTURBANCES

The first set of questions addressed with Cohort I was focused on substance use and related problems (Luthar & D'Avanzo, 1999), and descriptive analyses showed many signs of trouble among the suburban students. These youngsters reported significantly higher use of cigarettes, alcohol, marijuana, and hard drugs than did their inner-city counterparts, and also showed elevations in comparison with national norms. Suburban teens also reported significantly higher anxiety and somewhat higher depression than did inner-city youth. In comparison with normative samples, girls in the suburbs were three times more likely to report clinically significant levels of depression.

Also disturbing were findings on correlates of substance use. Among affluent (but not inner-city) youth, substance use was linked with depression and anxiety, suggesting efforts to self-medicate; this "negative affect" type of substance use tends to be sustained over time, rather than remitting soon after the teen years. In addition, among suburban boys (but not other subgroups in the study), popularity with classmates was linked with high substance use, suggesting that the peer group may endorse and even encourage substance use among affluent teenage boys.

In Cohort II, we saw no evidence of disturbance among the sixth graders, but among the seventh graders, some problems were beginning to emerge (Luthar & Becker, 2002). Among the older girls, for example, rates of clinically significant depressive symptoms were twice as high as those in normative samples. Whereas no boys in the sixth grade had used alcohol or marijuana, 7% of seventh-grade boys reported having drunk alcohol until intoxicated or using marijuana about once a month. Finally, results supported the earlier findings on correlates of substance use, which had significant links with depression and anxiety in this middle school sample, and with peer popularity among the seventh-grade boys.

In Cohort III, as well, preliminary data showed that suburban sixth graders scored below national norms on depression and anxiety, and also had lower scores than inner-city comparison youth. Once again, however, some signs of trouble began to emerge by the seventh grade, with popular students, for example, reporting significantly higher levels of substance use than others (Luthar & Sexton, 2004). We are currently examining different developmental pathways to problems and to well-being from pre- through midadolescence.

WHY MIGHT "PRIVILEGED" YOUTH BE TROUBLED?

In exploring pathways to maladjustment in affluent suburbia, we considered two sets of potential antecedents in our study of Cohort II. The first encompassed *achievement pressures*. Statistical analyses showed, in fact, that children with very high perfectionist strivings—those who saw achievement failures as personal failures—had relatively high depression, anxiety, and substance use, as did those who indicated that their parents overemphasized their accomplishments, valuing them disproportionately more than their personal character (Luthar & Becker, 2002).

The second potential antecedent was *isolation from adults,* both literal and emotional. Among upper-middle-class families, secondary school students are often left home alone for several hours each week, with many parents believing that this promotes self-sufficiency. Similarly, suburban children's needs for emotional closeness may often suffer as the demands of professional parents' careers erode relaxed "family time" and youngsters are shuttled between various after-school activities. Again, results showed that both literal and emotional isolation were linked to distress as well as substance use.

We next sought to explore family functioning in greater depth among sixth graders in Cohort III and, simultaneously, their inner-city counterparts. A common assumption is that parents are more accessible to high- than to low-income youth, but our data showed otherwise (Luthar & Latendresse, in press). We considered children's perceptions of seven aspects of parenting, and average ratings on four of these dimensions were similar for the two sets of students: felt closeness to mothers, felt closeness to fathers, parental values emphasizing integrity, and regularity of eating dinner with parents. Inner-city students did fare more poorly than suburban students on two of the remaining three dimensions—parental criticism and lack of after-school supervision—but at the same time, they did significantly better than suburban students on the last dimension, parental expectations.

Results also revealed the surprising unique significance of children's eating dinner with at least one parent on most nights. Even after the other six parenting dimensions (including emotional closeness both to mothers and to fathers) were taken into account, this simple family routine was linked not only to children's self-reported adjustment, but also to their performance at school. Striking, too, were the similarities of links involving family dining among families ostensibly easily able to arrange for shared leisure time and those who had to cope with the sundry exigencies of everyday life in poverty.

Subsequent analyses with Cohort III students and their inner-city counterparts when they were in the seventh grade revealed similarities in peer-group influences as well (Luthar & Sexton, 2004). Early adolescents at both socioeconomic extremes showed admiration for classmates who openly flouted authority. In the suburban context, high peer status was linked with overt displays of low academic effort, disobedience at school, aggressiveness among girls, and substance use among boys, and in the urban context, high peer status was associated with aggression and substance use among both boys and girls. Also noteworthy were startlingly strong links between physical attractiveness and peer popularity among affluent girls. This variable alone explained more than half the variation in their popularity scores, suggesting particularly high emphasis on physical appearance among this subgroup of girls (the links between attractiveness and popularity were substantially weaker among inner-city girls and among both groups of boys). All in all, the substantive message was that affluent adolescents, just like their inner-city counterparts, valued some peer attributes that could potentially compromise overall competence or well-being.

195

DOES REBELLION AMONG AFFLUENT
TEENS REALLY "MATTER"?

All adolescents might be drawn to overt forms of rebellion, but it is quite plausible that wealthy youth, unlike their poor counterparts, can dabble in drug use or delinquency without any substantive damage to their life prospects, given various safety nets (i.e., concerned adults and access to high-quality treatment services). To examine this possibility, we returned to our high school Cohort I data, as older teens reflect more variability on such forms of behavioral deviance than middle school students do. Once again, our findings showed that youth at the socioeconomic extremes were more similar than different (Luthar & Ansary, in press). In both settings, we found a distinct subgroup of teens who manifested multiple behavior problems—substance use, delinquency, poor interest in academics— and had school grades that were significantly lower than the average. Although the findings on urban adolescents were unsurprising in light of prior empirical evidence, the results on affluent youth were noteworthy in indicating that, despite the resources ostensibly available to them, nearly 1 of every 10 teenagers in this cohort exhibited high levels of behavior disturbances across multiple domains, and concurrently experienced significant risk for poor grades during the sophomore year of high school.

We also examined substance use among this subgroup of suburban sophomores annually through the remainder of high school (McMahon & Luthar, 2004). Twenty percent of these students showed persistently high substance use across time. Furthermore, across all three assessments, this group also showed relatively high levels of depression and physiologically manifest anxiety (e.g., nausea, difficulty breathing), as well as poor grades and negative teacher ratings. For as many as one in five of these affluent youth, therefore, high substance use, coexisting with depression, anxiety, and both behavioral and academic problems, was sustained up to the age of 18 years.

IMPLICATIONS FOR INTERVENTIONS

All is not necessarily well among children of the affluent. Across three suburban cohorts, a nontrivial proportion of youth reported diverse adjustment problems, and disconnectedness in families and pressured lifestyles constituted discernible challenges (for parallel evidence among adult samples, see Csikszentmihalyi, 1999; Kasser, 2002; Myers, 2000).

Why do affluent youth have these problems—despite all the mental health services ostensibly available? One possibility is that although high-income parents are generally willing to place overtly troubled youth in psychotherapy or on medication, they are less eager to delve into the less "conspicuous" problems in their children, in themselves, or in family processes more generally. Research has shown, for example, that parents in general tend to be aware when their children are depressed, but tend not to seek professional help unless symptoms include those that inconvenience adults, such as disobedience or asthma (Puura et al., 1998).

Upper-class parents can be particularly reluctant to seek help for the less visible problems because of privacy concerns, as well as embarrassment. Affluent adults are often very concerned about keeping family troubles private; this is not surprising, as misfortunes of the wealthy tend to evoke a malicious pleasure in people who are less well-off (a phenomenon called *schaden-freude*; see Feather & Sherman, 2002). Upper-class parents also can feel more compelled than most to maintain a veneer of well-being, feeling that "those at the top are supposed to be better able to handle their problems than those further down the scale" (Wolfe & Fodor, 1996, p. 80).

Then there are realities of everyday lives that impede change. In the subculture of affluent suburbia, overscheduled days are often the norm for young people, with high school students participating in numerous activities, which can then be logged on college applications. The careers of many parents, similarly, do in fact demand long work hours: Job sharing and flexible hours are not an option for chief executive officers or university presidents. At the same time, these careers do bring many personal rewards, including the gratification of mastering substantial professional challenges, and of providing well for stellar educations and leisure activities for the next generation. Few people would blithely repudiate such rewards.

Also relevant is practitioners' perseverance—or lack thereof—in pursuing nascent signs of trouble. School psychologists, for example, often hesitate to express concerns to high-income parents, anticipating resistance and sometimes even threats of lawsuits. Consequently (and paradoxically), wealthy youth can end up having less access to school-based counseling services than do students who are less well-off (Pollak & Schaffer, 1985). Clinicians may also minimize problems they see among the wealthy. The same symptoms are more often viewed as signs of mental illness among the poor than among the affluent; by corollary, the rich are more often dismissed as "not needing help" even when they report distress commensurate with that of others typically judged to be needing assistance (Luthar & Sexton, 2004).

Even if affluent youth do, in fact, receive high-quality psychiatric care, it should be emphasized that this is no substitute for strong attachments with parents. Decades of work on children's mental health policies have established that psychotherapy to address crystallized maladjustment is largely unproductive as long as the child's everyday life continues to present major challenges to adjustment (Knitzer, 2000).

In the future, an expedient first step toward addressing these issues would be to raise awareness of the potential costs of overscheduled, competitive lifestyles (Luthar & Sexton, 2004). This can be done effectively via books comprehensible to the lay public, such as those by Kasser (2002) and Myers (2000). Although obviously not panaceas, such dissemination efforts could begin to sensitize caregivers to risks in the context of affluence—risks that they (like developmental scientists) may have been only faintly aware of in the past.

Consideration of these issues is important not only for the families themselves, but also for society in general. Many children of highly educated, affluent parents will likely come to assume positions of influence in society, and their own equanimity of spirit may have far-reaching ramifications. Depression vastly impairs productivity. And people who are unhappy, with a fragile, meager sense of self, can be more acquisitive than philanthropic, focused more on gaining more for themselves than on improving the lot of others (Diener & Biswas-Diener, 2002).

CONCLUSIONS

Until the 1970s, developmental scientists had largely ignored children in poverty, and it is critical to correct the neglect of another group of youngsters heretofore invisible in psychological science: those in high-income families. Systematic research is needed on the generalizability of research results obtained thus far. Scientists need to establish, for instance, whether elevated distress or pressured lifestyles occur in wealthy metropolitan locations, and not just in suburban communities. It will also be important to determine whether these problems are discernible in nationally representative samples (assuming, of course, that high-income families are appropriately represented in them). Also critical are prospective studies that can indicate (a) whether problems such as depression or drug use generally represent temporary blips of adolescent angst among the wealthy or are early signs of continuing problems and, conversely, (b) if factors such as prolonged isolation and pressure within families do, in fact, set apart those teens who carry adolescent adjustment disturbances into adulthood. Finally, practitioners and parents must be alert to the risks potentially attached to wealth and status. The American dream spawns widespread beliefs that Ivy League educations and subsequently lucrative careers are critical for children's long-term happiness. In the sometimes single-minded pursuit of these goals, let us not lose sight of the possible costs to mental health and well-being of all concerned.

Recommended Reading

Csikszentmihalyi, M. (1999). (See References)
Kasser, T. (2002). (See References)
Luthar, S.S. (2003). The culture of affluence: Psychological costs of material wealth. *Child Development, 74,* 1581–1593.
Luthar, S.S., & Sexton, C. (2004). (See References)
Myers, D.G. (2000). (See References)

Acknowledgments—Preparation of this manuscript was supported by grants from the National Institutes of Health (RO1-DA10726, RO1-DA11498, RO1-DA14385), the William T. Grant Foundation, and the Spencer Foundation.

Notes

1. Address correspondence to Suniya S. Luthar, Teachers College, Columbia University, 525 West 120th St., Box 133, New York, NY 10027-6696.
2. We are currently examining effects of varying affluence across neighborhoods subsumed in wealthy townships.

References

Csikszentmihalyi, M. (1999). If we are so rich, why aren't we happy? *American Psychologist, 54,* 821–827.
Diener, E., & Biswas-Diener, R. (2002). Will money increase subjective well-being? *Social Indicators Research, 57,* 119–169.
Feather, N.T., & Sherman, R. (2002). Envy, resentment, Schadenfreude, and sympathy: Reactions to deserved and undeserved achievement and subsequent failure. *Personality and Social Psychology Bulletin, 28,* 953–961.

Kasser, T. (2002). *The high price of materialism*. Cambridge, MA: MIT Press.

Knitzer, J. (2000). Early childhood mental health services: A policy and systems development perspective. In J.P. Shonkoff & S.J. Meisels (Eds.), *Handbook of early childhood intervention* (2nd ed., pp. 416–438). New York: Cambridge University Press.

Luthar, S.S., & Ansary, N.S. (in press). Dimensions of adolescent rebellion: Risks for academic failure among high- and low-income youth. *Development and Psychopathology*.

Luthar, S.S., & Becker, B.E. (2002). Privileged but pressured: A study of affluent youth. *Child Development, 73*, 1593–1610.

Luthar, S.S., & D'Avanzo, K. (1999). Contextual factors in substance use: A study of suburban and inner-city adolescents. *Development and Psychopathology, 11*, 845–867.

Luthar, S.S., & Latendresse, S.J. (in press). Comparable "risks" at the SES extremes: Pre-adolescents' perceptions of parenting. *Development and Psychopathology*.

Luthar, S.S., & Sexton, C. (2004). The high price of affluence. In R.V. Kail (Ed.), *Advances in child development* (Vol. 32, pp. 126–162). San Diego, CA: Academic Press.

McMahon, T.J., & Luthar, S.S. (2004). *Substance use, psychopathology, and social competence: A longitudinal study of affluent, suburban, high school students*. Manuscript submitted for publication.

Myers, D.G. (2000). *The American paradox: Spiritual hunger in an age of plenty*. New Haven, CT: Yale University Press.

Pollak, J.M., & Schaffer, S. (1985). The mental health clinician in the affluent public school setting. *Clinical Social Work Journal, 13*, 341–355.

Puura, K., Almqvist, F., Tamminen, T., Piha, J., Kumpulainen, K., Raesaenen, E., Moilanen, I., & Koivisto, A.M. (1998). Children with symptoms of depression: What do adults see? *Journal of Child Psychology and Psychiatry and Allied Disciplines, 39*, 577–585.

Wolfe, J.L., & Fodor, I.G. (1996). The poverty of privilege: Therapy with women of the "upper classes." *Women & Therapy, 18*, 73–89.

Section 6: Critical Thinking Questions

1. Think about the times you have been happiest, or unhappiest, in your life. Did you always bounce back to a more moderate position? How would it affect your life if you believed that it is impossible to become happier than you are now—would it change your approach? Perhaps by giving up striving and attachment (as in the Buddhist approach) we can at least reduce our negative feelings, if not create more positive feelings. Do you agree with this interpretation of the Buddhist message?

2. Most of us think we would be happier if we had more money. Of course, the affective forecasting article suggests that such beliefs are often wrong, as does the article on the children of affluent parents. Is money like a craving that can never be satisfied, which creates more problems than it solves? Or, is striving for more money OK, as long as this striving does not become too central in one's life? What is your position on this issue?

This article has been reprinted as it originally appeared in *Current Directions in Psychological Science*. Citation information for this article as originally published appears above.